RESTAURANT BASICS REVISITED

Why Guests Don't Come Back ... and What You Can Do About It

Bill Marvin

The Restaurant Doctor℠

Hospitality Masters Press

Gig Harbor, Washington

Library of Congress Control Number: 2013913885

ISBN: 978-1-893864-02-3

ATTENTION ASSOCIATIONS AND MULTI-UNIT OPERATORS:
Quantity discounts are available on bulk purchases of this book for premiums, sales promotions, educational purposes or fund raising. Custom imprinting or book excerpts can also be created to fit specific needs.

For more information, please contact our Special Sales Department
Hospitality Masters Press, PO Box 280, Gig Harbor, WA 98335
e-mail: bill@hospitalitymasters.com
Phone: (800) 767-1055, Fax: (888) 767-1055
Outside the US and Canada: (253) 858-9255, Fax: (253) 851-6887

Original Artwork: Kevin Cordtz, Cordtz Studio, Colorado Springs, CO.

Contents

Foreword

In all my years as a hotel and restaurant professional, I associated with thousands of staff people. I don't think I've known more than two or three who were possessed of an innate sense sufficient to qualify them as having a complete understanding of that extraordinary world of "MONUMENTALLY MAGNIFICENT TRIVIALITIES." This book is not for them!

The doors of this world opened for me at the earliest stages of my career while in school in Lausanne, Switzerland. It was during this time I experienced my first of the great restaurants of France: Maxim's of Paris and La Pyramide in Vienna.

Both were legendary, and the latter was owned by one of the few really creative restaurant geniuses who ever lived ... Fernand Point. I was struck by the credo by which he lived and which became indelible in my mind for all the years which I would face in the exercise of my profession. He said, "Success is the sum of a lot of little things correctly done."

Among those truths which never change is that man is a gregarious animal who needs to belong. The individual counts most and all must be designed to fit the individual's scale ... human scale. Human needs, human emotions and human sensitivities remain basically unchanged.

Ellsworth M. Statler once said, "The majority of complaints in a restaurant or hotel are due more to the guest's state of mind than to the importance of the things about which he complains."

Otherwise stated, more often than not, the reason for the complaint is trivial. However, this triviality achieves a level of such monumental importance to the one who comes forth with the need to complain that we suddenly and unwittingly become confronted with a phenomenon which has never ceased to fascinate me ... that of monumentally magnificent trivialities.

These trivialities abound in our restaurant business and they surround us like millions of molecules. Most are so obscure and so taken for granted that the restaurant owner-operator pays little heed to how critically important they are or is even unaware that they must be accommodated in context, with consequences of failure or success.

This is what this book is about.

It is an assemblage, a compendium of a whole wide range of MONUMENTALLY MAGNIFICENT TRIVIALITIES. Surprisingly this book is not yet finished and it never will be. The list of "trivialities" is infinite and never ending.

As a source book and reference guide, the listings which follow are of inestimable value in the successful carry-through of one's restaurant business. Success will come to those who develop the disciplines and motivate others to recognize the tiny little details and to bring them to some form of order so that the results really are the sum of a lot of little things correctly done.

> ... the ever present menace of mediocrity
> calls for untiring vigilance.

– James A. Nassikas

Introduction to the Second Edition

Restaurant Basics was my first book, originally published in 1993. At the time, the Internet was a plaything for a few geeks and academics, cell phones were a rarity and smoking in restaurants was still common practice. What a difference a few years can make.

Since then, I've addressed thousands of operators all over the world. I have worked one-on-one with dozens of excellent restaurateurs ... and those aspiring to excellence. I've conducted countless talks, seminars and workshops, written another twelve books, authored dozens of articles for the industry trade press and produced two weekly e-letters for different segments of the industry.

The knowledge and understanding I've gained from this work, along with the reflection it takes to keep tapping into fresh insights, has deepened my grasp of our wonderful industry and what makes it tick. As I am fond of saying, when I had my restaurants I learned how to run restaurants. It was only when I finally got away from the day-to-day of it that I finally started to *understand* what made it all work.

So while the basics of the business are still basic, it seemed time to re-visit the material in that first book and update it where necessary to reflect the realities of the time and my current thinking about what it takes to be a place of hospitality in a new millennium.

Our industry is ever-changing and the expectations of our patrons evolve over time as well. So, as James Nassikas noted twenty years ago, a work like this is never really finished, merely paused from time to time for re-examination and reflection. Twenty years from now, perhaps someone else will revise it yet again.

Bill Marvin
The Restaurant Doctor[SM]
Gig Harbor, Washington

"The reader will take from my book what he brings to it. The dull witted will get dullness and the brilliant may find things in my book I didn't know were there."

– John Steinbeck, *East of Eden*

Preface

...You Wonder How These Things Begin

Many years ago now, I was doing a consulting project for a hotel in California. The property's Food & Beverage Director shared a little card with me – a wallet-sized list of 25 details the hotel had learned were important to their guests. All their managers carried one as a reminder to take care of the little things. I added the card to my library and didn't think much more about it at the time.

Five years later, on a visit to Cape Cod, I went to dinner with my dad. The restaurant was one of his favorites ... but they weren't having a good night. As the evening went from bad to worse, we discussed what was happening and why. I was noticing details the restaurant staff was missing, the lost opportunities to salvage the evening and, I confess, delivering a bit of a lecture on Service 101.

The staff was trying hard but they were seriously "in the weeds" and just didn't realize how they were alienating their guests. As the train wreck unfolded, we agreed that had the restaurant handled the small points better, our experience would have been much different. "You should write a book about this," my father suggested. "Someday I just might," said I, and went on to other projects. (By the way, he told me he never went back to that restaurant!)

While assembling material for a seminar a few years later, I thought of the little card I had received from the hotel. I added a few thoughts of my own and got the list up to 75 points, the sheer length of which looked staggering at the time! Later I thought more about it and added more items to the list. When I got to 200, I was certain I must have covered nearly all the potential problems!

However, as the list continued to grow, I found I had a tiger by the tail. Being more sensitive to what some might consider minutia, I noticed nuances I had overlooked before. The list turned into a project.

As I talked about what I was doing, people both inside and outside the industry offered more observations. Everybody, it seems, had a few pet peeves about restaurants.

It also became obvious there were many more reasons why people *don't* go back to restaurants than reasons why they *do!* As the list neared 1000 entries, it became the book we joked about at dinner those many years ago.

Restaurant Basics Revisited is about common, ordinary, simple-minded things that can trip up even the best operation. We're not talking about rocket science, complexities of food chemistry or nuances of French Burgundies. This is basic restaurant blocking and tackling.

Hopefully, most of the items in the book are details you already have under control, but perhaps there will be a few you haven't thought about that will give you a way to be even better at what you do.

Terminology Traps

In reading the book, you will notice I don't use some of the words you may expect to see. I also use some terms that may sound different to you. The language we use unthinkingly may contribute to many of our problems in these areas. If you want to change your results, start by changing your words. Here are some examples of what I mean:

Customer
The word suggests a relationship based on the transfer of money and is less delight-oriented than using the word "guest." Customers are just people who walk in the door with money in their pockets. They all get the same treatment. Guests, on the other hand, are special people to whom you extend courtesy, hospitality and an experience more closely tailored to their particular needs.

Employee
Employee is another word based on the transfer of money. I prefer "staff" although many companies talk about the "crew," the "team" or their "associates" with good results. Team-oriented words help create a more empowering work climate.

Service
The word service is dangerous because it can be too easily defined just from the perspective of the provider.

("I can't understand why Table 36 is complaining. I gave them good service!") The fact is that, in the end, good service can only be defined and determined from the guest's point of view.

Even "satisfaction" isn't a powerful enough word – it only means guests got what they expected. Simply meeting expectations is not enough to make you a legend in today's market.

Doubletree Hotels, for example, wants to provide service that "astounds" you. Play the word game. Focus on "gratifying" or "delighting" your guests and see what happens!

Manager

If you call someone a manager, they may think their job is to manage the staff. This attitude can easily lead to issues of control, manipulation and destruction of incentive. I much prefer the word "coach" because I think it better represents the model for effective leadership in a restaurant. A manager looks for problems, a coach looks for strengths. Think about it.

Waiter, Waitress, Server

Using these job titles may cause your crew to think their job is to wait or to serve – a costly misunderstanding for your restaurant.

Consider the possibilities if you gave that position the title of "sales person" or "service manager." Their role is truly to manage the process of merchandising products, making sales and delivering a memorable service experience to your guests.

What if you described the position as being a "story-teller?" Your staff can best help build long term sales by telling guests stories about your operation and its menu items. The back story about what makes you better and different – stories guests will, in turn, tell their friends.

Whatever direction you take with your words, give it some thought. As I said, language is powerful.

How this Book Is Organized

For ease of reference, I divided the material into chapters by general subject matter. This allows you, for example, to identify items relevant to the kitchen staff without having to wade through points that mainly concern the service staff.

Because restaurant positions are so interdependent, there is often no clear choice about where a particular point belongs. Where an issue speaks to lapses in more than one areas, I may mention it in more than one place. Don't be put off by the repetition. I don't want anyone to miss an important detail because they looked in the wrong chapter!

While the emphasis of this material may be toward full service restaurants, there are specific suggestions for cafeterias, fast feeders, caterers and most other types of foodservice operators. Conscientious restaurateurs (and managers of most any service-oriented business for that matter) can extract numerous insights and opportunities from this material, regardless of their operating style.

My problem has always been when to stop adding to the list. For as much as it contains, it is still incomplete. I'm sure you'll notice points that I missed. When you do, I encourage you to jot them down and send them along to me for future updates of this material.

Why share some of your best insights and secrets?

- because all of us are smarter than any of us. Cataloging the collective wisdom of the industry is a powerful resource.

- because your direct competitors already know what you're doing anyway (but they probably aren't reading this book, so they won't know the rest of the tricks.

- because it is in our collective best interests to assure dining out is a universally positive experience. Inept operators only educate the public to stay home.

The better the dining experience, the more people will dine out. The more firmly ingrained the dining out habit becomes in the public, the more we all will all benefit.

Acknowledgments

There are so many people that contributed to the original book that it's hard to know where to start. Several of these folks have passed on now and I suspect most the rest have changed jobs, but their attitudes, insights and ideas were instrumental in shaping my understanding of how our wonderful business really works.

My wife Margene still remains my head cheerleader. Most wives would have insisted I get a "real job" years ago! My late father and stepmother, Ed & Jeanne Marvin, unwittingly gave me the idea for the book and even paid for dinner the night the idea was hatched!

My deep thanks to Toni Lydecker, Lisa Bertagnoli and Mike Bartlett at Restaurants & Institutions and Claire Zuckerman at John Wiley & Sons for believing in the original project and making it happen. Carol Cartaino was a valuable counselor and resource from the beginning.

I am indebted to Sandy Spivey, Carroll Arnold and to George and Kristi Blincoe for their many suggestions. Bill Main and his class at USF provided at least a chapter's worth of good ideas. I am grateful to Rich Keller, Robin Cyr and George & Mary Atwell for their technical advice. Bob Wade and his staff at Wade's Westside helped more than they realize.

Thanks, too, to Brad Moss, Lee & Lynn Sterling and the staff at the Colorado School for the Deaf and Blind. I appreciate the advice of the staff at Silver Key Senior Services and to Michael and Chrissie Nemeth and their friends. Dru Scott and Gary Penn, among others, have some wonderful ideas that are reflected in my thinking.

And finally, I can't say enough about Sydney Banks, Ken Burley, Mike Hurst, Don Smith, Robert Kausen, George Pransky and the many others who have been my teachers and mentors over the years. I am profoundly grateful for their insights, support and patience. I hope they will consider this book as part of their legacy.

1
Momentous
Minutia

Hotelier James Nassikas coined the term "monumental trivialities" to reflect his obsession with details. He built one of the most respected hotel experiences in the world, the Stanford Court in San Francisco, on his passion for attending to the little points he knew were important to his guests.

Industry observers note the distinguishing feature between legendary operators and mediocre managers lies in their absolute belief in mastering the basics. Many failed restaurateurs have learned this lesson the hard way. What they thought was trivial turned out to be monumental in the minds of guests who didn't come back.

What Makes Minutia Momentous?

To understand how the little things can destroy your business, it helps to understand why people are likely to have a good time and why they might not. The answer is not as obvious as it may appear. It is, however, surprisingly simple.

You know from personal experience that when you're having a bad day, *everything* looks like a disaster ... and when you feel wonderful, the whole world just seems to work more easily for you. The events of the day don't change, but their impact changes significantly!

It works the same way for businesses. If you enter a business that has a depressing environment, it starts to bring your mood down. In your lower mood, minor events seem to take on more significance. You tend to be less trusting of people. You are more likely to find fault and complain. You definitely become harder to please.

Because they are unaware of the importance of the atmosphere they create, many businesses foster an environment that almost guarantees their patrons won't have a pleasant experience. Think of the last time you went to the Post Office, the bank or the supermarket! How likely is it that *anyone* will feel delighted and well-served in an IRS office?

Fortunately, restaurants have a natural advantage over many other types of businesses. People go to restaurants *expecting* to have a good time, so they usually arrive in a pleasant mood. Their higher state of mind predisposes them to enjoy themselves. You see, people will tend to enjoy themselves anytime they are in a high state of mind; anytime they feel good.

When they're in a good mood, they're more forgiving, more generous. The food tastes better and they spend more. They tend to be more open to recommendations. They'll tip better and are more likely to tell their friends what an exciting restaurant you have!

All you have to do is create and maintain an atmosphere where people will stay in a good mood and they'll almost always have an enjoyable experience. It seems too simple!

How Minutia Becomes Monumental

People enter your restaurant focused on having a good time. Anything that snags their attention can be a distraction, and distractions change a person's mood. Every distraction, every minor irritant that affects your guests, is like tying a small weight onto the helium balloon of their good mood.

These little annoyances add up, pulling your guest's mood down. As their mood drops, their thoughts become more negative. Their sense of well-being goes down. They tend to be more critical and abrupt with your staff. They become more difficult to please.

In turn, your staff can easily become less responsive to these "suddenly" impolite people. The experience can spiral down quickly for everyone. When a guest is in a lower mood, even the finest food and service can draw complaints. You can't fix it. it's just the way people view the world when they are in a low state of mind

It's really quite simple: Guests will inevitably experience an increasingly worse time as accumulated distractions drop them into lower states of mind.

And the worse it gets, the worse it gets. Here's an example:

For some people, bright red nail polish on the hands of a server bothers them. Many people don't notice but for some it's a big deal. But if you went out to dinner and the only thing wrong was the red nail polish on your servers hands, it probably wouldn't be a major problem.

But let's say you called the restaurant and got someone in the kitchen who spoke no English, then dropped the phone twice and put you on hold for five minutes. You finally get directions to the place but they're wrong, so you drive around in the rain for 45 minutes until you find the place.

Your car bottoms out in a pot hole coming into the parking lot and you have to park in the middle of a big puddle. There's water running off the roof onto the walkway as you approach the door, which has loose hinges. There are fingerprints all over the glass and the lobby is full of dirt and leaves.

The greeter is talking with a girlfriend on the phone. Without looking up from her conversation she waves you off to a table by the kitchen door. There's duct tape on the carpet, a draft from the air conditioner, the lighting is bad, the table is wobbly, there's a burn hole in the linen and coffee stains on the menu.

As the server approaches your table, she is chewing gum, scratching her head and has her fingers wrapped around the top of your water glass. At that point, red nail polish is a BIG deal!

I don't know why these people even *came!* I would have been ordering a pizza long before this. But even when they came, they were spoiling for a fight from the minute they walked in the door. You will work your buns off on a party like that, they'll stiff you on the tip and tell their friends never to waste their time at your place.

The point is that things you'd hardly notice in a good mood become intimidating in lower moods. Yet, without the accumulated weight of these distractions, people are most likely to remain upbeat and enjoy themselves. This is how minutia destroys your business.

Many of the distractions that impact the moods of your guests are seemingly insignificant items like a dirty menu, dead flies on the windowsill or lipstick on a water glass. Throughout this book, you will find seemingly insignificant items – momentous minutia – that can distract your guests and negatively impact their moods.

Picky, Picky, Picky

Is this list picky? You bet it is! No one who's ever been in the business would deny that foodservice is a game of details. It's just that nobody has ever set down what those details are!

The size of this (incomplete!) list can be intimidating. Still, the price of success in our industry is attention to the small points. The first step in solving a problem is always to realize the nature of the problem.

A few of these details are obviously sudden death. For example, if you send guests to the hospital with food poisoning, don't expect to see them back as patrons. If your staff embarrasses a businesswoman in front of her clients during an important luncheon, she's history.

Most of the points are not as terminal as that. They are just distractions and petty annoyances. But remember the idea of weights on the balloon or the straw that breaks the camel's back. If you want to be a legend, you can't afford to dismiss anything as too trivial.

Why Guests Don't Come Back

I mentioned that the overall feeling of value comes from exceeding the guests' expectations. It may help to think of the quality of your guests' dining experience as a game.

Because people expect to have a good time when they go out to eat, you start this game with a relatively high "score," say 90-100 "points" that equate to the diners' expectations.

As guests approach your building and progress through their meal experience, you gain or lose points depending on what they notice and what their experiences are. Most of these distractions are things for which you'll *lose* points if they happen but won't necessarily *gain* points if they don't. On the plus side, personal, unexpected touches can gain points and improve your score.

There's no particular point value to anything other than the value arbitrarily given by the guest. For example, something one person might not even notice could cause someone else to walk out in a rage!

This happens because perceptions are a function of someone's mood – the way they are thinking in the moment. The lower the mood, the more serious and threatening life appears to them The more onerous something appears, the more points it will cost you. It's not fair, but it's the way human nature works.

Your guests aren't aware of it, of course, but they keep a mental score. As they leave the restaurant, they assign a subconscious point total to their experience. The more positive their experience, the higher your score. When the final result equals or exceeds their expectations going in, you win big!

Your point total also has relevance in comparison to your competition. So if, for example, you provide a 75-point experience when your competitors are scoring 70, you'll have an edge ... but let a competitor get 80 points and you'll be in trouble. It may go without saying, but people have higher expectations of a $150 dinner than they do of a fast food lunch ... and they should!

Exceeding expectations creates delighted guests. If you score higher than people expect, they will love you, at least for the moment. If you score less than they expected, no matter how good a job you do, you won't be on their A List.

Worse yet, if you are inconsistent – good one time and sloppy the next – your guests won't trust you. When people mistrust your restaurant, you must score higher just to reach the same level of guest satisfaction. For every person (in relation to every individual restaurant), there's a score so low it will cause them never to patronize the place again.

What You Can Do About It

It is hardly reasonable to expect that none of these lapses will ever happen in your restaurant. Still, you can significantly reduce minor irritations through heightened awareness, effective staff selection, continual coaching and passionate attention to detail.

It's critical your guests sense how important the details are to you and your staff, that they see how your entire operation focuses on their satisfaction and know you are making a sincere effort to correct any minor lapses. This level of focus and caring creates and maintains an environment where guests will have a high sense of well-being.

Personally, I appreciate it most when an error is swiftly and skillfully corrected. It often shows me more than if the mistake never happened in the first place. Perhaps it is the human frailty and personal concern shown. If your heart is in the right place, you won't usually lose points for occasional oversights.

Don't get me wrong, I'm not advocating making errors just so you can correct them. As you will see, there are plenty of opportunities to blow it without doing anything intentional!

Restaurant Basics Revisited deals with minutia from the guests' point of view – the only perspective that really counts. Practices stated in the negative are likely to lower people's moods; those likely to delight guests are stated in a positive manner.

This is consistent with the idea that our primary job in the restaurant industry is to give our guests a wonderful experience. Unless guests enjoy themselves, nothing else really matters.

As odd as some items may appear, everything in this book has actually happened in a dining establishment. Not all details are issues to every one of your guests, of course, and many won't even apply to your restaurant. Still, each has the potential to weigh down someone's good mood and you pay a huge price any time that happens.

I suspect you will find yourself at odds with some of the ideas in this book. When that happens, be careful. I don't suggest this material is any sort of gospel. However, it is consistently oriented from the guest's perspective of the dining experience.

I know, I know ... for every item on the list that irritates one person, there is probably another who likes it just the other way. Some people want their iced tea constantly refilled; others don't want you to touch the glass.

Reading the Table

The ability to "read the table" is a priceless skill to develop ... and it is easier than we make it out to be. The secret is called *Presence* and simply stated, it just means quieting your mind and being totally *with* someone when you're with them.

When you slow down to the speed of life and just connect as people, you're much more likely to sense the needs and concerns of others.

Coupled with an awareness of practices that can set some people off, you'll be more likely to make the right moves at the right time. It also helps you keep the focus on what your guests need rather than on your own needs and wants.

Any time you're serving your own interests to the detriment of the interests of your guests, you're working against yourself, so beware of dismissing any of these notions too quickly. Items that look like they'll take too much work, cost too much money or involve too much training to correct are most likely to be in your blind spot.

While tips are the primary income for most servers, I still suspect the majority are motivated by wanting to do a good job and wanting their guests to have a good experience. Nobody on your staff is out to see how badly they can screw things up ... but since these mistakes still happen, it suggests many on the service staff are simply unaware of the impact such lapses have on their guests. Whose fault is that?

You can't avoid every potential problem, but you can try. There are items on this list you won't do anything to correct, but you could. There are even items that will annoy you just by being mentioned at all. (Those are usually the ones that hit too close to home!)

I'm also not suggesting you should make it a hard and fast rule never to be guilty of any practice on the list. That's not only unnecessary and unrealistic, but far too heavy-handed. After all, you want to create a place of hospitality, not a police state!

That said, though, I urge you to think long and hard of the potential risks before you decide a particular point is unreasonable or that you can afford to overlook it in your training and coaching.

If you start to think of your operation from your guests' perspective; if your priorities shift a bit; if you see a few new ways to become more responsive to the needs of your guests; then this book will have served its purpose (and, most likely, your bottom line as well!)

Now let's get to work!

2
Outside Oversights

Your building and your outward appearance deliver a message far more clear than your advertising. Your point total starts changing as soon as your guests start traveling toward your restaurant.

Do you get a head start on a great score or start at a disadvantage? In a business where creating and exceeding people's expectations is essential, does your exterior appearance make potential guests excited or apprehensive?

Does it make them feel good about their decision to dine with you or cause them question their judgement? Does it honestly reflect the care and attention they can expect inside?

The difficulty with outward appearances is that the focus of the management and staff is typically inside the building. The staff often enters and leaves through a back door and seldom sees their operation from the perspective of their patrons.

Compared to the dynamic environment inside, it is easy to think of the exterior of the restaurant as relatively unchanging. While some aspects of the outside don't require daily attention, there are many others that do. Assign responsibility for monitoring the outside appearance of the property in the same way as any other job.

Design Deficiencies

These are problems created by the physical design of the building and grounds as well as the realities of land area and access. You cannot correct all design deficiencies, but you can work around many of them if you are willing to do the work.

Poorly Lit Parking Areas

If guests feel uneasy about their safety, they'll go elsewhere. Dim shadows in the parking lot make perfect hiding places for muggers and create anxiety in your guests. I doubt this is the sort of first or last impression you want guests to have of your restaurant.

Install bright lighting in your parking lot. Go one step farther and add accent lighting for your landscaping. It will provide more light on the grounds and make the restaurant more attractive at night.

Difficult or Inconvenient Access to the Property

If you're too hard to get to, the public won't bother. An interesting exercise is to have an out-of-town friend drive you to the restaurant without any guidance from you. See how easily they can find the place and make their way into the parking lot. Remember, you are not an impartial judge of how easy it is to find your restaurant.

Inadequate or Inconvenient Parking

How often are you in your parking lot at the height of the rush? Do you really know if guests have trouble finding a place to park? If they can't park easily, eventually they won't try to park at all.

After business hours, is there available parking space in the lots of nearby businesses? If so, make a deal with them to use the space, don't just let guests commandeer it! Often a trade for meals is enough of a gesture to maintain good neighborhood relations.

If your parking area is some distance from the restaurant's main entrance, you also have a problem, particularly in cold climates. Inconvenient parking can discourage business and cause your guests to get in the habit of going elsewhere.

To make it as easy as possible for your guests, you may want to consider valet parking. Let the valet run down the block. Don't ask your guests to do it. Consider offering complimentary valet service. Sure, it will add a cost, but you won't make a dime unless guests come in to dine in the first place!

Improper Parking Lot Drainage

Poor drainage creates puddles. In wet weather, portions of your lot could turn into small lakes and become unusable. Worse yet, a guest could arrive when the lot was dry only to find their car marooned in the middle of a small lake due to a sudden rainstorm.

Standing water in the lot also leads to major maintenance problems. The next time the weatherman predicts a thunderstorm, bring your umbrella and boots to work and take a walk around your parking lot. You may be surprised. I remember one restaurant in Tennessee where the main drainage flow was right down the middle of the parking lot. I arrived during a heavy rain storm and there were literally white water rapids in front of the door!

Inconsistencies Between the Exterior Appearance and the Reality of the Restaurant

If what guests see is not what they get, you'll have a problem. There are many examples of good restaurants that failed because the exterior of the building and the operation inside were at odds.

I remember a restaurant in San Diego that looked like an elegant supper club from the 1930s – pale pastel with a sweeping covered entry for arriving cars. The only problem? It was a coffee shop! People looking for a formal meal were disappointed when they got inside and those looking for a casual meal never thought to stop.

There would be a similar problem if you looked like an Italian restaurant from the outside and were serving Mexican food. This disconnect can easily happen when a new operator takes over an existing restaurant and makes no major changes to the exterior.

Unclear Entry into the Building

I was at a restaurant in Pennsylvania, an interesting building with several porches. I tried four different doors before I found the entrance to the restaurant! It didn't even look like a likely entry. I'm not sure I would even have seen it if some others hadn't been leaving. When I got inside, I was already frustrated! A simple sign could have avoided the problem.

Quarterly Questions

Quarterly questions require some level of action several times a year. In most cases, seasonal attention is sufficient. In harsh climates, they may need to be monitored more closely.

Poorly Marked Parking Spaces

Maintaining proper spacing in the parking lot reduces the chance of damage to guest vehicles. It also helps assure you get the full number of cars into the lot. Your climate will determine how often you need to dress and re-stripe the pavement.

Potholes in the Parking Lot

This includes any hazard that could damage a guest's car. Watch limbs and branches that could scratch a car's paint. If potholes develop, fill them with gravel until you can make permanent repairs. Remember, potholes never get smaller and never go away by themselves.

Be aware of any sharp grade changes between the parking lot and the street that could cause a guest's car to bottom out. If you can't fix these grades, your guests will appreciate a sign at least warning them of the hazard. Guests will remember the repair bill long after they've forgotten your restaurant.

Broken Sidewalks

You don't want to create personal injury or discomfort for your guests. If your part of the country experiences continued freezing and thawing, your walks will take a particular beating. Ice melt compounds can pit and scar the surface. Concrete may last forever, but it still needs maintenance and attention. Monitor the condition of your walkways and plan for periodic repair or replacement.

Old, Dirty or Stained Menu in the Window

Your menu is a sales tool. Be sure your posted menu looks as fresh and appetizing as the ones in your dining room. Remember the sun will take a toll on a posted menu. Does the menu display cabinet have any leaks? Is it well-lighted at night?

Pay as much attention to the decor of the menu display case as you do the decor of the restaurant. It's a sneak preview of what people can expect inside. If your restaurant is up a flight of stairs, consider some professional color photographs or a closed circuit video feed to show potential guests what to expect.

Faded Exterior Paint

Particularly in climates that enjoy intense sunlight, paint fading can sneak up on you. Fading happens gradually and our sense of time gets distorted. For example, we have an addition to the family home put on in 1960 that's still called "the new room!" Take a critical look at the building at least once a quarter. Pick a sunny day. Look from several different angles and see if the building looks fresh.

Handrails That Give Guests Splinters

With continual exposure to the elements, the grain on wooden handrails opens and becomes a hazard. Make it a habit to slide your hand up and down the railings to test their condition. Sand and re-apply a sealer regularly. Don't wait until you have a problem.

Grass or Weeds Growing Through the Pavement

If you have grass or weeks growing through your sidewalks or in the parking lot, people might think you don't do any business! Fortunately, a few well-placed shots of a grass or weed killer can keep this problem under control ... if you do the work!

Water Dripping off the Roof onto Guests

Of course this only happens on rainy days or when snow is melting, neither of which is a time when you really want to be wandering around outside! If the cause is not a design problem, it may be a maintenance issue. Make sure gutters and down spouts are always in good repair and free-flowing.

Jumble of Newspaper Racks

I've had newspaper vendors place racks on my property without even asking permission! Look at this area with fresh eyes every so often. Make vendors replace dented or faded racks. Have unwanted racks removed and if you have several different papers, consider combining all those separate racks into an integrated unit.

No (Or Inaccurate) Hours Posted

To make it easy for guests to patronize you, they have to know when you're open. This is particularly true if you are closed when they pull up! Posted hours also enable them to arrive when they can avoid the rush (and give you their business when you are most able to take it.)

If you usually enter the restaurant through the back door, change your pattern now and then. You'll be surprised at what you will notice ... like the fact that the hours posted on the front door don't reflect the changes you made six months ago!

You won't make any friends if guests arrive during posted hours only to find the door locked. Make it a habit to open ten minutes early and close ten minutes late. Who needs an argument over whose watch has the correct time?

Disorderly Cluster of Decals on the Front Door

Decals and stickers on the doors accumulate over time and become almost invisible to operators. They are not, however, invisible to your guests. A neat display of current decals from the Restaurant Association, Chamber of Commerce, etc. can be a plus. Replace any that are torn or faded and remove those that have expired, remove them. If you're no longer a member of an organization, remove its sticker from your door.

Faded or Broken Sign

Wind, weather, vandals and the forces of nature will have their way with your signs. Take a close look every few months and see if it projects the image you want. Often, just washing it can make a big difference, but when it needs to be re-painted ... just do it.

Posters and Handwritten Signs All Over Front Windows

I'm all for supporting activities in the community, but you are still a place of business, not a community bulletin board. Anything in view of your potential patrons should professionally promote the image of *your* business, not someone else's.

Daily Duties

There are actions you must take every day to stay on top of potential problems. In some cases, you may want to check on some of these points even more frequently.

Trash in the Landscaping

The wind is your worst enemy in this regard ... and the wind isn't going to go away. It is critical to pull papers and other debris from the plants every morning. Be sure to get it all, not just the pieces that are easy to reach. It doesn't take long for abandoned pieces of paper deep inside shrubbery to become unremovable lumps of pulp!

Missing Lights in the Sign

This condition presents an uncaring image to the passing public. Of course, you never look at the signs in the daytime and when the signs are on at night, everybody is going crazy inside the restaurant! You may not be able to do much on a Saturday night, but Thursday evening might be a perfect time to assure the integrity of the lights in the signs. Keep spare bulbs on hand, particularly if they are a special size. Also be sure to have a long ladder or bulb-changer to make the job faster and safer.

Bottles, Cans or Broken Glass in the Parking Lot

You don't have control over what happens in your parking lot after the restaurant closes. Nonetheless, whatever happens during the night becomes your responsibility at sunrise. The cleanliness of your parking lot clearly tells your guests about the care they can expect inside. Clean all debris from the parking lot every morning.

Doors That Are Hard to Open

Even doors that work easily most of the time can be a real struggle in damp weather. Be aware of how easily the door swings when you open it. Watch your elderly guests to see if they have problems. Ask them if it's difficult for them. Better yet, have someone on your staff there to open the door for arriving and departing guests.

Dirt or Debris on the Walkways

Keeping your walkways clear and inviting is as important as vacuuming your carpets. Besides the liability and public safety issues, a spotless exterior delivers a strong message about your caring. Sweep away dirt, leave and cigarette butts every morning. Do people notice outdoor cleanliness? Ask Disney World!

People Loitering on the Property

Unsavory groups hanging around can be intimidating. How can you discourage the congregation without a confrontation? Often just increasing the lighting will make you a less attractive hangout.

Encourage local police to drop by for coffee. If the neighborhood is marginal, a security guard can make your guests more comfortable and discourage the flock on the street. Yes, it will cost money, but you have an obligation to assure the safety and comfort of your guests. Fail at that and lose them forever.

Overflowing Trash Cans or Dumpsters

This is particularly annoying when it can be seen from the parking lot. Trying to save some money with fewer trash pickups is false economy. Remember that lost business has a far higher cost. Do all you can to reduce the bulk of your trash. Use a disposer for food waste, bale your cardboard and recycle glass and plastic. Remove trash before it accumulates enough to detract from your image.

Loose Door Hardware

The heavier the door, the more strain it places on the hardware. Check the integrity of latches, locks and hinges every time you open the door and regularly tighten the screws that hold everything in place. Don't wait until they become noticeably loose.

Unkempt Landscaping

You can't afford to spend good money for quality landscaping and let it deteriorate. Particularly during the growing season, the look of your shrubbery can change quickly. Assign responsibility for keeping your landscaping neat, either to a member of your staff or a landscape service. When planning new landscaping, it is better to have low-maintenance than high-maintenance plants.

Lobby Full of Leaves, Dirt or Debris

Every time a guest opens the front door, anything that is blowing around outside has the chance to blow inside your restaurant. Assign someone to keep an eye on this and stay ahead of it, particularly on stormy or windy days.

Dirty Glass on Entry Doors

You must clean the glass on your front doors several times a day, particularly if you serve children. To save some work, clean the glass thoroughly and apply a clear silicon (not wax) auto polish. It will dry clear and for several days afterward you can just wipe away fingerprints! Much faster than Windex and paper towels.

Reader Board with Old or Incomplete Messages

A reader board is a constant caretaking job. Always have a message on your reader board ... and be sure to remove your St. Patrick's day message on March 18th!

Every day, you have to check for uneven or missing letters. The appearance of your reader board delivers a message about your attention to detail and your restaurant, good or bad. It can be a real asset if you're willing to invest the time to use it properly. It will help sink you if you don't stay on top of it.

Reader Board Without the Proper Letters

Reader boards can gain you points, but they can also work against you if you try to use a "5" where you need an "S" or hope an inverted "3" will work as an "E." Your reader board should also advertise your concern with details, not just your daily special.

Flies in the Trash Containers

A mass of insects is incompatible with creating guest comfort and enthusiasm. Reduce the amount of wet garbage in the trash and always keep containers tightly covered. Clean the trash containers regularly, remove refuse frequently and spray as necessary to keep this problem under control.

Policy Perils

Some problems exist only because you've chosen to have (or not have) a policy about something. If you elect to change the policy, you can eliminate the potential irritant.

Parking Spots by the Front Door Taken by Staff

The restaurant is in operation for the enjoyment of guests, not the convenience of the staff. Make it as easy as possible for guests to patronize you. As part of your staff orientation, tell your crew where to park their cars and why. Follow up with violators until they get the message. Make an escort available for any staff member concerned about walking alone to their cars after dark.

Charging Guests to Park Their Cars
In some cities, valet parking fees are the norm. In other areas, it's an annoyance for your guests. If a charge is needed to maintain the legal separation between yourself and the valet service, credit the cost against the guest's bill. The goodwill and repeat patronage will more than pay for any additional costs.

Damage to Guests' Cars While Dining
In a strict sense, you may not have control of what happens in your parking lot. Still, you can reduce the potential for damage and have a plan to deal with a problem if it arises.

Check with your insurance carrier to see if your liability coverage extends to cars in your lot. If not, see if they could provide coverage. "It's not my responsibility," is not the answer you want to give a guest whose car has just been broken into while parked in your lot!

No Menu in the Window
It won't make a difference to guests who have been there before, but if you want people to come *back*, you must get them to try you in the first place. Seeing the menu and prices before walking in the door can be the deciding factor for first-timers or people who are just strolling past.

Bonus Points

Everyone likes pleasant surprises. These little unexpected touches are opportunities to improve your score and put your guests in a better mood. They help make up for any lapses in the operation and give people something to talk about to their friends.

Complimentary Valet Parking
I asked one operator why he offered complimentary valet parking rather than letting people park themselves. Wasn't that just an unnecessary expense? With parking in the area limited, he figured each car in his lot was worth $95 in sales to him ... and he could fit more of those cars in the lot if he did the parking. Brilliant!

If the people in those cars would otherwise be patronizing your competition, the numbers have to work out in your favor. Besides, it means you can deliver cars to departing guests that have already been cooled down in the summer or heated up in the winter. Now *that* is hospitality!

Complimentary Umbrellas in Inclement Weather

Use large golf umbrellas with your restaurant's name prominently silk-screened. The gesture will be so impressive that you'll probably have little problem with people returning the umbrellas. If you are concerned about guests keeping your umbrellas, offer a coupon for a complimentary glass of wine with their next meal. That would do your guests a favor and build repeat business at the same time.

Or ask guests to drive past the front door on their way out so a staff member can retrieve the umbrella from their car. Even if they keep the umbrella, you get free promotional exposure each time it rains!

When the weather is stormy, you might schedule an extra person to walk people to their cars with an umbrella. Bad weather makes many people reluctant to go out at all. A service like this (or the free valet idea) can draw business you would otherwise not get.

Guest's Names on the Reader Board

People love to see their names up in lights and you could give them their fifteen minutes of fame. You have as much to gain by using your reader board to make your guests feel special as you do by using it to advertise your specials.

When guests make a reservation, ask if there is an occasion that brings them in. (Warning: it could be a group gathering following a funeral, so asking, "Is this a celebration?" could be embarrassing).

If the occasion is festive, though, ask if they would like you to put it on the reader board. You could easily become *the* place in town to celebrate!

Pleasant Surprises

The staff at a McGuffey's Restaurant in North Carolina had some time on their hands one day. Noticing guests' cars were getting covered with blowing dust from an adjacent construction project, their solution was to wash the cars in the parking lot while their diners were having lunch! Can you imagine the goodwill you would create by an unexpected gesture like this?

What is the potential for taking the sting out of waiting in line at a quick serve drive-up window by washing guests' cars? You could have a school group do the work as a fund-raiser except that *you* pay them for each car washed, not the guest. You could even get a few points just by cleaning windshields!

Orchestrate the Experience

"Orchestrate" probably sounds like a strange word to use, so let me offer a story to illustrate what I mean:

I remember listening to an interview with a Broadway producer on the thinking that goes into creating a hit show. He said the show actually started well before the curtain went up. Every detail of the play-going experience was carefully thought out and coordinated to produce the desired end result. Nothing happened by accident.

What did they want people to see as they came down the street and approached the theater? What colors were used? How was it lighted? Was there music playing on the street? It all needed to enhance the right expectations and set the stage appropriately for what awaited the patrons inside.

Then they looked at the lobby. What was happening when people entered? What were the colors? What were the smells? How was the staff dressed? How was it lit? What sounds were in the air?

When people got to their seats, how was the theater lit? Where there smells in the air? Was it warmer or colder? What was there to look at? Did the program match the experience that lay ahead?

When the orchestra started to play, it was all carefully coordinated with the lighting so as curtain time approached, the lights gradually came down, the music built and the audience was in exactly the right mood when the curtain rose.

They gave the same attention to the sights, sounds, smells and such during the intermission. They considered the restrooms and what was going on in the theater itself when most of the patrons were taking a break.

Finally, they planned out the experience as guests left the theater after the play. He contended the show wasn't over until guests got home. He took responsibility for everything from the original idea to attend the event to the conversation on the way home.

That's a lot of careful planning, but millions of dollars were at risk in that very risky business. Before you write off the benefit of so much work to help assure success, consider that restaurants are also major investments in a business that is similarly fraught with peril. Can you afford to be any less deliberate?

If you want results your competitors are not going to get, you must do the work your competitors are not willing to do. *Do the Work!*

3
Annoying Impressions

Your point total starts changing again when your guests enter the restaurant. What they see, what they smell, what they hear and what they feel will affect how they think ... and that determines how they evaluate the experience.

Their first and last contacts with your staff are usually in the lobby area. This presents incredible opportunities to create good will ... or a major chance to drop the ball. How you use those opportunities and what you get from them is up to you.

Personal impressions arise from actual contact with your staff, making them even more critical than impressions garnered from the outside of your establishment. The good news is that all these shortcomings can be eliminated through conscientious staff selection, thorough training and consistent coaching.

The bad news is that, to the extent they exist in your operation, they indicate lack of management attention. If awareness is the first step toward solving a problem, here is the first step to improve your point total in the area of initial guest contact.

Telephone Trauma

For many of your guests, the telephone is the first contact they have with your restaurant. Your advertising urges them to call, so what happens when they take you up on that offer? The answer may determine if they arrive feeling hopeful, cautious ... or not at all.

Poor Telephone Practices
This is particularly important if the phone may be answered in the kitchen. Train everyone in the restaurant on telephone manners and why they are so important. Coach your staff on what to say, how to say it and what to do with questions they can't answer. Everyone on the staff should know the procedure for taking reservations and be able to take complete and accurate messages.

Talking on the Phone While Dealing with Guests

Only undistracted, focused attention will cause your guests to feel served. By trying to do two things at once, you're telling guests that their arrival isn't the most important event of the moment. I've seen parties walk out when faced with this mindless behavior.

If you are involved in something else when a guest arrives, at least acknowledge their presence with eye contact and a smile. Let them know that *you* know they're there and that you'll be right with them. Complete your call within one minute and welcome your new guests properly.

Treating Telephone Calls as an Intrusion

Everyone develops a routine and tends to resent breaks in that pattern. Continually remind your staff that guest service is the only reason the restaurant exists. Pay particular attention to the tone of voice your staff uses on the phone. Remember, your guests have many other dining options.

Wrong or Unclear Directions

Develop concise descriptions of how to get to the restaurant. Work up a set for all major directions of approach and test them. Post them by the phone and coach all your staff in delivering the instructions cheerfully. An interesting exercise is to sit (silently) in the car while an out-of-town friend drives you to your restaurant. Make sure they have no other directions besides what your staff told them on the telephone.

Putting a Guest on Hold for More than 30 Seconds

If you can't get back to a caller promptly, take a number and call them back within three minutes. It pays to be organized when you do this. Make notes of their name, telephone number and the time they called. You can pick up points for smooth handling of the situation. You'll surely lose points if you promise to call and don't.

Letting the Phone Ring More than Four Times

When guests call, they're trying to do business with you. Why make that difficult? Give some thought to how easy it is for your staff to answer your telephone, particularly before the restaurant opens for the day.

If you can't guarantee responsive coverage, consider forwarding your main number to another phone during those periods. Perhaps there is someone at a central office or a former staffer at home with a young child who can provide the level of service you need.

Answering the Phone With Nothing but "Hold, Please"

No matter how busy you are, it takes only a few seconds to be polite. Take a second to thank them for calling. Explain that you're on another call and will be back to them within 30 seconds. If you can't meet that schedule, take a number and call right back. If you are abrupt on the phone, you're telling the caller they are not very important to you.

Not Knowing Operating Hours, Daily Specials, Etc.

Guests who call don't know who is answering the phone. All they know is whether they were treated respectfully and whether their questions were answered courteously. Every staff member must be able to answer basic questions about the restaurant and its offerings to avoid inconvenience to callers.

Lobby Lapses

Guests' first and last contact with your staff is usually in the lobby area, setting the stage for the evening or creating a final memory.

Cluttered Entry

Many restaurants are a central point for information on what's happening in town. Your operation may serve this purpose, but that doesn't mean you can turn over your entryway to everyone's flyers, posters and free newspapers without exercising some control.

The issue is not *their* material, it's *your* first impression. Approve all materials before anyone places them in your restaurant. Remove dated flyers and posters promptly after the event and assure the display is neat and tasteful. Build a rack for free newspapers and put up a bulletin board for notices. Look at it critically every day to see that it reflects well on your restaurant.

Greeting Guests While Seated

Many greeter stations have a stool for the hostess to rest on – not the most professional look. But when guests arrive, the greeter must rise, smile warmly and welcome them to the restaurant within thirty seconds. Ideally, the greeter would be moving toward the new arrivals with a smile.

Greeting guests while seated delivers a message that your personal comfort is more important that the patrons who just arrived. A good general rule is to always "stand and deliver."

Being Greeted with a Number ("Two?")

Greeting guests with a number does nothing to reinforce their sense of connection. Your first words should thank the guests for coming and welcome them to the establishment. After that, deal with the details of how many in the party. Asking if there is anyone else joining them might be a less trite way to learn the size of the party.

Clutter and Junk at the Greeter or Cashier Stand

This first impression can set the tone for the evening. Periodically, enter your restaurant by the front door and see it from the viewpoint of a first-time guest. What catches your eye? What degree of caring does the look of the reception area create?

Decor That Doesn't Fit

This challenge always presents itself when converting an existing operation to a new concept. You must make the look and feel of the new restaurant completely fresh and consistent. If not, you will only remind your guests that you don't pay much attention to detail.

Inconsistent elements affect your patrons, even if they don't know why. They will leave with a slightly uncomfortable feeling that something was wrong, not exactly the sort of lasting impression you want to encourage. Recycling restaurants can be profitable, but do yourself a favor and spend the money to do it right.

A Greeting That Focuses Only on the Needs of the Greeter

Welcoming a guest to your restaurant by asking "Smoking or non-smoking?" is as bad as greeting them with a number. Fortunately this is a moot point in most places now, but as we discussed, first make them feel welcome, then get other necessary information.

Unclear or Absent Signage at the Entry

People don't like to feel incompetent or inept. For maximum peace of mind, they want to know where to go and what to do. Should they wait for a greeter or seat themselves? Is there a non-smoking section and where is it? Ideally, the greeter will be at the door when guests arrive, but cover yourself by having clear, professionally-made signs on display for those times when the staff is elsewhere.

No Indication of Form of Payment Accepted

Do you honor credit cards? If so, which ones? Do you accept personal checks? Is your operation cash only? How are your guests going to know this? If they only get the answer when the check is presented, you're setting up another potential irritation.

Why create a problem that can be so easily avoided? Let your guests know the rules before they get too far into the meal. All credit cards provide decals you can place on the front door. A discrete sign in the lobby or on the menu outlining your policy on accepting checks will avoid embarrassment or awkwardness at the end of the meal.

Interiors and Staff That Don't Look like Your Ads

If your website, print ads or television commercials picture smiling staff in crisp uniforms, be sure that's the way your restaurant runs. Don't create an image you can't deliver or you'll disappoint your guests, even with an otherwise pleasant experience.

Being Greeted with Arm and Hand Signals

Many greeters could easily have a second job parking airplanes! They wave, they point, they make a variety of signals that have no meaning at all to the guest. I assume there is some element of imagined efficiency behind this, but it usually comes across as uncaring and impersonal.

Attitude Atrocities

The way your staff interacts with the guest is critical. The quality of this interaction is determined by a combination of their innate personal characteristics, their level of coaching and the effectiveness of your operating systems.

Not Being Acknowledged Within 30 Seconds

For better or worse, your initial contact with a guest will set the tone for the rest of their dining experience. Many people have a natural insecurity when entering a business for the first time and their first impression suggests if they made a good decision or a mistake.

Nobody is comfortable when they think they have blundered ... and few will happily stay if they feel their presence is not noticed or appreciated. When you have a line of guests waiting for service – whether at the front desk or the bar – eye contact and a smile will let *them* know that *you* know they're there and they will relax.

Calling a Guest by the Wrong Name

Nothing is sweeter to someone than the sound of their own name. At the same time, using the wrong name is rude and disturbing. Make it a game to get to know the regulars. Use their names often ... and correctly.

Inattentive Greeters
Drop *all* routine sidework and welcome guests to the restaurant as soon as they walk through your door. Sorting guest checks or doing paperwork is *always* less important than creating a positive first impression for paying patrons. If your actions give the impression that something routine has a higher priority, guests will become irritated and you'll be playing catch-up all night.

Grossly Inaccurate Estimates of Waiting Time
You can't get it right every time, but you can make a game of seeing how close you can be. At the least, you should keep guests informed of the status of their wait so they won't feel abandoned.

False Familiarity
The wrong name issue also extends to false familiarity. This usually happens when the server gets the guest's name from the credit card and calls the guest by the first name on the card, despite the fact there is no previous relationship.

For example, my legal first name is William so that's what it says on my credit cards, but nobody who knows me ever calls me that. If I receive a phone call asking for William, it immediately signifies a telemarketer on the line. Last names are constants, though, so you are much safer to refer to guests as Mr. or Ms until or unless they ask you to be less formal.

Sitting Down on the Job
We all get tired, but you can never take a break when you're on stage. The staff should always look like they're ready to respond to the needs of their guests, so give some thought to where and how often your crew can get off their feet and re-charge.

Insincere Smiles
A smile with no true feeling behind it is worse than no smile at all. When you put the same attention toward creating as positive an atmosphere for your staff as you do for your guests, smiles will become more natural and spontaneous.

Bad Attitude at the Greeter Station
The old cliché is that you don't get a second chance to make a first impression. Nowhere is that more important than when guests first walk in the door. A disinterested greeter – or worse, one who is rude or abrupt – drops the guests' mood immediately, setting the tone for the way they'll view everything that happens afterward.

Not Keeping Guests Informed of the Status of Their Wait

Delays happen and most people understand that the restaurant doesn't have total control of how long people stay at the table. Make it a policy to check back with waiting parties several times.

Visit them about halfway through their quoted wait time to let them know you remember they're there. Let them know whenever their wait is likely to be a few minutes longer than quoted. Advise them when their table is getting ready to leave. To *sell* the wait you must *manage* the wait. Guests appreciate and remember your concern.

Mumbled Communications

People can get uninspired attention lots of places. Clear your head, make eye contact, smile and say what you need to say clearly and concisely. Be sure they know you're glad they came.

Unintelligible Speaker at the Drive-up Window

Few things are as frustrating as an inability to communicate. When your guests can't understand what is being asked of them or if they can't make themselves understood easily, they get irritated ... and an angry guest is unlikely to become a happy guest.

Not Thanking Guests as They Leave

How would you feel if you left a friend's home after a pleasant evening and they didn't even say goodbye? It's no different in our industry. A positive last impression validates the guests' experience and makes them feel good about the money they've spent.

Coach your greeters to thank guests for coming and invite them back. Do *not* ask, "How was everything?" The answer to that inane question is always, "It was fine." Mindless questions will only lead to mindless answers.

Be more creative and personal in forming your questions and you will receive more meaningful answers. The most important point is to make sure your thank-you is as warm and sincere as your hello.

Policy Perils

Some negative first impressions result from management policies. If you see a guest annoyance that can be eliminated by changing your position on something, do it. After all, enough can go wrong without creating more problems for you and your patrons.

Not Honoring an Advertised Policy

For example, if you advertise that you accept reservations, guests will be annoyed if you refuse to do so. Whatever you include in your ads is a commitment. Your ad in the Yellow Pages commits you for a year. The information on your website is a promise. Once you've gone public with a policy, it's hard to modify it. If you have changed a policy, your staff needs permission to use their initiative should a problem arise.

Not Accepting Reservations

I respect the reasons why some restaurants don't take reservations, I just understand you'll alienate some people if you don't. A survey of Amex cardholders in South Florida determined the ability to get reservations was a prime reason they selected a restaurant.

Trying to reserve *all* your tables can easily get you backed up when a party lingers, but perhaps you could take limited reservations during the evening and seat everyone else as they arrive.

Some restaurants only accept limited reservations (via a private phone number) for their VIP members. Others address the issue by allowing guests to call the restaurant and place their names on the waiting list, shortening the wait when they get there.

Sticky Situations

There are several scenarios that can get the dining experience off to a rocky start. They may be created by house policies, lack of training or just by chance, but whatever the cause, it's not as much what happens as how skillfully you handle it.

Asking about Reservations in an Empty Dining Room

Obviously, with an empty dining room, whether the party has a reservation is irrelevant. You may want to know if they're on your reservation list, but don't make that your first question. Instead, on the way to the table, asking if they'd previously called in can be a smoother way to get the information you need.

Accepting a Reservation, Then Making Guests Wait

Guests may tolerate a short wait, but anything over five minutes defeats the purpose of making the reservation and suggests a system problem. Until you have a solution, you must do something to make it right for those who had an unexpected delay. Often a complimentary cocktail or appetizer can help smooth things over.

Having to Wait Hours for a Table

In the industry, we see a waiting line as a positive, but it's not a high point for many of your guests, even if it does attest to your popularity. If you must make a guest wait for a table, sell the wait.

Coach your greeter to be sensitive when they explain where guests can wait and what you can do for them until a table is ready. If you have an appetizer menu in the bar, suggest a couple of choices. If you have a drink special, point it out. Give them a dinner menu to study. Assure the guest you'll remember they're waiting. They must feel personally served, not efficiently processed.

Waiting in Line When Empty Tables Are Visible

I understand why this might happen, but there's no reason you can give that will make any sense to your guests. Seat them at once, get them a menu and a drink and get on with the evening!

Snobbish Seating

Don't reserve "VIP" tables that sit empty for hours while you divert paying guests onto cramped two-tops in the middle of the dining room. No guest is more important than the one you're serving at that moment.

Reservations are one thing, but when you hold back special tables for special people that may or may not show up, the message you deliver to everyone else is that somehow they're less important to you. Snobbish seating is a disrespectful practice that can only carry a huge cost in lost business over time.

Lost Reservations

It's not worth a confrontation with a guest. Even if you suspect the person is not being truthful, smile and do your best to make it right. Tell them what you *can* do for them, not what you *can't*. A loud argument will bring down the mood of the everyone within earshot. Better yet, design your reservation system with enough slack to be able to accommodate the unexpected.

No Place for Guests to Wait

If you provide takeout service, where do people wait to pick up their orders? Is there a place for non-smokers to wait other than a smoke-filled lounge? Must smokers wait outside in the weather? Can families or elderly guests sit somewhere comfortable until their tables are ready? Remember that serving the guest also applies to those who are not yet eating.

No Place to Hang a Coat

This isn't a disaster but it *is* an inconvenience. Invest in a few coat trees, put some hooks in the walls or even convert a closet for this purpose. If there's no space in the lobby area, carry the coats to the manager's office. Bring them back when guests are ready to leave.

Seating Snafus

Just when you thought it was safe to go into the dining room, I must warn you about losing points in the seating process.

Racing Off to the Table, Leaving Guests in the Dust

This is probably the fault of a job description that focus on activities instead of results. If you tell a greeter her job is to seat people, you can get mechanical compliance. If you define a job in terms of what you want to accomplish, you'll get something different.

What if you told the greeters their job was to create a positive first and last impression? What if the greeters had the responsibility to assure that guests feel cared-for and welcome? What if part of the job was to see if they could learn something about the guest or tell them something about the restaurant (if they were receptive to it?)

What if you defined an appropriate table as one the guests would enjoy? It changes everything and involves the greeter in the process of guest gratification.

Dropping Menus and Leaving Before Guests Are Seated

The greeter's job is to create a positive first impression, not just to deliver menus to the table. That means assisting with the seating, taking coats as necessary and setting the stage for the server's arrival. Coach your staff on the human aspects of their position as well as the mechanical ones.

Seating Smokers Near Non-Smokers

If your state still permits indoor smoking and you don't have separate dining areas, expect complaints any time you seat smokers and non-smokers in close proximity. Despite the best efforts of your ventilation system, it seems smoke will always move toward those who can't tolerate it!

If there is an issue, smokers will feel attacked and non-smokers will feel violated. When a dispute arises (and you can count on it), both groups just get irritated and have a less pleasant experience.

Accepting a Bribe for Preferential Seating

This is extortion that only serves the ego of the person asking for the spiff. Have a clear policy against this and dismiss those involved if it happens. Also be sensitive enough to make it right with any other guests who may have been inconvenienced by the incident.

Seating a Guest at a Dirty or Unset Table

There's no excuse for seating a guest before the table is ready. No matter how busy you are, you must clean and set the table before you can start the meal service anyway. You don't do yourself any favors by putting a party down too soon.

In a cafeteria, guests seat themselves, so if there is a breakdown in prompt table clearing, guests may be *forced* to sit at an unclean table, particularly during the rush. Stay ahead of it or suffer the backlash.

Seating a Guest in a "Black Hole"

A black hole is a table that's not on anyone's station. The problem, of course, is that nobody knows it has happened until it happens. Take extra care at pre-shift meetings to assign all stations and that every table is clearly someone's responsibility. Be sure everyone knows which tables are on their station. (The occasional pop quiz can help.) Do a walk-around if necessary. Watch carefully during shift changes and pay attention to station adjustments as newly-arriving staff comes on the floor or as duties consolidate when the rush is winding down.

Seating Guests at a Table with a Tip on it

It is unprofessional to seat guests at a table that's not completely theirs. With children, it can even be dangerous because they'll put the money in their mouths! Give bussers permission to pick up tips and give them to the appropriate server. If a server has a problem with this, handle it individually.

Not Allowing Guests to Change Tables

To be successful, the restaurant must exist for the enjoyment of the guests, not the convenience of the staff or management. There is seldom a justifiable reason not to accommodate so simple a request, particularly in a half-empty dining room.

Handing Guests the Wrong Menus

If you have separate menus for each meal period, be sure your staff can distinguish between them. While having to exchange menus is not a "hanging offense," it does show a lack of attention to detail and is a distraction you can easily avoid.

Buffet Boo-Boos

A few important elements influence a guest's first impression of your cafeteria or buffet before they even experience your wonderful food. Take another look at your operation and see if you are creating any of these problems for yourself.

Confusing Traffic Flow
Your guests' experience is more pleasant when they have a clear idea of how the line is arranged. If you cannot change the layout, consider signs that clearly identify the start of the line and indicate where guests can find specific types of foods.

Serving Lines That Look the Same Every Day
You can become the destination of choice even when people don't have a choice! The danger of a built-in clientele for an operation like an employee cafeteria is that you continually need to show a new face to prevent boredom. An unchanging routine is also boring for your staff. The only sure way to sustain this variety over time is to get your staff involved in finding new and different ways to present your fare. Their good ideas will surprise you!

Long Delays at the Cashier Station
While guests are waiting to pay, their food is getting cold. Even the most skillfully prepared and attractively presented dishes will not make people happy when they're lukewarm.

You are in the service business even in a self-service environment, so schedule enough cashiers to meet the requirements of the crowd. Delayed guests are unhappy, and unhappy guests soon start dining elsewhere ... or bringing their own lunches.

Not Being Able to Bypass Portions of the Line
It's frustrating to wait in a serving line behind people who are taking time over something you don't want. Give some thought to how patrons can bypass bottlenecks and get their meals faster.

Bonus Points

Everybody likes pleasant surprises. These little unexpected touches are opportunities to improve your score and put your guests in a better mood. They help make up for any lapses in the operation and give people something to talk about to their friends.

Using the Guest's Names Respectfully ... and Correctly

No matter how casual your restaurant is, it is impolite to address guests by their first names until and unless they ask you to do it. You will never lose points by being too polite. The more often you use the guest's name, the more often you will see the guest.

Opening the Front Door for Guests

Olive Garden once had a staff person whose sole job was to open the door and greet guests enthusiastically. Christopher's in Phoenix went one step farther and had their captains walk guests to the valet stand. They found it an excellent way to provide personal service and learn what guests *really* thought of the evening.

Finding a Seat for Waiting Guests

When a guest has to wait, too often they're just waved off in the direction of the bar. Consider having one of your staff escort them to a place where they can wait comfortably. It may be in the bar or just a spot in your waiting area. This offers one more chance to sell the wait, offer drinks or appetizers and reinforce your commitment to their well-being.

Free Beverages During the Wait

The Pacific Café opened in San Francisco back in the mid 70s. It was in a residential neighborhood out toward the beach and the weather was often cold and foggy. On top of that, it was a small place and had virtually no space inside for guests to wait.

The night they opened, the manager saw a waiting line extending down the sidewalk. Feeling sorry that his guests had to wait in the cold, he offered free wine to everyone in line until he could seat them. Needless to say, the waiting patrons loved it and word of the practice spread quickly.

The next night, the waiting line was back and the manager gave away more wine. A tradition had been established. Pacific Café's popularity (and the complimentary wine) continues to this day.

Somewhere there's an accountant going crazy! Yes, Pacific Café has given away a lot of wine, but they've also set themselves apart, had a line out the door for forty years ... and sold a lot of dinners!

4
Table Transgressions

When guests reach the table, what they see and feel is an important part of their impression of your restaurant. If you don't stop and read the silent messages delivered by your tables and the items on them, you're leaving yourself open for potential problems.

Many tabletop issues can be traced to poor training of the bussers. Particularly since bussers are typically filled by workers in their first jobs, you can't assume anything. They must understand *what* you want done, of course, but they also need to know *how* you want it done and *why* it's important things be done that way. The more they understand about their role in overall guest gratification, the better they will do.

Setup Shortcomings

When guests arrive at the table, the condition of the table settings is their first clue about your professionalism and how seriously you address the details.

Silverware Set Askew
The ability to quickly reset a table is an important skill for a busser to master. Still, if the settings aren't neatly and accurately placed, speed is irrelevant. Be sure they know how you want the place setting put down and that they do it that way consistently.

Since you reset tables in view of your guests, watch the moves and develop a little choreography if necessary. The process should be smooth, silent and sanitary. Train bussers to handle silverware only by the handles, to pick up glassware only by the stem or the lower third ... and to never, ever put their fingers in the glasses!

Forks with Bent Tines
Given how many people handle silverware from the time you clear the table until you reset it, it's discouraging this problem exists at all. Train your dish crew to be aware of the condition of the silver as they load and unload the dish machine and coach your bussers and servers to check each piece of silverware before they place it.

Tabletop That's Not Picture Perfect

Particularly if service is slow, guests may find themselves with nothing else to do but study and critique the tabletop. When setting the table, it's not enough just to get it done, it must be done neatly and accurately. Be sure they (and you) understand what that means.

Tables Set with Napkins in the Glasses

I appreciate the look this can bring to the dining room. The problem arises if the glasses are later used for water or wine. The napkins have been well-handled before they're placed into the glassware, transferring that handling to the inside of the glass.

If you later use the same glass for water or wine, guests can (rightly) question its sanitary condition. If napkins in the glassware are part of your tabletop, don't stop the practice. Just be sure to remove the glasses when your guests have unfolded their napkins.

Unevenly Folded Napkins

If you go to the expense of a linen napkin, be sure it is neatly and evenly folded. Many napkins are far from rectangular when they return from the linen service. If this is an issue for you, use a different napkin fold that lessens the problem.

Wrinkled Paper Napkins or Placemats

Paper is more delicate than linen. Once paper has been crumpled, you cannot smooth it out again, so be sure to properly store and protect your paper supplies. You won't gain any points if your napkins look like they've already been used!

Flimsy Flatware

Lightweight silverware feels cheap in the hand. It may be less expensive to purchase initially, but it conveys a second-class image. Besides, it bends more easily and has a shorter working life than more substantial stock. Be sure your flatware is at least as heavy as what your guests are likely to be using at home.

Stained Paper Napkins

It is common practice to store paper napkins in the service stands with the coffee and condiments, but one spill on a stack of napkins sends the whole pile into the trash. Rearrange your service stands to store napkins well away from anything that could spill. A high shelf is safest. Alert bussers and servers to watch for stained paper napkins and never set a table with a napkin that is less than perfect. Be sure there is enough light in the service stands to identify stained napkins before they get taken to the table.

Tables Not Completely Set When Guests Are Seated
Were you ever checked into a hotel room where the beds still hadn't been made or the bathroom was still dirty? How did that make you feel? No matter how busy it is, you don't save any time by seating a party before the table is ready for service. You can't serve the table before everything is in place anyway and it delivers a message to guests that they're not that important to you.

Mismatched China or Silverware
If this is part of your concept, fine ... but if guests don't know you're doing it on purpose, they'll think you don't know the difference! Be sure to keep the pattern numbers of your china and flatware to avoid mismatches on future orders. Every few years, you might consider upgrading your china to a new look, just to break the monotony for your guests and staff.

Flimsy Disposables
If single service plates or utensils are part of your operating plan, get the highest quality products you can afford. Outdoor dining requires serviceware substantial enough that the wind can't blow it around. This situation could also require you to install wind screens or abandon disposables entirely, but guests won't have a pleasant experience if they're chasing their serviceware around your patio.

Wet Ashtrays
Where smoking is permitted, clean ashtrays are essential ... but when a guest places a cigarette in a wet ashtray, everyone loses. The guest has a soggy cigarette and you have an angry guest as well as a mess to clean up. Wipe out ashtrays with a dry cloth, paper towel or cocktail napkin just to be sure.

Wet or Sticky Tabletops
I know your Mom taught you not to put your elbows on the table, but you know everybody does it. If their arm (or their wallet, notebook, purse or newspaper) *sticks* to the table, watch out! How are they going to clean themselves up? What are they thinking about you while they are doing it?

Aggravating Accessories

When you become aware of the impact your table decor has on the dining experience, you should automatically pay more attention to it in your purchasing, training and coaching.

Dead or Wilted Flowers on the Tables

Fresh flowers require attention. At least every morning, inspect all the flowers to be sure they still enhance the look of the table. If they're getting a little weak, replace them. Trying to stretch them a day too long will undo all the good they do you in the first place.

Incomplete Table Appointments

Have you ever been at a table that had a salt shaker but no pepper? How about two peppers and no salt? This usually happens after you've combined several tables to seat a large party and are quickly returning them to their normal positions.

If staff isn't paying full attention when resetting tables, condiments can be switched around. This creates a real annoyance for guests whose meals get cold while they're trying to flag down someone who can get them some salt!

Poor Quality Artificial Flowers on the Table

Whatever you put on the table should reflect favorably on your restaurant and enhance the dining experience for your guests. Saving a few dollars with cheap plastic flowers tells your guests you take shortcuts and don't care too much about how things look.

They may make some assumptions (right or wrong) about how much you care about the other aspects of your operation. If you use artificial flowers on the table, find high quality silk ones.

Unadorned Tabletops

At the least, have *something* decorative on the table in any restaurant or cafeteria. Remember that people don't go out to eat just because they're hungry. A candy bar at their desks will take care of hunger! Dining out should have a more special feel. The decor doesn't have to be elaborate or expensive, just something that reminds them they aren't eating at home!

Centerpieces That Obscure the View

Be sure your decor doesn't interfere with conversation. Vases of tall flowers are often a culprit. Once you get the table looking just the way you want it, have your staff sit in all the chairs. See if it is possible to carry on a conversation. Often the table looks different from a seated position than it does when you are standing.

Physical Follies

This is about the design deficiencies of your seating. Like other design problems, avoid them through awareness and proper planning.

Chipped or Worn Laminate on Tables or Countertops
If your operation has exposed laminate tops, keep an eye on them. When the edges get chipped, repair them. Chipped laminate is a safety and cleaning problem.

When the finish on the top gets worn, replace the top. Worn tops make your entire dining room look rundown. If you have a problem with this, just think the money you're saving on linen. If you *still* have a problem, think of how annoyed your guests get when they have to eat off a shabby table.

Table Tops Too Small for the Service
Just because a table has four sides doesn't mean it can seat four people. Determining the proper table top size takes some planning. There must be room for the place settings, of course, but is there room for the guests to rest their arms? What else are you going to place on the table during the meal and where is it going to go?

You need space for shared appetizers, wine bottles, side dishes, etc. Pizzeria tables must be large enough to accommodate the pizza pan. Cafeterias must allow for trays. The additional money you might make by picking up a few extra seats with small tabletops is not usually worth the points you will lose by crowding your guests.

Chairs That Don't Slide Easily
For guests to be seated, chairs must be pulled out and pushed in. During the meal, guests may wish to change position or leave the table. Be sure the legs of your chairs have casters or slides that make movement as easy as possible. It's annoying to wrestle with a heavy chair that refuses to slide across a dining room carpet.

Tight Booths
The advantage of booths is that you can get more seating in a given area than you can with tables and chairs. Of course, if you can't get your guests *into* the booths, that extra capacity doesn't do you much good. When planning booths, be sure the spacing between the back of the bench and the edge of the table is adequate for the typical adult. Having to eat in an unpleasantly tight booth makes for an unpleasant meal. Better to have fewer seats and happier guests.

No Wide Chairs for Wide People

A friend of mine was a former heavyweight judo champion. As you might expect, he was a *big* guy! One of his pet peeves was that restaurants often had no chairs he could fit into.

Standard armchairs are often too tight. If the restaurant has armless chairs, the situation is a little easier, but not much. Booths were nearly always out of the question.

There are enough wide people out there these days that it's worth having a few wider chairs available. They will appreciate it and are likely to become regular patrons. Remember that wide people often got that way by having larger-than-average appetites!

Uncomfortable Seating

Sometimes the physical design of a chair just isn't comfortable. Even chairs that *look* comfortable can be unpleasant to sit in for long periods. Before you buy, get a sample and it an extended "butt test." Is the height right? Is it easy to get in and out of? Is it comfortable?

If you're after fast turnover, you may not want your chairs to be *too* comfortable. The rule of thumb is that the higher the average check, the longer guests expect to stay and the more comfortable the seating must be.

Table Tops That Aren't Level

There's a difference between wobbly tables and table tops that are not level. Off-level tables are often very solid. Even the most out-of-level tabletop will still hold place settings. The problem is that an off-level surface causes people to feel like something is wrong. This minor annoyance will color their entire dining experience and it will be more difficult for them to fully enjoy their meal.

Booth Seats That Pitch Forward

This is usually a symptom of home-built booths. Improper pitch causes your guests to slide toward the table and spend the entire evening pushing themselves back. When the seat pitches forward, it takes constant muscle tension for guests to maintain a comfortable dining position.

By the end of the evening, they may be exhausted from the struggle! Usually, we want the dining experience to be more relaxing than that. If you have the problem, either rebuild the seats or install new cushions that correct for the slope.

Condiment Calamities

You fuss over the food that you prepare in the kitchen but have you thought about the edibles that already are on the table - condiments, crackers and such? Here are some aggravating points to watch for.

Salt and Pepper Shakers Sticky, Greasy or Half-Empty
Make wiping down the shakers a regular part of the table setup process. This is also the time to check to be sure the tops are on tight, particularly if you have playful younger guests!

Pepper Shakers So Full They Won't Pour
This was the phenomenon that originally piqued my interest in the minute details of the guest experience. It seems counter-intuitive but it's true: fill a pepper shaker to the top and it won't work. Make your staff aware of this fact and train them to leave about half an inch of space at the top of the pepper shaker.

Ketchup Bottles Coated at the Neck
This applies to almost every condiment container that you refill and is everybody's complaint. Make sure to wipe the necks clean every night and every time you refill the bottles. Better yet, find another way to serve ketchup, such as ramekins or small portion cups.

Condiment Containers That Are Nearly Empty
Condiment containers often gets overlooked in the heat of the rush. Check *all* condiments as part of your regular sidework. Take those that are less than one-third full out of the dining room. Either use them in the kitchen or donate them to a shelter or food bank.

> **NOTE:** While refilling condiment containers is common practice, be aware that condiment bottles are single use containers. Most health departments do not allow them to be refilled because they can't be properly cleaned and sanitized. There is also the potential for cross-contamination when you pour product from one container into another.

Empty or Partially Used Packets in with the Full Ones
This is most often an issue with crackers and sugar packets. Check for used packets every time you reset a table or take a cracker basket to the table and make it standard practice to empty the cracker baskets at the end of the day and start fresh the next morning. Save the crushed packets for use in the kitchen. It's also a good idea to regularly empty and clean the sugar caddies.

Salt or Sugar Crusted Inside Dispensers
This problem arises when you've washed the shakers and refilled them before they're completely dry. If possible, wash shakers in the evening and leave them inverted overnight before refilling. Be sure they are on a rack where water can easily drain and where there is free air circulation.

Separated Mustard
Get in the habit of giving the container a shake before taking it to the table. (Make sure the top is on tight first!) Be alert for caked mustard on the rim of the jar. Wipe the mouth of the container clean every night and replace the containers when they get low.

Stained Labels on Condiment Bottles
Nothing detracts from the look of a table like a messy condiment bottle. If you insist on refilling condiment containers (see note on the preceding page), refill the bottle that has the cleanest label , not just the one with the most in it.

Salt or Sugar Too Caked to Pour
This can be a problem in areas of high humidity. A little uncooked rice in the salt shaker will help. Sugar is a little tougher. Either use a sugar shaker that seals tightly or switch to individual packets.

Wet Sugar Packets
If a guest places a wet packet back in the sugar bowl, the next diners will get an unpleasant surprise. Quickly check sugar bowls and packets as you reset the table.

No Sugar Substitute on the Tables
Given the national obsession with weight, sugar substitute is as necessary a condiment as salt or pepper. Stay in touch with your guests to be sure you're offering the brands they prefer.

Loose Tops on the Condiments
Be sure condiment tops are on tight when you bring the container to the table. If a guest absent-mindedly shakes the bottle, you don't want them (or the dining room) sprayed with steak sauce!

Crystallized Honey
Honey dispensers can be an annoyance when the honey is starting to crystalize and turn to sugar. This happens when honey comes in contact with water. When cleaning honey containers, allow them to dry thoroughly overnight before refilling. Any crystallized honey can be used in the kitchen.

Devilish Details

There are a variety of small points that can arise at the table with the potential to distract your guests from having a good time.

Napkins Too Small to Cover the Lap
When a napkin is so small you need one on each knee, you have an irritant! Within limits, the larger the napkin, the more luxurious the experience for the guest. Whether paper or linen, napkins should be substantial, large enough to cover the lap easily and of a material that won't slide onto the floor every time the guest changes position. You usually get what you pay for.

Silverware or Unwrapped Straws on a Bare Tabletop
Guests may assume the tabletop is clean but is it sanitary? Place settings belong on a place mat, napkin or tablecloth, not on a bare tabletop. If additional silverware is needed at the table, place a plate or napkin underneath it. This may appear minor but if it can bother a guest, it should bother you as well. Wrapped straws are not a problem ... and I suggest you *only* serve wrapped straws. If you automatically place a straw in every drink, your usage will be a lot higher than it needs to be.

Ashtrays with More than Two Butts in Them
If you allow smoking, watch ashtrays and regularly replace them. Cover the dirty ashtray with a clean one when you lift it from the table to keep ashes from flying about. Replacing an ashtray that contains a lighted cigarette requires you to handle the cigarette, a practice you definitely want to avoid. Either wait until the guest has the cigarette in their hand or has stubbed it out.

Napkins In the Dispenser Backwards
Filling napkin dispensers is a simple task, yet how often have you tried to take a napkin only to find there was nothing to grab? This is a symptom of inattention to detail. Coach your crew to not over-fill the napkin dispensers and on the importance of making sure the napkins are placed in the proper position. Make it a practice to remove one napkin after re-filling a dispenser. You'll know at once if you've filled it correctly.

Chewing Gum Under the Table, Counter or Seat
This is like gravity in our business. Whether you enjoy gravity or not, you can't fight it! At least twice a week you need to scrape the chewing gum off the bottom of tables and chairs. Just do it!

Ashtrays That Don't Hold a Cigarette Firmly
Some ashtray designs won't hold a cigarette off the bottom of the ashtray. This causes the cigarette to burn unevenly and annoys the smoker. State and local ordinances aside, it is your decision whether to permit smoking in your establishment or not. If you do, make sure that what you do works for smokers.

No Clean or Safe Place for a Woman to Put Down a Purse
Picture a busy bar in the middle of the Friday night crush. People are everywhere and the floor is awash with spilled Margaritas and beer. What's a woman going to do with a $200 handbag? If she must keep it in her hands, under her arm or in her lap, she'll be uncomfortable. Screw small coat hooks under the table and bar tops to provide a safe place to hang valuables. The ladies will love you!

Knives Too Dull to Cut
My father always impressed upon me the need to use the right tool for the right job. Restaurant knives are no different. Be sure the knives you provide guests will work for the purpose intended. The coward's way out is to use only steak knives in the place setting. A steak knife will cut anything on your menu (I hope), but is not very impressive for spreading butter.

Placing Items on the Table Carelessly
Always *place* items on the table rather than *put* them on the table. Coach your staff to take the extra second required to place items carefully, quietly and respectfully without interrupting a guest's conversation. It's only being considerate.

No Provisions for Wheelchairs
Disabled guests deserve the same comfort and ambiance as other patrons. Make sure some tables near the door can accommodate a wheelchair without the chair sitting in the middle of a traffic lane. It's just common courtesy for people who deserve it.

Bonus Points

Everybody likes pleasant surprises. These little unexpected touches are opportunities to improve your score and put your guests in a better mood. They help make up for any lapses in the operation and give people something to talk about to their friends.

Interesting Flower Arrangements

This may only be practical in more upscale restaurants, but an impressive, professionally-designed floral piece at the entry is both unexpected and memorable. If it helps keep you prominently in the minds of your guests, it is worth your consideration.

Attractively Coordinated Tabletops

Often, the look of tabletops in independent restaurants are not the result of planning or conscientious design, it just happens, driven by whatever seems to look the best when you browse the restaurant supply store or look through a catalog. There's nothing wrong with those sources, but you're likely end up with what everyone else has.

Take a clue from the better restaurants and hotels and consider your tabletop as a complete picture. Coordinate china, glassware, silver, table coverings, napkins and accessories to create a unified look that will have real impact on your guests.

Ask your supplier for catalogs that include items they don't keep in stock. In the end, the cost may not be too much different from the piecemeal approach, but you will have a signature look that will elevate your image in the eyes of your guests.

5
Environmental Apathy

There's been much talk about the condition of the environment and what we must do to protect it. What about the environment in your restaurant? What condition is *it* in and what are you doing to save it?

We call the internal environment of a restaurant atmosphere or ambiance – the "feel" of the place. It is a major decision factor when people go out to restaurants. The difficulty in managing atmosphere in your dining room is that you quickly become too familiar with it. After awhile, you just don't notice the details.

Your environment is a feast (or famine) for the senses. Sight, sound, smell and touch all combine to create the stage setting for the dining experience. Don't leave it to chance.

Unsightly Scenes

Most environmental irritants relate to what your guests see as they look around your restaurant. Fortunately, not all your guests will notice every one of these points. Still, how many of these potential annoyances will you allow to persist?

Table Linen with Small Holes, Rips or Burns
People dine at "white tablecloth" restaurants for a refined dining experience. It makes no sense to spend large sums on the finest ingredients and the most skilled chefs only to have the diner distracted by holes in the linen. If you're not getting the quality of linen you need, make a fuss about it. You don't have to accept everything the linen company sends you. Tell suppliers what you expect and refuse product that doesn't meet your standards.

Flickering Lights
I've been in several restaurants where the lighting level fluctuated repeatedly. Surges happen occasionally but recurring brightening and dimming will drive everyone crazy! If you notice this problem, consult your electrician or public utility to find a solution. Allowing it to continue will eventually empty your restaurant.

Clutter and Junk

Cleanliness is a critical factor in guest satisfaction. Junk and clutter make cleaning impossible and contribute to a dirty feeling in the restaurant. Your guests could conclude that you maintain your kitchen in the same condition and choose to dine elsewhere.

Lighting Too Dim to Easily Read the Menu

Your guests cannot order what they cannot read. This is a particular annoyance for older diners who dislike reminders that their eyes are less sharp. The options are to raise lighting levels, issue flashlights to all your servers or have some menus with larger type.

Sometimes, changing paper or ink colors on the menu will improve the contrast and make it more readable. Every so often, watch your guests as they read your menu. Be alert for signs of difficulty and take any necessary corrective action.

Sun or Glare in Diners' Eyes

Large windows can be a real attraction for your guests. However, sun in a guest's eyes will always distract them both from their meal and their companions. If your windows face the sun, you must invest in window shades.

Tinted glass can help reduce glare and reduce the potential fading sun can cause to furnishings. Often, more solid shades are needed. If you have solid shades, be sure to lower them when the sun strikes the dining room and raise them when the problem has passed. It is distracting to have the shades down when they're not needed.

Personal Items of the Staff in View

Your guests come to the restaurant for a complete change of environment. Personal articles are a distraction from that escape. The most satisfactory solution is to provide staff lockers for personal items. If space is tight, perhaps you can put lockers along one wall of a wide hallway. Where there's a will, there's a way.

If you can't do that, create a secure space for personal articles out of sight of the guests. Bear in mind you can't store personal items in food preparation areas. Personally, it even bothers me when I find purses stored in the service stations. Your guests won't see it but it's still a poor sanitation practice.

Poorly Lighted Stairways or Hallways

Dim lighting causes people to feel less secure and can lead to more accidents. Carefully design and control the lighting throughout the restaurant to enhance the sense of well-being for guests and staff.

Light Glaring from the Kitchen

Lighting sets the mood of the dining room while lighting levels in the kitchen are far brighter. You must baffle kitchen light carefully to prevent destroying the dining atmosphere for your guests. This problem becomes more acute if you have an exhibition cooking area or an open pass-thru window from the kitchen.

Harsh Lighting

Lighting that glares or casts harsh shadows makes both people and food look bad. Control all the lights in the restaurant by dimmers so you can adjust the lighting intensity to the most flattering levels. Bear in mind you need light from the sides as well as from above and continually adjust lighting levels throughout the day.

Seasonal Decorations Still up Weeks after the Holiday

You know how tacky it looks when campaign signs are still in place weeks after an election? Your restaurant is no different. Unless out-of-season decorations are part of your concept, the celebration is not over until you've packed the decorations and safely stored them away for next year.

When it comes to holiday decorations, timing is everything. Ideally the decorations are removed the morning after your main holiday celebration. This is when your staff is least likely to want to take them down, but life is like that. Be sure your planning includes scheduling the timely removal of seasonal items.

Chipped Paint on Windowsills or Door Frames

The trim takes the most abuse and it can easily get away from you. At least quarterly, examine the windowsills, baseboards and door frames with a critical eye. Scrub or repaint as necessary to keep the room looking fresh and attractive. Door frames take a particularly heavy beating. Clean them regularly to prevent them becoming soiled or sticky.

Messy Pile of Newspapers or Magazines in the Lobby

Particularly if your restaurant is a breakfast destination, you will accumulate newspapers earlier guests leave behind. Making these available to other diners is a homey touch that can be a plus.

The problem is not having a place to keep used newspapers neatly available. The greeter is the most likely staff member to handle this task. Support their efforts with a rack, box or table where they can neatly place the reading material. Recycle it at the end of the day.

Carrying Trash Through the Dining Room During Meal Hours
My first restaurant in San Francisco was on the third level of the shopping arcade in a major downtown development. The only route from the kitchen to the trash was through the dining room, across the patio and down the service elevator. My second restaurant was on the second floor of a building in Sausalito where the only route for trash was down the main entry stairs.

Believe me, when you have this challenge, scheduling is essential! You must remove all trash during the slack periods, no matter how small the quantities might be. If you don't stay on top of this, you can find your production capacity literally choked on garbage in the middle of the rush with no pleasant way to fix it!

Bus Tubs Full of Dirty Dishes
This is particularly annoying next to guest traffic lanes. If you use bus tubs, see how creative you can be about keeping them out of sight. Admittedly, concealing bus tubs may create additional cleaning requirements. Still, you can control cleaning more easily than you can control the reactions of your guests when you keep garbage on display in the dining room.

Uneven Pictures on the Wall
Maybe it's the rotation of the earth that causes picture to tilt after awhile. Of course, you can solve the problem by screwing pictures directly to the walls, but if you hang pictures more conventionally, use two wires and two hooks about eight inches apart. Check the pictures regularly to be sure they remain level. Small pieces of adhesive velcro between the picture and the wall can also help.

Fluorescent Lights in the Dining Room
Fluorescent lights can be terrific in the kitchen but disastrous in the dining room. You can't dim them without very expensive controls, so you have no control of your lighting levels. Worse yet, the blue-white light spectrum from some fluorescent tubes can make your food look off-color and unappetizing. Don't use them. Period.

Un-Cleared Tables
The most attractive decor in a dining room is fannies on chairs, not dirty dishes on tables. The excuse I often hear for an un-cleared dining room is that the rush just ended. If so, why isn't the crew busily clearing and re-setting tables? When the rush is over, only the amateurs take a break. The pros get the room ready for the next rush before they relax.

Jumbled Pile of Tray Stands in the Dining Room

Constant use is no excuse for disorderly storage of tray stands. The solution is to make sure there's a specific place set aside for tray stands and that staff promptly returns all stands to this spot.

Be sure the spot you choose is convenient or you'll only make the problem worse. Your dining room staff can identify the best spots. Once you've determined the location, do your best to make the stands less visible to your guests. Perhaps placing a tall plant on each side of the spot will be enough. The answer depends on your decor and traffic patterns.

Inconsistent Elements of Decor

Would you feel right about a Moroccan restaurant in a log cabin? (I actually know of one, but was never drawn to try it.) I usually see this issue when a restaurant has been recycled from another concept and the owner has tried to spend as little money as possible. The theory is good; the practice, however, is not.

Inconsistent decor creates is false economy and creates a disconnect in your guests. If they don't perceive your operation as a completely new or credible restaurant, you may remain saddled with the sins and bad reputation of the previous operation.

Continual Renovation or Construction

Constant upgrading is important to keep you competitive, but do the major work as quickly as possible and preferably when the restaurant is closed. You are investing the time and money to create guest comfort, not inconvenience.

Dining in a construction zone is not most people's idea of a relaxing evening and they may take their business elsewhere until you complete the project. If the work drags on, they may develop other dining habits.

Soiled or Faded Drapes

We take draperies for granted because their changes are so subtle. Over time, draperies exposed to strong sunlight will change color, so keep a fabric sample on file and periodically compare it to the condition of what's in use.

All drapes become soiled. Slap them with your hand. If you see a cloud of dust, it's time to vacuum or send them out for cleaning. Drapery cleaning is not an overnight project, so have it done when you close the restaurant for a short time for other reasons, a rare occurrence for most operators.

Plan B: When you plan the restaurant, make all windows in a room the same size and buy a spare set of drapes. This allows you to rotate draperies and clean them one at a time. You'll never have to close for cleaning and your drapes will last longer.

Shades Hanging Unevenly in the Dining Room

Assign someone the responsibility to monitor the appearance of the dining room throughout the day. You might want to make this a task for the last person who reported for work. New arrivals are more objective than someone who has been in the room all day. Remember your guests are always new arrivals and will notice anything that's out of alignment.

Draperies Hanging off the Track

Make this inspection part of your morning routine. Most drapes attach with simple hooks that can come loose if anyone disturbs the material. Operate each drape before the restaurant opens to check the integrity of the mountings and take care of any problems at once. It is a small detail in a business where you measure success by attention to small details.

Broken Wallboard or Plaster

You must maintain the physical integrity of the building. You don't always have control over the events that cause damage to the walls but you always have control over the repair efforts. In the food preparation areas, broken walls are a health hazard. In guest areas, broken walls tell the world you run a shoddy operation.

Make all repairs at once. If a guest sees the same problem two visits in a row, you may not get a third chance. After you make the repair, analyze the cause of the accident to see how you can prevent a recurrence. Rolling carts cause many wall problems. Often bumpers on the carts or corner protection strips will avert future damage.

Staff Disturbing the Dining Room

A staff break room is just a dream for most operators. If the crew eats standing up in the kitchen, it is a health department violation, so the only option may be to use the dining room.

If the staff eats in the presence of your guests, they must conduct themselves in the same manner as your guests. If they are raucous or disruptive, it will reflect poorly on your restaurant. Guests will sense a "Jekyll and Hyde" nature to your crew and trust them a little less.

Sloppy, Handmade Signs

Wall signs may be appropriate in some casually-themed operations but are rarely proper in more upscale spots. If you choose to have signs in the dining room, be sure they have the same level of finish as the rest of the decor. Have signs professionally made, even for those you only plan to display for a few days. The cost is small and you can reuse signs for any daily specials that repeat periodically. Always verify spelling with a culinary dictionary or web search.

Burned-out Light Bulbs

Checking and replacing light bulbs is a daily duty whether you like it or not. The difficulty is usually that you don't know if a bulb is out until you need to turn the lights on and when it's time to do that, it's often too late to replace the bulbs.

To stay ahead of burnout, you must keep a supply of bulbs on hand. If access is difficult or awkward, such as with recessed lights in a high ceiling, invest in a bulb-changer – essentially a suction cup on the end of an extension pole. Bulb changers allow you to replace inoperative bulbs without dragging a ladder into the dining room.

Obviously Amateur Repairs

Do-it-yourself repairs are an economic necessity for many operators. If local building codes allow and the repair meets professional standards, save the money and do the work yourself. But if the work is illegal or poorly done, it represents expensive savings. Everything in your restaurant must meet the same professional standards. You don't cut corners on your food, don't cut corners on the physical integrity of your building.

Leaks in the Ceiling

Unfortunately, the only way you typically discover the roof leaks is when the water comes through the ceiling! You seldom see the roof, so you rarely think about. While it's fresh in your mind, call a local roofing contractor to find out how often your particular roof needs re-coating. Include this expense in your long term capital budget, regularly put money aside for it, and repair the roof before it can become an annoyance to your guests.

Disintegrating Carpet

There comes a time in the life of every carpet when it must be replaced. Conscientious operators make the replacement before the need is too obvious. Trying to stretch an extra six months from a deteriorated carpet may defer a few thousand dollars of capital costs, but at the expense of alienating a few thousand guests.

Duct Tape Holding Carpets Together

Thank God for duct tape! Without it, most restaurants would fall apart! A roll of duct tape should be included in every restaurant tool kit. (You *do* have a decent tool kit, don't you?)

But did you know duct tape is available in other colors besides the standard silver? If you must use tape for a temporary repair, pick a color that closely matches the material you're repairing. At the same time, make a call to someone who can make a permanent repair. Duct tape will work as a temporary fix in emergencies, but it's only an acceptable long term solution on ducts!

Deferred Maintenance

Deferred maintenance is a polite way of saying you've let your place slide to a point where its condition has become noticeable. Decisions to delay upkeep activities always make sense at the time.

The problem is that eventually the work must be done. As the old TV ad said, "Pay me know or pay me later." The longer you delay, the more expensive the repair is likely to be. Meanwhile, your business just feels shabby.

Guests don't feel good about being in a drab restaurant. The longer the condition persists, the fewer guests return. The fewer guests return, the less likely you can afford the repairs. The only way out is never to get into this position in the first place. Do what you have to do to make your restaurant reflect your professionalism.

Broken Tiles on the Floors or Walls

Broken tiles are unsightly and pose a cleaning and sanitation issue as well. Take a minute to examine the physical integrity of the tiles at least once a week. Repair cracked tiles promptly. Be sure to keep some spare tiles and grout on hand for future repairs.

Broken Windows

You must replace broken glass immediately. Aside from being yet another distraction you don't need, broken glass can cause injury, encourage break-ins and give your place a shoddy reputation.

Since the odds are that you'll have to replace some glass eventually, it's prudent to establish a relationship with a glass company before the need arises. Have them survey your restaurant to get familiar with what you might need. If you learn replacements for particular windows are a special order item, at least you won't be shocked if/when you have to place that order.

Offensive Decor
Avoid decor that might alienate your guests. Many people are disturbed by stuffed animals, snakes and such. They may have an objection to killing animals or an allergy to the fur. They may think the trophies are dirty and present a sanitation problem ... and they may be right on all those counts. Remember that offensiveness is in the mind of the beholder.

Obnoxious Noises

Gathering spots usually have a higher noise level than an operation designed to be a sanctuary from an active world. There are extremes in both directions and finding the right sound level requires you know your guests. Here are a few considerations to keep in mind:

Background Music That Intrudes on Conversation
Whether your music is foreground or background, the appropriate music level depends on the type of restaurant. Still, even a lively place can have sound so loud it causes people to complain.

People go to restaurants for social reasons and every element of the operation should enhance that social motive. If the music interferes with conversation, it will only be attractive to people who don't want to talk. Needless to say, the more formal the venue, the more subdued the appropriate sound level.

Radios Blaring from the Kitchen
Is there something genetic about kitchen workers that requires music blasting in their ears at all times? This is a constant struggle in many restaurants, particularly where the production crew feels disconnected from the activity in the dining room.

Help them understand the reason to modulate or prohibit kitchen radios is the noise pollution it creates for guests. The solution may be to extend the restaurant sound system into the kitchen. The use of digital players with headphones takes the listener out of the communication loop ... and you may be held liable for hearing loss.

Loud Entertainment
The bar is usually the loudest area of a restaurant. If you want simultaneous activity in the bar and the dining room, consider some serious sound baffling in the walls between the two areas. If your bar gets busy after the dining room closes, a sliding partition will let you to expand into the dining room.

Kitchen Noise That Reaches the Dining Room
Commercial kitchens are noisy by nature. Clanging pots and pans, shouted orders and whirring machines all add to the noise level. If you have exhibition cooking, this problem can be even more severe.

In new construction, you can position the kitchen to reduce the problem or sound transfer. In existing operations, the answer is more elusive. If you have a problem with noise transfer, insulate the dividing walls or place acoustical tile on the kitchen ceiling. Check the mountings of dishwashers and ventilation fans to be sure they don't vibrate and cause extra noise.

Harsh Acoustics in the Dining Room
There's a difference between loud sound and harsh acoustics. Loud sound is a function of volume. Harsh acoustics arise when you have poor quality sound to begin with and hard surfaces that bounce those sound waves back into the dining area. Distortion is irritating at any volume level.

If your place has blank walls, hard floors, large windows and bare tabletops, your dining room will likely be an acoustic nightmare. The solution is to break up the reflective surfaces. Discuss the most effective way to do this with an acoustic specialist.

Television Sound and Background Music Simultaneously
This is noise pollution in the extreme. Many people cannot bear the cacophony created by two conflicting sound tracks. If you want everyone to hear the television, pipe the TV sound through the house sound system so all guests can hear the television without the sound blaring. Otherwise, mute the televisions. This assures only one source of sound is heard at a time.

Crying Babies and Disruptive Children
The more you understand what children want and provide it for them, the fewer potential problems you'll have to deal with. You can't stop children from being children, but you can take steps to reduce disturbances.

Don't seat families next to couples or elderly diners. If unruly kids create a disturbance for your other guests, though, you must restore order in the dining room. Ask the parents for their help in quieting their children. They know they're creating a disturbance. It's uncomfortable, but failure to act can alienate your other clientele. Chapter 16 offers more suggestions for making your establishment responsive to the needs of families with children.

Dropping China, Silver or Glassware
Accidents happen, but the crash of breaking dinnerware is particularly jarring. If the staff applauds the accident, it only shows their insensitivity to the impact of excessive noise on the diner's enjoyment (along with their insensitivity to the cost of serviceware and its potential impact on profitability).

Coach your staff in proper methods for handling serviceware and the importance of not trying to carry too much at once. Perhaps carts are a workable solution for your operation. It might also be worthwhile to create an incentive for your crew to reduce breakage.

Clattering Dishes
Train your staff how to clear and set tables quietly. The noise is distracting to everyone in the dining room. Working silently is especially important when clearing extra place settings from a table occupied by a single diner. Clattering dishes only call attention to the lone diner and may make them uncomfortable.

Blaring Television Sets
The speaker system is the weakest part of a television set. When you increase the volume, acoustic distortion can cut some people like a knife. If you want to broadcast television sound throughout a room, tie it in through the sound system. The easiest way to do this is to route your television signal through a DVD player and tap the audio outputs on the back of the device into your sound system. The quality of sound will be better and you can service all your guests without irritation.

Unsettling Odors

The only smells you want wafting through your restaurant are the enticing aromas of your food. When other smells and fragrances enter the air, the result can be unsettling.

Sour Smell in Dining Room or Bar Carpets
The smell comes from bacteria acting on spilled food and beverage and indicates the carpet needs cleaning. Carpet is an inappropriate flooring choice in areas where spills are a regular problem. In a high volume bar or a restaurant catering to families, hard flooring will be far easier to clean and maintain. Regardless of your flooring material, clean up all spills immediately. Mop the floors or vacuum the carpet daily and have a schedule for regular carpet shampooing.

Unpleasant or Antiseptic Smell in the Restrooms

Any smell in the washrooms other than a *very* light un-perfumy scent will make your guests uneasy. You want the facilities to *look* sparkling clean, of course, but not *smell* like they've been freshly cleaned. Fortunately, unscented cleaner/sanitizer solutions are now more available than they once were.

Murky or Smelly Water in the Bud Vase

A vase of fresh flowers on the table is a delight in many restaurants. However, if the same flowers sit in the same water for a few days, the vase starts to smell like low tide in Boston Harbor! If you use fresh flowers, make changing the water in the vases part of your daily sidework and you'll be fine.

Frustrating Feels

The final dimension of dining room atmosphere determines how your guests feel while they are dining. We have discussed several of these points before and they are important enough to mention again here.

Sharp Edges on Tables, Booths or Chairs

Nobody wants their clothes ruined on a social occasion. Even if you do a superb job of handling the situation, the inconvenience of a clothing snag can leave the guest with a bad memory of their experience ... and that can't be good.

If you are responsible for damage to a guest's clothing, there are two things you must do: 1) You must pay the value of a replacement article on the spot. Be generous and don't negotiate the price. 2) You must also consider the "hassle factor" – the inconvenience of having to shop for a replacement article.

The operable rule is Replace Plus One. This could be a free meal or a gift certificate, perhaps both. The actual cost is minimal and will help maintain the guest's habit of dining with you.

Wobbly Tables and Chairs

If you thought matchbooks or cocktail napkins were invented just to help level dining room tables, you know the problem. Wobbly tables and chairs are constant distractions throughout the meal. The discomfort can even overshadow the memory of your fine food and service. Self-leveling feet are available for dining room tables. Ask your restaurant supply or look for them at a trade show.

Slippery Floors
Slick flooring makes guests fear for their safety. Unmarked slick floors can cause physical injury. Neither situation enhances the dining experience. Except for emergency cleanups, only mop floors during slack periods and always put out warning signs to alert guests and staff to a potentially slippery surface.

Overcrowded Tables and Chairs
In some concepts and in some cities, crowded tables are the rule and guests hardly notice. However, a Denver restaurant with New York City seating density will be uncomfortable and unnerving. Guests not accustomed to other diners within inches of them will feel their privacy has been violated, particularly in more upscale concepts.

Overcrowded tables usually mean tighter traffic aisles that create problems for all diners. Passing patrons and staff can constantly bump and jostle a guest seated next to the aisle. Guests in wheelchairs may find the dining room inaccessible. Whatever seating increases you may gain from crowding tables together is likely more than offset by guests who will not return.

Being Seated at a Bad Table
Many restaurants have "good tables" and "bad tables." The good tables are usually by the windows; bad tables are beside the traffic lanes, the kitchen door or the restrooms. Not surprisingly, guests seated at good tables are far more likely to enjoy themselves than guests relegated to the less desirable spots.

If you have an undesirable table, either find a way to make it cool or change your layout to eliminate the problem. If you can't do either, remove the table and put in a plant! You can't afford to seat guests unless you can give them a quality experience.

Torn Coverings on Seats or Booths
The physical integrity of your guests' dining environment can have a bit influence on their dining experience. Inspect booths and chairs for damage every business day. Order immediate repairs when you find a problem. Rips and tears will only get bigger and more ugly over time.

Ask your upholsterer to recommend a good repair kit for temporary patches to vinyl seating. When ordering new seating, design the cushions to be removable and order a few spares. This will let you keep all your seating in service while repairs are made.

Dining Room Too Hot or Too Cold

Proper temperature in the dining room is essential to guest comfort. As the room fills or as guests become more active, there will be an increase in temperature due to body heating. Be sensitive to these changes and adjust your system to compensate.

Be alert for guests who don sweaters or jackets. Watch for patrons wiping their foreheads. When in doubt, ask your guests if the temperature is comfortable for them.

Small Table in the Middle of a Big Room

The smaller the table, the more important that you place it against a wall or a divider. A small table floating in the center of a large room can make guests, particularly a single diner, feel set adrift, conspicuous and uncomfortable.

If your clientele is predominantly couples and you have a lot of two-tops, break up the dining room with low divider walls or planters and place the smaller tables against the dividers. This anchors the table, provides the necessary intimacy and can often increase your seating capacity. In any event, uncomfortable seating makes for an uneasy meal experience.

Broken or Rickety Chairs

If a guest thinks their chair may be unsafe, they'll either have to ask for a replacement or spend the entire meal on edge, hoping it won't collapse under them. In either case, their dining experience will be unnecessarily compromised.

When considering new seating, ask for contact information for other restaurants who are using the same chairs. Ask the managers of these operations for their experiences with the product before you make a final commitment to purchase.

Remove broken chairs from service immediately and replace them with a spare. (You *do* have spare chairs, don't you?) For your own sanity, send broken chairs out for repair or discard them at once. Otherwise, they pile up in the storeroom and choke your operation.

Bonus Points

Everybody likes pleasant surprises. These little unexpected touches are opportunities to improve your score and put your guests in a better mood. They help make up for any lapses in the operation and give people something to talk about to their friends.

Individual Light Dimmers

Many people need brighter light to read the menu and prefer more subdued lighting during the meal. Some solo diners like to read or work while they eat. Obviously one preset level of illumination will not be universally satisfactory.

Particularly if your dining room has high-backed booths, consider wiring the table lighting through individual dimmers. This will allow each guest to have their lighting just the way they want it.

Individual Volume Controls

When we designed the new dining room for the Olympic Training Center, we put two big screen television sets at the end of the room. They were easily visible from every table so we wired the television speakers into the sound system. There were thirteen sets of speakers in the dining room, each set with its own volume control.

Athletes could turn the volume up to hear what was playing or down if they didn't want the interruption. We didn't have to turn the television volume up to the threshold of pain to project to the back of the dining room ... and the sound quality was much better.

Divided Dining Areas

Smaller dining areas create a sense of intimacy and comfort that most guests don't experience in a more open room. Low dividers, half walls, planters, plants and level changes give the dining room visual interest and break up the space.

Private Dining Rooms

There are many reasons for dining out that could be enhanced by privacy. Small business meetings, special occasion celebrations or a romantic evening can become more enjoyable and unique in a private setting.

Private dining rooms can open new markets for business. You can close them off when they're not needed to make the dining area appear comfortably full with fewer people. You can book them for catering functions or open them into the main dining room for use during peak periods. All in all, they are an effective way to make odd spaces more productive.

If you plan to remodel your dining room or build a new operation, give this idea some thought.

6
Menu Missteps

The menu is your blueprint for profit. It determines your image and defines your concept – the shopping list your guests use to spend their money. Often it's your best (or worst) sales-maker.

Your menu is a merchandising tool. It should help you sell the things you want to sell and be well-written: entertaining, informative and representative of your restaurant. Often, prospective guests may decide whether or not to visit solely on the basis of seeing your menu somewhere. What it says to them and what it contributes to your success is a critical factor in your profitability.

Poor Presentations

What you see is what you get in menus. Placing the menu in your guests' hands sets the mood for the evening. If the menu is exciting and interesting, the evening will have more promise. If it creates confusion, diners will be more apprehensive.

Menu Print Too Small to Read Easily
Your guests can't order what they can't read. This is particularly annoying for older diners who dislike reminders that their eyes are less sharp. The options are to either raise the lighting level or use larger type on the menu. Sometimes, changing the paper or ink colors on the menu will improve the contrast and make it more readable. Watch your guests as they read your menu. Be alert for signs of difficulty and take any necessary action.

Menus That Are Difficult to Understand
What are you? Many menus are so disorganized that it's difficult to understand exactly what sort of place the restaurant is. When you create a confusing image in the minds of your guests, they don't know where you fit in their mental Rolodex. People are bombarded with thousands of messages every day. To be memorable, you must stand out in their minds. A clear menu is a major advantage in creating that mental positioning.

Printed Menus with Handwritten Changes

Image is everything. If you make a change, print a new menu. This includes changing the vintage year on wine lists. Handwritten changes and cross-outs are unprofessional. Fortunately, color laser printers and clear café-style menu covers make menu changes much easier. If you have a more graphic menu and still want the ability to make your own changes, print four color shells and overprint the individual items and prices on the computer.

Specials Board Showing Yesterday's Offerings

Promoting expired specials suggests you're not paying attention. Make it a routine responsibility after the meal to erase the specials from the board. This is just part of shifting your perspective to see everything in the restaurant from your guest's point of view.

Illegible Blackboard Specials

Using a blackboard to list specials can be an effective marketing aid. It is an easy solution, but only if your guests can read what's on the board! Be sure the person writing your specials has a neat, easily readable hand. Don't make patrons guess or it could negate the merchandising value of the board.

Recitation of Daily Specials that Goes on Forever

Limit verbal presentations of daily specials to two or three items. Guests can't remember any more information than that anyway, so presenting more choices just wastes the server's time and makes the diner impatient.

I recommend a mini menu explaining the day's specials to leave on the table after the verbal presentation. This way you can advise guests of the details and prices of your specials and they won't feel uncomfortable when they can't remember what you said.

No Daily Special Insert

Everything you do in the restaurant must reflect your concern for guest gratification, attention to detail and professionalism. When one menu at the table has the daily special insert and another doesn't, it creates an additional annoyance for your guests (and the staff who have to correct the error). Coach your greeters to check each menu to be sure the inserts are in place.

Consider changing the color of the menu inserts each day to make it easier to spot outdated ones. You don't need the embarrassment and your guests don't want the inconvenience of getting it wrong.

Menus Too Big to Handle Easily

Menu size should be in relationship to the amount of information you need to present and the size of your tables. It is awkward for guests when the menu is too large to set down on the table.

Misspelled or Grammatically Incorrect Menu Copy

Menu writing is more than simply listing your entrées. Verify the spelling of entries with a culinary dictionary and have a third party carefully proofread the final copy. Avoid long and glowing descriptions in favor of a simple listing of ingredients. After all, who really believes "broiled to perfection" anyway?

Photocopied or Flimsy Menus

If your menu looks like the tenth copy of a copy, you'll look like an amateur, no matter how skillful your menu-writing skills or the quality of your food and service. At the least, a self-printed menu should be a sharp, original laser copy.

Unidentified Items on the Serving Line

The days of "mystery meat" are long past. Guests won't order what they can't identify. Unlabeled items mean you miss an opportunity to merchandise the items on the line.

Admittedly, it can seem like a full time job to stay on top of item labeling, particularly if you make frequent substitutions. Decide if the results are important enough for you to make the extra effort. In my book, if it increases your sales and makes your guests happier, it is always worth doing.

No English Translations

Formality is one thing, snobbishness is another. When a menu does not describe the items in the native language of the guest, it is pretentious and rude. Even if you just explain the items in subtitles, a menu English-speaking guests (or French, Spanish, or whatever the native language of your diners) can read is common courtesy. Unless you have more business than you can handle, you really can't afford to alienate any potential patronage.

Antiquated Menu Presentations

If your menu looks like 1950 and your restaurant doesn't, you have a problem. Outdated menus can lead to an image that you are an outmoded restaurant. I'm not suggesting you should change the items on your menu, just look at how you are presenting them. Often a fresh look can give your operation a boost in the market.

Soiled or Wrinkled Menus or Table Tents

Menus with creases, stains or beverage rings look unappetizing. Those that are greasy, dog-eared or sticky get the meal off to a bad start. The condition of your menus speaks to your attention to detail and can cause patrons to draw conclusions about the cleanliness of your kitchen. If that conclusion is unfavorable, everything you do will be suspect. Inspect all menus before the meal and discard all those that are not perfect.

Listing Items Guests Can't Order at the Time

It is annoying if your guests have to consult their watch when reading your menu. When it's noon and the menu lists items that are not available after 11:30 or items that aren't available before 5:00, you lose points. Be sure your menu tells your guests what you *can* do for them, not what you *can't!* I understand the desire to save some money on printing, but at what cost?

Discrepancy Between Menu Board and Items on the Line

You know how it happens. The items on the line and the menu board are in perfect agreement when you open. As the meal progresses, you sell out of some items and replace them with others.

The switch happens on the line but nobody takes the time to change the menu board. How are your guests going to know what to order? If the menu board lists Lamb Stew when you're actually offering Beef Stroganoff, guests will notice something is wrong before they notice how good the Stroganoff looks.

The easiest solution is to have an electronic menu board or one that uses pre-printed strips instead of changeable letters. It will make changing the board easier. Easy jobs tend to get done while difficult jobs are put off. Do yourself a favor and make it as easy as possible to do the job easily and correctly.

Entrées That Don't Look like Their Photos

For certain concepts, full color photographs on the menu, table tents or wall posters can effectively market entrées. Photographs create expectations in your guests and entice them to order ... but they must be professionally done. It is almost impossible to take a picture yourself that will present the food in all its glory.

Setting enticing expectations is a good thing, but if the item you serve doesn't match the photo or if the portion served differs from its advance visual billing, guests will be disappointed, no matter how good the item turns out to be.

No Dessert Menu

When it's dessert time, presentation is everything. Oral descriptions can only do so much. Guests are unlikely to remember more than two or three items presented verbally. Desserts on the dinner menu are useless. People won't order dessert when they order appetizers and the entrée information is irrelevant to the dessert decision.

Even in casual restaurants, I recommend a separate dessert menu that will merchandise not only desserts, but after dinner drinks and special coffees. You have more to gain than you have to lose. Even with an attractive dessert tray, a separate dessert menu can still be a valuable sales aid.

Menu Jargon

Food Network junkies notwithstanding, not everyone knows what *gastrique* or *gremolata* is ... and the typical diner may not be able to visualize the difference between a *confit* and a *coulis*. Why risk making a guest feel stupid? Technical precision is one thing, but there's no shame in utilizing parenthetical explanations or better yet, just writing menu descriptions in plain English!

Policy Problems

Management policy actually creates many menu problems. Whether the decision is overt or by omission, the way management chooses to operate the restaurant can create irritations for your guests. Have any of these diner disasters ever happened in *your* place?

No Children's Menus

Children appreciate having something just for them because they're always stuck with material designed for someone else. At the same time, parents appreciate the simplicity of knowing what you have in children's portions.

Ordering the Item *Description* and Getting Something Else

Be sure menu copy properly describes the item and makes it sound attractive to your patrons. Because menu descriptions often tend toward the flowery, the wording is often misleading. Phrases like "grilled to perfection" are trite and rarely accurate. If your guests take what they read literally, they'll be disappointed when they don't get it. Omit full sentence descriptions entirely. Instead, give your entrées an exciting name and simply list the ingredients that are the major flavor components.

Not Enough Menus for All Guests

Asking guests to share menus makes a poor first impression. The first step in the solution is to realize lack of menus slows service and makes your guests less trusting of your professionalism. Find out if the shortage is because of too few menus or simply a failure to get them back to the greeter after the guests have ordered.

Peak demand determines how many menus you need. During the rush you have the least flexibility and that's when menu shortages most impact on your timing. Before the rush each day, count your menus to be sure you still have enough in service.

Keep an emergency stock of spare menus in a sealed package. If you must break into the reserve package, you'll know to have more menus printed. Also, if you find you're losing menus to souvenir seekers, print small, high quality promotional menus. They give you the exposure and save money at the same time.

Small Portions at Big Prices

People may not go out to eat just because they're hungry but you can bet they won't go out to eat if they *aren't* hungry! Small portions at high prices may work briefly in trendy restaurants but how many 20-year-old trendy restaurants have you seen? You must provide value or lose your patronage. On the other hand, smaller portions at *smaller* prices are working well for many operators.

Only Dinner-Sized Portions at Lunch

Most Americans still eat their larger meal in the evening. We are conditioned to accept larger portions (and the accompanying higher prices) later in the day. Failure to offer more traditional luncheon-size portions at midday effectively makes you non-competitive and renders the menu unworkable. In that case, the guest is in a no-win situation – they must either order more food than they really want or get up and leave.

Menus That Completely Change Daily

A completely fluid menu can confuse your market about what to expect from your restaurant. This general idea has worked in some small restaurants but the danger is still there. If you think this style has promise for you, consider a weekly menu instead. Perhaps two or three solid signature items guests can always count on backed up with four daily specials can satisfy your need for a limited menu without confusing your regulars.

Fixed Price Menus with Surcharges

If you advertise a fixed price menu, that's what your guests expect. If your "fixed price" becomes like buying a car with all the added extras, you'll be remembered about as fondly as the typical used car salesman! Fixed price menus can be attractive to diners but charge what you need to charge and don't run the risk of making your guests feel cheated by trying to run up the tab on them.

Charging Extra for Blue Cheese Dressing

I know items like blue cheese dressing may cost a little more than the average, but other dressings choices cost less. To keep from confusing (and annoying) your guests, base your prices on the average and keep it simple. If you want to tip the scales a bit, develop a tasty, low cost signature house dressing.

Failure to Offer Meatless Options

There are a growing number of people in the country who choose to reduce or eliminate meat consumption. Additionally, many more are watching their fat and cholesterol intake by choosing meatless entrées. By reflecting this preference on your menu, you become a viable destination for these diners. An added advantage of meatless entrées is that your profit margins are often more attractive.

No Healthy Choices on the Menu

All things being equal, I believe many diners would prefer healthier choices *provided* those choices are tasty. It takes experimentation to modify menus to lower fat, cholesterol, sodium and calories without losing taste, but it can be done if you're willing to do the work.

With the nutritional content of restaurant food under suspicion, three or four healthy choices on your menu can help you become the restaurant of choice. Surprisingly, long haul truck drivers are particularly concerned with nutrition. As a result, you are apt to find more low fat choices at most American truck stops! For more information on the subject, contact your local Heart Association.

Violations of "Truth in Menu"

In many areas, the law requires you present an accurate picture of your menu offerings. The law aside, honesty is always the best policy. If you must lie to your guests to keep their business, you're living on borrowed time anyway. You need to earn the trust of your patrons to succeed and you won't earn that trust by misleading them. Make sure everything you say is 100% accurate.

Negative Comments on the Menu

I once had lunch at a restaurant whose menu contained all of the following notations at the bottom of the menu:

- We reserve the right to refuse service to anyone.
- Sales tax will be added to all taxable items.
- Not responsible for lost or stolen items.
- Please refrain from smoking pipes or cigars.
- Sorry, we do not accept checks.

I was struck by the negativity. I'm sure this wasn't their intent but it was the result they got. There may be legal reasons your menu must include certain statements, but whatever you need to say, pay attention to how and where you say it. Put it all in one place and you may be making a different statement than you intended.

Boring Menus

If price increases are the only menu changes you ever make, you risk restaurant death by boredom. When your menu becomes stale, your entire operation gets dull. Adjust your menu at least twice a year. Quarterly is even better to coincide with the changing season. Remove less popular (or less profitable) items. Feature ingredients that are in season to add variety. Don't mess with your core menu, just tune things up a little. Your staff will appreciate the change as much as your guests.

Useless Information

The trend toward more locally-sourced ingredients is a good thing ... until it becomes distracting. I heard of a menu where one full page listed 58 of the restaurant's suppliers and even gave a shout-out to "the indigenous Mapuche people of Patagonia" for making their bread baskets.

All that credit is great, but if you have all that extra space, why not use it to tell diners how you cook your Copper River salmon? If you really want diners to know which farm you buy your beets from, put it on your website. They'll find it.

Unfocused Menus

The only sure recipe for failure I know is trying to be all things to all people. Be clear about who you are – and are not – and don't clutter the menu with lame dishes just there to please picky eaters. These days, most diners have looked at your menu online and selected you because you have what they're hungry for.

Too Many (Or Too Few) Items on the Menu

Most menus I see are far to large to be profitable. Your menu should offer enough of variety to give guests a reasonable choice, of course, but not so many items that it becomes confusing.

An enjoyable and effortless dining experience creates the good time your guests want. Logic says that the more choices you give a guest, the more likely they are to be get exactly what they want, but guests don't come to your restaurant to become students of your menu.

Giving people unlimited choices does not enhance their dining experience. In fact, it may only allow them to (eventually) select about what they'd eat at home ... and a restaurant meal should be more special than that. Remember, the faster they find a choice that interests them, the sooner you'll get the table back!

No Signature Items on the Menu

What are you famous for? What are your guests going to tell their friends about? Signature items create a unique identity for your restaurant in the minds of your market: a unique house dressing, special soup, an entrée they can't find anywhere else in town, a distinctive side dish and a famous dessert. It's easier on the kitchen, faster for the service staff and more interesting for the guest.

Advertising bombards people with thousands of slick advertising messages every day. They tune most of them out. Signature items helps them remember you when they make the dining decision and help them justify giving you their business ("I go there because ...").

Signature items don't need to be your most expensive menu items. They don't even have to relate directly to your main menu theme. They just have to be special preparations that you do better than anyone else ... and that your guests rave about. Ultimately, it is your guests who will identify what you are famous for. Pay attention.

Wine List Weirdness

A menu by any other name is still a menu. Wine lists may be the object of intense study, an afterthought prepared by a wine salesman or somewhere in between. A full discussion of wine list design could be an entire book but one that would apply to a limited number of restaurants. For now, here are a few common errors to consider.

No Wine Descriptions

Unless your guests are wine experts (most are not) they may want some help in choosing wines that are unfamiliar to them. Wine lists are typically arranged by color, import/domestic, country of origin and sometimes by the type of grape. This is a start, but of little help to those unversed on the wines you offer.

Guests understand the distinctions between sweet, dry, delicate and full-bodied. If your patrons are generally not very wine literate, consider restructuring your wine list along these lines.

A user-friendly wine list will encourage diners to experiment and they become more comfortable with their choices. The more at ease your guest become with wine, the more they will develop the habit of drinking wine with the meal. Combined with thorough staff training and tastings, this can increase wine sales significantly.

Lack of Balance

An effective wine list will offer something for all tastes. Specific requirements for cellar composition depend on your menu, of course, so a steak house would likely offer more red wines than a seafood cafe where the list would favor whites. Balance requires a range of choices and a tier of prices with selections for every budget. Having your most popular wines available by the glass or offering free tastes is also a plus.

More than Three Items Not in Stock

If you're going to offer it – and expect to sell it – you must have it in stock. Maintaining a wine list is a continual process. The more extensive the list, the more time required to support it. This is another area where you can present a more professional face to the public by computerized inventory tracking and the ability to update your wine menu when your stock shifts. If you cannot reprint the list as wines or vintages change, choose wines where you can count on a more consistent supply.

Few Moderately-Priced Selections

Many operators shoot themselves in the foot by trying to price wine with the same percentage markup they use for liquor at the bar. Wine is the only item in the restaurant offered in the same form as your guests can purchase it themselves. If they know they can buy a particular wine for $25 at the wine shop, they will resent your trying to sell the same bottle for $85.

Reasonably-priced wines will increase sales and you can only pay the bills with dollars, not percentages. A fair pricing formula you might consider is to start with the *retail* price of the bottle. (Your price, of course, will be less) and add a standard dollar amount, perhaps $10-15 to provide your profit. The sales price will be fair, higher priced wines will be more of a bargain and your reputation will spread among wine lovers.

Too Many Selections

Like menus, wine lists can offer so many choices that they become a full time study in themselves. Carefully created and maintained wine cellars are a delightful enhancement of fine dining. Those restaurants with the clientele and staff to appreciate and maintain the wine list make a special contribution to our industry. For most operators, though, the care and feeding of an extensive wine list can be a struggle, complicated by not-in-stock items.

The wine list must complement your food items. Many operators at the lower end of the market can make due with interesting house wines. Most casual-theme operations only need a modest list that's within their ability to understand and service. Upscale restaurants can justify a more extensive list. As with any menu, the attraction of a wine list is not what you write but what you can deliver.

Bonus Points

Everybody likes pleasant surprises. These little unexpected touches are opportunities to improve your score and put your guests in a better mood. They help make up for any lapses in the operation and give people something to talk about to their friends.

Menus in Braille and Foreign Languages

You wouldn't offer your English-speaking guests a menu written in Chinese. Yet we think nothing of presenting an English language menu to a newly-arrived Chinese guest. It is only courteous to give your guests menus they can understand.

Your local organization for the blind can help you prepare Braille menus. Ask your multi-lingual guests to help you translate your menu into other languages. [Hint: have the translation done by someone for whom that language is their mother tongue.] Include English subtitles so your staff can follow along. It is a small gesture of respect for a small segment of your market but a true measure of your passion for guest gratification.

Extensive Heart-Healthy Menu Options

With the right recipes, food items and equipment, you can prepare low fat dishes that are as tasty as any conventional offering. Of course, not all selections have low fat versions, but I've designed a well-balanced casual menu where 75% of the items met Heart Association standards, including hamburgers and french fries! All it takes is wanting to do it ... and a willingness to do the work.

Imaginative Dessert Selection

There's always room for dessert. It's only the *idea* of dessert that gives guests pause. It is interesting that many diners will carefully order low calorie entrées and follow up with a massive dessert! You can most always sell a dessert for two diners to split, provided you capture their imagination.

To do this, offer some signature desserts – items so unique and mouth-watering your diners just can't refuse. Present them either in person with a dessert tray or in heartfelt word pictures.

Assume nobody can pass up your special double chocolate bread pudding. This mind set is easier if you make your desserts on the premises instead of purchasing them from outside sources. Back all this up with an attractive dessert menu. Most people don't bake exotic desserts at home, so there is real value in offering your guests something truly special they can't get anywhere else.

Basic Nutritional Information

Your guests want to know what they're eating. Any nutrition student can do a general analysis of your recipes and most hospital dietary departments have sophisticated computer programs for recipe analysis. You may well be able to trade gift certificates for services rendered.

So make a few friends in the right places and you may be able to provide information to your guests that will give you a competitive edge. This type of analysis also helps you see ways to improve the nutritional content of your entrées without impacting taste or cost.

Smaller Portions at Smaller Prices

Dieters and elderly diners appreciate this option and it can work to your advantage because you can offer half the portion for 60-75% of the full menu price and still maintain a respectable profit margin. This approach allows many entrées to be attractive as appetizers. Half portions can also make you more attractive to the growing number of diners who prefer grazing to ordering a full meal.

Mini Desserts

Want to sell more desserts? Think small: two bites, two bucks, 100 (or so) calories. You know that the first two bites of a dessert are the best. After that, it's just work. Seasons 52, a Darden concept, was one of the first to offer shot glass-sized desserts. They present an array of nine choices – from key lime to cheesecake – and, I'm told, sell dessert to over 75-90% of their diners! More often than not, a party of four will just take all nine!

There are certainly desserts that can demand the $8-10 tab some restaurants ask, but in many cases, that's just too much, both in terms of dollars and quantity. However, another two bucks for a little something sweet at the end of the meal is an impulse decision and an easy choice to make.

Not-On-the-Menu Items

People like to know things others don't know and they like to be able to do things others can't do. To tap into this human tendency, tell guests a secret – something that isn't public knowledge. What secrets can you let people in on?

Drive-thru chain In-N-Out Burger has a "secret menu." Those in the know can order a "3x3" or get their burgers "Animal Style" – combos not found on the menu board.

I know of restaurants where the best-selling item on their menu is not on their menu at all ... and never has been! But if you know to order it, you can get it. Human nature being what it is, once you know the secret, you'll order the item simply because you *can!*

7
Service Stumbles

Y our service staff has the largest responsibility for guest gratification since they are the principal point of contact – the ones who orchestrate the dining experience. Their attitude, presence and skills will highlight or destroy the efforts of the rest of your crew.

It's easy to lay the blame for service problems at the feet of the service staff, but their behavior only reflects the attitudes they see in their managers. Operators who deny this relationship are the ones with high staff turnover and perpetual guest relations problems; the ones who believe it's impossible to find qualified workers even as other operators in the same market have a waiting list for job openings.

It's not easy to acknowledge your own role in problems. Still, by taking responsibility for staff attitudes, you can change your level of guest service. We call this phenomenon "the shadow of the leader."

The good news is that you can change yourself – in fact you're the *only* person you can change. When your outlook changes, the outlook of your staff follows suit, something we talk about more in the next part of the book. I mention it here only to give you something to think about as we explore the many well-intentioned actions that can innocently destroy the guest service experience!

Remember your primary job is to give your guests a good time. Unless guests enjoy themselves inside your four walls, nothing else matters.

Annoying Attitudes

Attitudes are mindsets. A "bad attitude" is just a belief that your needs and convenience are more important than the needs and convenience of others. It's a contagious disease. Here are a few signs that this virus has started to infect your organization:

Needing to Be the Center of Attention
The need to be the focal point of everything suggests an individual with an ego problem. It implies that what is happening for them is more important than what is happening for anyone else. These people cannot make your guests feel important until their priorities shift. Fortunately, their attitude can turn around if they adopt a guest-oriented stance to their jobs ... and that change can happen for them as soon as it happens for you (and not before!)

An "I'm Doing You a Favor" Attitude
It's easy to find arrogance and indifference in the world. People don't need to come to your restaurant to experience it. Besides, guests are doing you a favor by patronizing your place. They have many other choices ... and they *will* make other choices if you don't earn – and show them you appreciate — their business.

Socializing with Some Guests While Ignoring Others
Good service is fair and equal. Human nature being what it is, you will insult the slighted guests and they are unlikely to return. The solution is eyeballs in the dining room, compassionate coaching, continual training, and constant support to help your staff become more sensitive to the needs of *all* their guests, all the time.

Being Too Familiar or Excessively Chatty
Guests come to the restaurant for their own reasons. When a staff member personally interjects themselves into the guest's world without permission, they are an intruder. Undue familiarity creates withdrawal and resentment, while the staff member probably thinks they're just being friendly. Remember, good service is always defined from the guest's viewpoint, so know when to open your mouth ... and when to shut it!

No Sense of Humor
There are many unexpected events in the restaurant business and a sense of humor is often the lubricant that makes an evening flow smoothly. That's why it's important to at least have guest contact staff who can take a joke.

Mike Hurst, late owner of Fort Lauderdale's 15th Street Fisheries always asked job applicants, "What's the funniest thing that's ever happened to you?" He asked the question with a straight face and watched their reaction. The answer wasn't important. He wanted to see a laugh and an animated response, figuring that people who can laugh at themselves were the "sparklers" he wanted to hire.

Making a Fuss about a Dropped Dish
Accidents happen and nobody likes to be embarrassed. If you call attention to a guest's mishap, you'll drop their level of well-being immediately. This usually guarantees their outlook will be negative for the rest of the meal.

The most effective way to handle a spill is to treat it as the everyday occurrence it is. If you must say anything, a passing comment like "Don't worry, it happens all the time," takes the pressure off and helps salvage the evening for everybody.

Visible Reaction to the Amount of the Tip
Nonverbal statements are often the most devastating because every guest in the room can read them, so it's appropriate to coach servers not to display a reaction to the amount of a tip.

A better question is why their first action would be to look at the tip? Be sensitive to the possibility they may be under some financial stress or feel underappreciated on the job. There's always more going on than you know about.

Making Light of a Guest's Complaint
How a restaurant handles complaints says more about its service orientation than almost anything else. Giving guests what they want is important to your success. Take all complaints seriously (the guest does!) Service staff who fail to treat every complaint as a significant opportunity to assure guest satisfaction will discourage the very feedback essential to their success.

Refusing to Take Payment to the Cashier
This attitude reflects an organization (or an individual) where guest service is an imposition. The fault most likely lies with the attitude of management. Precede any staff discipline actions with serious self-examination ... but address the attitude as soon as it appears.

Protecting the House
This happens when the guest has a legitimate complaint that goes against a house policy. The staff person ignores the well-being of the guest and defends the policy, probably because there are more rewards for following the rules than for pleasing the guests.

While you have every right to set restrictive policies for your own business, you must also be prepared to pay the price arrogance may bring. Not only could it cost you patronage, but you could lose your service-oriented staff members as well.

Rushing Guests Off the Table or Out of the Restaurant

Don't spring the check the second the final fork drops. Ask if a guest is ready for the check before you drop it on the table. People might want dessert, another drink, or a minute to linger after the meal. Turning tables may mean more sales, but people deserve a bit of time to digest before the bill arrives.

If you hurry a party out just so you can get an additional seating at the table, you may never see them again. Worse, their negative word-of-mouth will offset the good comments of five other parties. The implications of the math aren't difficult to grasp. Remember you are selling the overall experience, not just the food.

Repeat as necessary:

This restaurant is run for the enjoyment and pleasure of our guests, not for the convenience of the staff or the owners.

Expecting Guests to Know the Restaurant's Procedures

It's easy to get irritated when a guest asks about something that, to you, is obvious. We assume that what is basic knowledge to us must be equally evident to everyone. It isn't. The safest attitude is to treat every guest like a first-timer and take personal delight in telling them details they didn't know about your restaurant.

Calling the Guest by Their First Name

Using a guest's first name can sometimes be a plus ... provided you know them personally and they've asked you to use their first name. However, the practice is offensive when there's no prior personal relationship and the staff member gets the guest's first name from a credit card.

For example, my legal first name is William but I don't use it and I don't know anyone who does. Those who know me call me Bill. Call me William and instead of coming across as friendly, you'll impress me as arrogant. When you get a guest's name from their credit card, use only their last name and be safe.

Using a Condescending Tone of Voice

The message you deliver is always in your tone of voice. Elderly guests, the handicapped and minorities are particularly sensitive to a condescending tone. Just because someone is different doesn't mean they're broke, stupid or undeserving of excellent service. These groups often receive poor treatment and will appreciate your responsiveness and respect.

A Disgusted Look Following an Exchange with a Guest
This is an insult to the guest that everyone in the dining room can see. Remember that guests always have good (to them) reasons for their comments and questions. Mocking them only shows your ignorance, insensitivity and immaturity.

Different Treatment for Different People
Beware of prejudice in all its forms. Don't draw conclusions just because a guest is young, arrived with a bus tour, isn't dressed well or has a coupon. There are no second-class guests in a legendary restaurant ... and becoming a legend is a worthy goal.

Ignoring Obvious Attempts For Attention
Being ignored insults the guest and suggests a server who feels *they* are at the center of the dining experience, not the guest. They will not tolerate anyone telling them what to do. It is impossible for these individuals to give responsive service unless they can find humility. Help them straighten out their priorities.

Refusing a Request to Change Tables
Does this suggest a control issue? If guest gratification is truly Job One in the restaurant, this sort of problem is unlikely to surface. If it does come up, you know where to point the finger first.

Touching the Guest
Unless you have a prior personal relationship, the only touching that is considered professional is a firm handshake ... and even then, only when appropriate. Shoulder rubs or a playful hand on the arm are uninvited (and unwelcome) intrusions. Some guests are already nervous that you're touching the plate they're about to eat from. Don't allow implied intimacy – no matter how well-intentioned – to get out of control!

Invented Policies
Some servers feel the guest is there for the convenience of the staff, not the other way around. When a guest asks to do something a staff member just doesn't want to do, I have seen them invent a "policy" on the spot that discourages it, apparently trying to take advantage of the guests' ignorance.

The thin line between ignorance and arrogance was crossed when two of the four people at our table said they wished to split the bill evenly by providing two credit cards, a reasonably routine request. The waitress said, "We automatically add a 20 percent charge for that." Oh, really?

No Smile

Servers can work super long hours, as many restaurants have few regulations, or just bypass labor laws entirely. Double or triple shifts are fairly normal and that takes its toll on a server's mood. Still, that doesn't give anyone a free pass to be abrupt.

You may be tired, but you're paid to be courteous and welcoming to guests. Just got broken up with? It happens. Leave your baggage at the door and put a smile on. Even if its fake, at least it won't make guests feel horrible for asking you to bring them some bread.

Too Much Information

When you're at the table, don't over share about your day, your job, or your life outside the restaurant. If a guest asks, you should respond, of course, but limit the exchange to briefly answering their specific questions, not offering unsolicited information.

From the guests' perspective, the whole notion of someone bringing you food, cleaning up your dirty dishes, raking your crumbs off the table, and witnessing the breakdown of your marriage over a bowl of clam chowder is a totally weird part of modern life. Restaurants can be awkward that way.

Don't break the fourth wall and talk about how you are actually a marine biologist and you're getting ready to move to Alaska to study whales — or worse, tell a sob story about how another table stiffed you on a tip. Keep it professional and with luck, guests won't drag you into their arguments and ask you to arbitrate.

Making Guests Feel Like Criminals

Do you cop an attitude when a tables orders just drinks, or just dinner, instead of seven courses and four bottles of wine? Don't laugh. It happens all too often. Yes, the restaurant business is tough, and if the servers don't turn those tables the boss won't be happy, but that is ultimately not the diner's problem.

There are egregious acts of lingering, and those people who come in for a cup of coffee and start writing their new novel are clearly social misfits. However, just because they're eating light today, or not ordering the requisite amount of small plates that is deemed "appropriate for a party of their size," shouldn't mean they get treated like a problem.

Pay proper attention to fostering regulars. Treat guests equally well whether they spend $10 or $100, and things will probably work out better for everyone in the long run.

Preconceived Notions

You don't really know anything about another person. Even those you may have known for years can surprise you, so in the hospitality profession, making assumptions or projecting your own prejudices on another is not only disrespectful, but dangerous.

Forget the paternalistic assumption that older diners can't handle spicy food when they've specifically requested it or it's clearly labeled as such. Issue a warning if you must, but serve it hot when they want it that way or as the dish demands.

Likewise, never assume that certain groups will be poor tippers and therefore don't merit your full measure of service. People only tip well because they *want* to and it is not in your best interests to give them any reason to feel you are not worth it.

That said, certain demographics *are* more likely to tip better than others. A trio of businessmen in suits enjoying a few drinks will probably leave a larger sum than the group of students, but this doesn't mean both tables don't deserve the same quality of service.

Often groups of students will be completely ignored over other tables because of the belief that "students don't tip." There may be a chicken and egg situation going on here; students may not tip because the level of service they receive is terrible when compared to nearby tables. People only tip well because they *want* to and it's not in your best interests to give anyone a reason to feel you are not worth it. Give every guest your very best efforts. You never know who will be feeling more generous.

System Slip-Ups

Many problems point to breakdowns in the restaurant's systems. The only effective resolution is to identify weaknesses and fix them. Try to solve problems by fixing the people involved and you'll never receive another suggestion from anyone on your staff. No one will dare point out a problem if it they think they might be blamed for it.

Orders That Arrive Incomplete

You must get it right the first time or you'll throw off the timing of the entire meal. In fast-paced operations, an expediter can be invaluable in assembling and checking orders. Incomplete orders cost you points with your guests and create additional work for the service staff.

Bringing Food the Guest Did Not Order

People love surprises. Bringing them an unexpected extra at no cost is a good way to gain points ... but bringing them something by mistake only makes you look incompetent and bumbling.

Running out of China, Silver or Glassware

You can't talk your way around this! Small inventories can be false economy. The immediate problem is inconvenience to the guest and the potential loss of future business. When you finally buy the additional stock, if you can find it, it probably will cost more.

Also, having enough china, glasses and silver saves costly labor hours. If you don't have to wash dishes during the meal, you can "sandbag" soiled utensils, allowing the dishwasher to help in the kitchen and catch up on warewashing after the rush is over.

Wet Plates or Trays

If plates or trays are not air drying properly, it may mean your dish machine's final rinse isn't hot enough. If it's not a temperature problem, the dish crew may be stacking the pieces too quickly after they come out of the machine, either because of inadequate training or lack of adequate clean dish landing space. Whatever the cause, wet serviceware gets the meal off to a bad start.

Running Out of a Menu Item

First, you need effective forecasting and inventory control to reduce the problem of outages. On the other hand, never being out of stock may signal excessive inventory levels. The solution is attention to inventory management ... and the right choice of words.

Here's another case where your choice of words makes a difference. When you *run* out of something, guests think you don't know how to run your business. However when you *sell* out of something, it suggests you have highly desirable items that are freshly prepared in limited quantities. Of course, when you cannot provide what the guest orders, always suggest alternative choices.

Not Receiving Coffee Before the Dessert

Many desserts taste much better with a cup of coffee. Delivering coffee before dessert maintains the flow of service between clearing the main course and serving the desserts. It also assures your guests will gain the most enjoyment from the efforts of your pastry chef. Since it takes longer to drink a cup of hot coffee than to eat most desserts, you also may turn the table a little sooner.

Sitting at the Table Without Being Acknowledged

Most guests don't expect the immediate availability of the server. Guests just feel more comfortable when they know the server is aware they are waiting. Even if you're busy, it is important to at least let waiting guests know you noted their presence.

Approach the table within one minute of the guests' arrival, *stop*, focus your attention, give a short welcome and let them know you will be right back. Talking to the table while you're moving tells the guest you have something going on that is more important than they are. Be sure your system allows enough time for this important first step of good service.

Not Providing Service in Order of Arrival

Not unreasonably, people expect to be served before parties that arrived or were seated after them. Your greeter can help smooth out potential point loss by properly rotating parties between stations to keep the workload balanced, assuring a server will not get two or three new parties at the same time. If for some reason you can't avoid double seating, develop a means of communication that will let the service staff be clear on which parties arrived first.

Not Serving Guests Promptly

Hot food must be hot. If you don't serve all guests at the table at once, some guests will sit with their food cooling while waiting for their companions to be served – a socially uncomfortable experience that won't enhance your guests' enjoyment of their meal.

Meal Service Too Fast or Too Slow

Appropriate pacing varies with the type of restaurant and the meal period. In quick service operations, speed is always an important factor. In table service, rapid service is more of an issue at breakfast and lunch than in the evening.

Bringing courses out too quickly makes the guest feel rushed, too slowly and the meal experience drags. A good server will pace the courses to match the speed (and need) of the party. This requires reading the table and maintaining communication with the kitchen in general and the expediter in particular to be sure items come out at the proper time and can be served while they're still piping hot.

The higher the check average, the more time your guests expect to spend at the table. A possible exception is guests who are enjoying a pre-theater meal. They'll be watching the clock closely. The more you know about the motives of your guests, the easier it will be to adjust the pace of service to be responsive.

No Place for Meal Debris

Give some thought to what the guest is going to need to get through the meal comfortably and be sure they have it. For example, where are they going to put clam shells, bones, cracker wrappers, etc.? Always have a spare plate or bowl for bones and shells.

To solve the problem of cracker wrapper clutter, just place the full cracker basket inside an empty one. When bringing the crackers to the table, separate the two baskets. You'll create a receptacle for the trash ... and a pleasant point of difference from your competition.

Serving Food Ordered by Another Table

Getting the orders confused is embarrassing for everyone. The guest doesn't know whether to eat the food or not, the service staff shows its ineptitude and the guest who originally placed the order doesn't get served when they should.

The situation is further complicated by the problem of what to do when you realize the mistake. You certainly can't pick food up off one table and serve it to another.

The proper solution, if there is one, is costly. First acknowledge the mistake to both parties and apologize for the error. Leave the incorrect item as a complimentary gift to the party who received it and bring a complimentary replacement to the person whose order you misdirected.

Trying to talk your way out of the error or failing to correct the mistake will only alienate both parties. The cost of an extra entrée is far less than the cost of losing two groups of potential regulars.

Slow Service at Breakfast or Lunch

Guests are rushed in the morning and have limited time for lunch. If you can't regularly get them through either meal in 25 minutes, feature two or three dish-up items you can serve with a guarantee of timely service. Remember the critical timing is from the time your guests arrive until the time they walk out the door. This is different from the length of time it takes to deliver their order.

Endless Waits in the Drive-up Line

Fast food is supposed to be fast. Cordless headsets help improve communication between the guest, the order-taker and the production line (and avoids the need for shouting!) If slow service is a problem, involve your staff in identifying the lapses in the system and suggesting ways to improve your accuracy and speed. You may be surprised by their insights.

Waiting for Coffee to Brew

Everyone appreciates a fresh cup of coffee but nobody likes to wait for it. Particularly in fast-paced restaurants, you may want to assign someone to just brew coffee during the rush to be sure it will be made properly. The only thing worse than waiting for coffee when you need it is ending up with a cup of bad coffee!

Food Sitting Visibly in the Pickup Window or On a Tray Stand

This has to be a frustrating experience for restaurant guests. I have even seen guests get up and serve the plates themselves! If your system can't move hot food while it's hot, consider a runner system. Under this plan, servers rarely leave the floor. The next available runner delivers hot food to the server the instant it's up in the kitchen. If the waiter is occupied, the runner can serve the entrées following the seat number codes on the guest check.

Guests Having to Get Their Own Coffee

Americans expect prompt coffee refills. When their frustration reaches a point where they get it themselves, you've lost points. Either have enough staff to keep up with the demand or consider insulated coffee carafes you can leave on the table.

Condiments That Don't Arrive Before the Food

Don't make guests wait for a condiment while their food gets cold. An effective system always allows the necessary accompaniments to arrive at the table before the entrée is served. This assures that hot food won't sit on the table while you fumble around the service stand looking for the steak sauce!

Mis-Packed Take-out Orders

This is a big reason for dissatisfaction among quick service patrons. Statistics suggest that fast feeders improperly assemble one out of three orders. This is particularly irritating at the drive-up window since the guest won't discover the error until they are well away from the property.

Screwing Up the Order

When guests see a server without a notepad or something to write an order on, they are either impressed or just waiting for the server to return to table with, "Sorry, what was your order again?" It may look cool to simply remember orders, but the likelihood of making a mistake is much higher, especially on complex substitutions or large tables. Get it right the first time and write the order. A few seconds of extra effort will pay off in better tips.

Glacial Service

Be alert for what might be called the "Bermuda Triangle Effect." That's what you get when an empty restaurant also features service that moves at the speed of a glacier. Those two diners sitting alone in the dining room are still paying patrons. Some would argue their rarity makes them that much more precious.

Horrible Habits

A problem with hiring "experienced" servers is that you don't really know the exact content of that experience. Many experienced workers have only succeeded in learning someone else's bad habits and poor attitude. Fortunately, you can overcome bad habits through diligent coaching, provided you know what to watch for.

Lack of Eye Contact

One of my favorite pastimes, especially in coffee shops, is to see if a waitress can make it through the entire meal without making eye contact even once. It's discouraging to see how often it happens.

Coach your staff on the importance of smiling eye contact. The idea is simply to start the relationship with every new guest by looking them directly in the eye with a sincere smile. Nothing warms the heart like smiling eye contact. When it doesn't happen, guests can think you have something to hide. They trust you less, tip less and are more critical of both the restaurant and your service.

Snatching Away Menus

If you have the story of your restaurant on the menu, give the guest time to read it. The menu can provide information that helps make you unique in the market and offers an excellent way to tell guests of policies and priorities that are difficult to convey any other way.

Invariably, the server will pick up the menus just as the guest is getting interested in the story, leaving the guest empty-handed! If a guest is reading the menus, leave it with them. The more familiar guests are with your back story, the more reasons they'll have to return and the more they'll have to tell their friends.

Pointing at Each Guest with the Pen

Guests are not at the table to perform for you. Unfortunately, this is the impression you give when you point at each guest with your pen when asking for their orders. The habit is annoying and makes the dining experience less personal. Stop it!

Unlike verbal mistakes, pointing with the pen is an error others can detect from across the dining room. This also makes it easy for the managers to notice. Becoming aware that this unconscious habit can be irritating is an important first step toward breaking it.

Repeating Each Item as the Guest Orders

This is particularly annoying when you repeat the order back to the guest as a question.

> Guest: *"I'd like the club sandwich, please."*
> Server: *"Club sandwich?"*
> Guest: *"... with a side of french fries."*
> Server: *"French fries?"*

You sound like a broken record and it's annoying. If you're unsure what the guest said or meant, repeat the order back to them, but do it after they are finished ordering.

Naming Each Item as It's Served

No comment is necessary when you serve an item, but if you feel it appropriate to say something, pass along some information about the item or its preparation. Provided the statement is true, saying "The salmon came in fresh this morning and the dill in the sauce came from our own garden" can elevate a guest's mood and give everyone at the table a story to tell. Just saying "Here's your salmon" gains you nothing.

Thumb on the Plate During Service

Serious lapses occur when you don't pay attention. A need for speed never justifies careless or unsanitary service. Many guests won't say anything about a thumb on the plate, but that doesn't mean they haven't noticed the error.

Rather than risk a confrontation with you, they'll talk about it to their friends. If the rest of the meal experience was marginal, a misplaced thumb could be the reason they start dining elsewhere. Hold plates with the pad of the thumb, not the tip.

Not Facing Bills When Giving Change

This simply means all bills are face up and arranged in order of denomination. It's part of treating money with respect. A jumbled pile of currency makes the guest feel you are treating their money casually. Remember, the change is *their* money until and unless they decide to leave some of it as a tip. Proper currency handling shows professionalism and people will feel more comfortable entrusting you with their cash.

Addressing a Woman as "The Lady"

People are people, not objects ... so watch your words. Always talk to each guest individually and personally, regardless of gender or age. If the waiter says something like, "What would the lady like tonight?" it comes across as disrespectful. Make eye contact and address her directly.

Holding Glasses by the Bowl or Rim

Never allow your crew handle a glass by the bowl or rim. It not only leaves fingerprints, but it's like sticking your fingers in the guest's mouth! Many diners will send back glasses if you handle them this way, others just seethe quietly, but you don't need the aggravation ... and neither do they. Train your staff to handle glassware only by the stem or the lower third.

Entering Guests' Conversation Uninvited

If your guests want a buddy, they'll invite you over after work! If you overhear one person at the table say something you know is wrong, resist the urge to correct them. If they want your opinion on something, they'll ask for it. By the way, knowing the scores can be an important plus if you have a sports-oriented clientele, just don't offer information guests haven't requested.

Scraping Dishes in Front of the Guests

Once you remove a plate from the table, whatever you scrape off it is automatically considered garbage. You wouldn't bring trash to the table at the beginning of the meal, so don't do it at the end. Handle your garbage in the kitchen and avoid creating a negative memory for your patrons.

Approaching a Table with Dirty Dishes in Hand

This is like shoving garbage in your guests' faces. How receptive do you think they will be to your skillful dessert dissertation if they're looking at the remains of someone else's lunch while you are talking? Never address a table unless your hands are clear and you are entirely focused on the guests.

Leaning On or Over the Table

This habit may be seen as an invasion of privacy. You can safely reach slightly over to pick up a menu or serve a plate, provided you don't stay draped over the table. Leaning on the table at any time for any reason is always a poor practice. Show your respect by not violating guests' airspace.

Using Restaurant Jargon

Each restaurant has its own verbal shorthand. It means something to you but sounds like another language to others. You wouldn't address your English-speaking guests in Turkish, so why would speaking in jargon be any different?

For example, don't tell them you have a four-top by the window, just say you have a wonderful table with a view. If you say their Chick Sand is almost ready, they may think you are talking about women on the beach instead of a broiled chicken breast sandwich! You get the point. Using these phrases can be an unconscious habit until you become aware of your words.

Placing a Tray on the Table

If the tray is large, put it on a tray stand. Hold a cocktail tray in your hand. The table is the guests' private domain. You have permission to enter with food and beverage, but they will resent your claiming a portion of their space by placing a tray on the table.

If the table is empty, it's still poor practice to place a tray down. Other guests may not feel the bottom of a tray is particularly clean and that placing it on the table dirties the table top. (It probably does!) Just use a tray stand and avoid the problem.

Interruptions or Questions While Guests' Mouths are Full

This behavior is rude and can make your guests feel uncomfortable. If the restaurant is on fire, you have a duty to interrupt. Outside of that, there's nothing you have to say so important as to be worth potentially irritating your patrons.

When you approach a table actively engaged in conversation, it is far more respectful to stand there quietly until your guests stop talking and look at you. Then say what you need to say. If they ignore your presence, quietly move away and come back later.

Sweeping Crumbs Onto the Floor

If you only tell your staff to clear the table, this is what you may get. They must understand their responsibility to maintain the ambiance of the dining room. Crumbs on the floor will be a distraction to your guests for the rest of the evening and will lower their opinion of your restaurant. Eventually you must pick up the crumbs anyway.

Marvin's Law of Creative Laziness says to never do any more work than necessary to accomplish what you want. Why clean up the crumbs twice? If crumbs do get on the floor, use a carpet sweeper for a quick, quiet cleanup.

Loud, Harsh or Grating Voices

Some diner concepts can get away with an abrasive style of service, but unless this is part of your operating identity, you'll lose points with your guests if the server's voice is not pleasant and well-modulated. The more relaxed the pace of the restaurant, the more refined the appropriate style of speech.

Not Bringing Enough Change for the Tip

While it's poor form to assume a tip, it is also reasonable to be prepared for one. If a guest chooses to leave a cash tip, they will appreciate having the proper change to do it. It is embarrassing to have to ask for change for a $20 bill. It slows down the guest and requires an extra trip to the table for the service staff. When bringing change to a guest, consider what the guest is likely to need for a tip and structure the change that way.

Loosening Caps on Condiment Bottles

I'm sure those who do this think the practice is a courtesy. Not so much. The problem comes when a guest instinctively gives the bottle a shake before using it. You won't pick up any points when Worcestershire splatters all over your dining room!

Placing a Bus Tub on the Table or Chair

The situation is similar to placing a tray on the table. Bus tubs full of soiled dishes and food scraps are not clean. Dining room guests may think placing a bus tub on the chair will make the chair dirty and they're probably right. Then they start to wonder about the chair *they* are sitting on. Avoid lowering your diners' security level. Keep bus tubs on a cart or tray stand.

Language That's Too Formal or Too Casual

Incongruence makes guests feel something is wrong, though they may not know what. We've discussed the value of consistency in the execution of a restaurant concept. Language is another element of that consistency. The language expectations are different in a burger joint than they are at a white tablecloth restaurant. The more formal the operation, the more formal the language expected.

Fingers Inside Glasses, Cups or Bowls

We've discussed the dangers of fingers on the plates when serving the table. Proper handling of cups, glasses and bowls is even more critical. Mishandling these items places the fingers on a surface the guest may put in their mouth. Proper handling is essential when setting (and clearing) the table.

You can remove glasses faster when you put your fingers inside them, but then what? Other guests don't know if you washed your hands before you picked up their clean serviceware. How realistic is it to think you'll wash your hands in the middle of every clear and reset cycle? Guests are far more sensitive to poor sanitation practices than you may realize.

Handling Silverware by the Eating Surface

All guests notice this bad habit. Improper silverware handling can put your guests in fear for their health. Whether there's a real basis for their concerns or not, they may just decide not to chance it and take their business elsewhere. Thoroughly coach your staff on the correct (and safe) way to handle all serviceware.

Not Serving Everything from a Tray

People carry plates to the table in their hands at home. To make dining out a more distinct experience from eating at home, trays are a good place to start. The way it looks to your guests, trays are clean and professional while carrying plates by hand or stacked up the arm is not. How do you want to handle it?

Hovering

Being attentive is one thing, but being creepy is something else again. Keep an awareness of all your tables and where they are in the meal process, but do it from a distance that respects their personal space. Otherwise they will feel watched ... and that is quite a different feeling.

Note that you really become conspicuous when you stand still. The trick to remaining "invisible" is to stay in motion ... provided you move at the speed of the room. If the pace of the dining room is fast, move more quickly. If the dining room is relaxed, a more leisurely pace is appropriate.

The server/guest relationship is like dating someone: you want to see them, you want them to be around when you want/need them, but you don't want them hanging around *all* the time. Checking on a table periodically is crucial. Checking on a table every two minutes is smothering.

Nothing changes in two minutes. They haven't just started hating everything. Their experience is still positive (and will be unless you keep getting in everyone's face and not giving the table some "me time.") The opposite is also true: be aloof and unresponsive and it'll generate contempt. The trick is to be able to read the table.

Challenging the Guest's Judgement

It's both rude and foolish to refuse to acknowledge an improperly cooked steak/burger/etc. is overdone or underdone. There are objective ways to sort rare from medium rare from medium from well done from burned to a crisp ... but being right is not the goal. They guest may not always be right, but they're never wrong!

Telling Guests How to Order

It isn't the place of the server to dictate how the order will be taken, particularly if the guests have other wishes. When serving large parties, it is often helpful to ask permission to start at one end of the table and take the orders in sequence. The important point is to ask permission first and be open to alternatives. Dictating to your guests will only build resentment that can interfere with their enjoyment of your restaurant.

Asking a Man for the Woman's Order

Perhaps you could get away with this fifty years ago, but now this disrespect is sure to offend female diners. Treat all guests as equals, regardless of age, sex or physical condition. Anything less can just create more problems than you're ready to handle.

Taking Men's Orders First

Sexist though it may be, proper etiquette is to handle service in the following order: children first (since they won't wait), women (eldest first), then gentlemen with the host (if male), last. If guests want to give you their orders in a different sequence, don't argue about it. You have a seat number for every spot at the table anyway, right? Serve the entrées in the same order if you can. Some guests may consider it rude to alter this sequence.

Recommending the Most Expensive Items on the Menu

When guests ask for a recommendation, suggesting the priciest things on the menu will come across as insincere and self-serving, even if it *is* the best choice. Your mission is to earn their trust, give them a memorable experience and leave them eager to return ... not to pry every dollar you can from their clutching fingers tonight.

The safest approach is to give them your top three choices. Include at least one signature item of your restaurant – something they can't find anywhere else in town. One item on your list can be an upsell but in general you'll be farther ahead to play it safe and keep your suggestions in the medium price range. Make a friend tonight and they may opt for a pricier choice on their next visit.

Fussing over a Single Diner

Single diners just happen to be dining by themselves at the moment. They usually appreciate a little more personal attention from the service staff, but making a fuss only embarrasses them by calling attention to the fact that they're alone.

By all means, offer them reading material or a larger table if they brought some work with them. If they bring a book, get them a table with more light, but don't treat it as anything out of the ordinary. Give unaccompanied diners the care and respect they deserve and you can gain a loyal regular guest.

Personal Comments on the Check

In service, as in life, there is a fine line between attentive and unsettling. Middle school-style exclamations of affection, scrawled awkwardly on a post-meal guest check, are rarely rewarded with larger tips. Instead, these drawings can instill a type of fear usually reserved for backwoods gas stations. Next time you're thinking about adding a little personal pizzazz to the check, take deep breaths until the urge passes. Professionalism trumps all.

Cell Phone Use on the Job

There's no case you can make that whatever you are doing on your phone is somehow improving the dining experience for the guests seated in your station or waiting for food you should be preparing. The world will continue to turn just fine without you for a few more hours. If there's an emergency, instruct your family to call the restaurant manager.

What you do on your breaks or when your shift ends is your own business, but when you're on the job, *be* on the job. If it's not already a firm policy in your restaurant, just say no to cell phone use when you're on the clock.

Proselytizing

Be a pro and keep your personal ideologies to yourself. No possible good can come from expressing personal opinions to guests on any issue not directly related to your work in the restaurant, particularly when the content of your message is has overtones of religion or politics. Remember you are here to serve, not to preach.

The same may apply to advancing religious or political views to your co-workers. What you choose to discuss after work over a cold beer is your business, of course, but when you are at work, best to avoid pushing your personal views on non-work-related topics.

Not Washing Hands Frequently

Guests notice when you don't wash your hands, particularly when they see you serving food after handling cash without stopping by the hand sink. (Money is the dirtiest thing you're likely to handle all shift.) Make frequent handwashing a visible habit and your guests will rest easier. It can also create a point of difference when they notice poor sanitation practices in your competitors!

Moving Condiments from One Table to Another

If a table wants ketchup, get it from the service stand, not from the next table. It may appear more responsive but your guests won't see it that way. The table that just "lost" their ketchup feels diminished (you've taken something away from them) and the table you give it to will feel uneasy to get a "used" product.

For whatever it says of human nature, guests feel items coming from the service stand are clean, safe and acceptable. They view items taken from another table with suspicion and are uneasy when it happens, perhaps because they don't have the same level of trust with the stranger in the next booth.

Eating or Drinking While Dealing with Guests

You must always remain in character when you're on stage. This means not visibly engaging in any activities not in direct service to your guests. When you break that rule by allowing guests to see you eating or drinking at your work station, it makes them feel you have priorities other than seeing to their well-being. Not good.

You will eat and drink during your shift, of course, and the only acceptable way to handle this is to take your breaks away from your work station and out of sight of paying guests. Never drink while a guest is watching and never eat standing up. If you take your meal in the dining room, do it seated at a table away from the main traffic flow and conduct yourself as if you were a paying guest.

Squat, Take a Knee, or Sit Down at the Table

Unless this move is part of the historic fabric of the restaurant, there's no reason to get down to eye level to take an order. In fact, many guests find it incredibly weird. Ironically, small children can be particularly creeped out by the squat maneuver.

This unprofessional invasion of personal space only alienates your guests and has a negative impact on diners' inclination to leave a generous tip. A good general rule is to always "stand and deliver" with a smile.

Asking For A Tip

Leaving a tip is still a societal standard and you should expect one from most customers ... but not so much if you remind guests to do it. Phrases like "The tip isn't included," "The tip button is right there," or the audacious "Can you leave a tip please," are a slap in the face. Do you think they're not good for it or that they're just gonna run off without leaving a thing? Most North American customers know the tipping routine, so don't make them feel like cheapskates ... unless, of course, you don't want a tip at all.

Passing the Buck

There's nothing more unattractive than someone who blames others for their own failures. Blaming any and all problems on the kitchen – making the cooks sound like a bunch of incompetents – is just a little too convenient. Is it really their fault the food took an hour to come out, or did you just forget to put in the ticket? This goes back to the inherent problems that can arise when tips alone drive the level of service. When a place is working as a team, you seldom see people throwing their colleagues under the bus.

Assuming the Tip

When a guest pays in cash, it's arrogant to assume that any excess is your tip. If a guest gives you a $50 bill to pay for a $33 check, don't assume the extra $17 is yours or ask if they want change. To do so will all but guarantee an irritated guest , a smaller tip when the smoke clears, and probably a flaming review on Yelp as well!

Tips may represent the bulk of a servers compensation, but tips are still a voluntary transaction. It is presumptuous to assume the guest wouldn't want the change. Whether you get the tip they plan to leave now or in five minutes is irrelevant.

Frustrating Focus

Focus is another name for presence and presence is simply the absence of distractions. High presence makes others feel well-served, but when you are distracted – when your mind is on something else – the people you are with become annoyed. It's as simple as that.

Have you ever had a conversation with someone who was doing something else while you were talking? Even though they may have heard everything you said, how did their lack of attention make you feel? My guess is that found the experience irritating.

It's no different in the restaurant. If the service staff is thinking of something else while the guest is talking to them, the guest will feel irritated. They may not understand why, but their experience will be that the service wasn't good and they will be in no hurry to return.

When managers clutter their staff's minds with rules ("The 6¾ Steps of Good Service"), they sow the seeds of their own destruction. If a sales person is thinking about the "6¾ Steps," they can't focus on the guest. Even if they followed all those steps to the letter, the guest wouldn't experience good service ... and certainly not hospitality.

On the other hand, lack of distraction produces the feeling of being well-served in spite of the circumstances. When a staff member has high presence, the "6¾ Steps" are irrelevant.

Here are some examples to help you better understand the point. The same distracted state of mind is behind all these problems.

Inconsistent Service

Some restaurants seem to have "good days" and "bad days." Ever wonder why? Good days happen when the staff has nothing on their minds except delighting guests. Bad days arise when the crew is distracted and doesn't connect with patrons (or each other). Your place will always reflect the state of mind of the person at the top, so if your team is starting to lose it, look in the mirror.

The Feeling of Being "Processed"

Guests get this feeling when you do all the mechanical steps correctly but fail to connect with your guests on a human level. Coach your staff about the difference between hospitality and service, focus on the results you want and give as much latitude as possible for people to achieve those results in their own way.

Not Having Total Focus When at the Table

When your mind is somewhere else, it's impossible to give good service. Distraction in the server creates irritation in the guest. It is the feeling of glib insincerity you get when a server is mouthing words and you know they're thinking about something that has nothing to do you and your needs.

When you are at the table talking with guests, there's nothing you can do about bringing coffee to Table 17, emptying the bus tub or making an appointment with the dentist. Don't allow these thoughts to be distractions. It will cost you dearly.

Too Hurried to Be Attentive

Guest gratification comes from the quality, not the duration, of the contact. When you're distracted, others feel unheard and will continue to pester you until they feel that you actually got what they were saying.

On the other hand, if you slow down, clear your mind and give the other person your total attention, you can take care of business quickly. The difference is amazing. Here's an example:

> Imagine a two-year old is looking for attention and you're in the middle of something. As they tug on your pants you say "Later, kid, I'm busy" without looking up from your work. Do they say, "Sure, Daddy, I understand?" Not a chance!
>
> To take care of a two-year-old, drop what you're doing, get down eyeball to eyeball and give them five or ten seconds of your undivided attention. You'll buy yourself some time. You may buy a few minutes and you may get an hour, but if a two-year-old doesn't get that degree of attention, they will pull on you for the rest of their natural lives!
>
> It's no different if they're twenty-two or sixty-two. People want to know that you "got it" – that what they had to say actually got through to you ... and this can't happen if you are distracted.

The only difference between dealing with children and adults is that kids are more honest – they won't pretend that they have your attention if they don't. Adults are usually more socially correct, but no less observant.

Appearing Stressed or Out of Control

Lack of focus causes the events of your life to look overwhelming and you easily find yourself "in the weeds." As we discussed earlier, feeling stressed or out-of-control is just a symptom of a busy mind. When you learn to drop distractions, you automatically start to take things more in stride. There are no skills to learn, events will just look different and you'll instinctively know what to do.

The first step toward dropping distractions is simply to become aware of your busy mind. When you find your mind cluttered with thoughts or you feel yourself getting stressed, recognize what's happening. Relax, take a deep breath, clear your head and get on with your day. If you recognize your own thinking for what it is and don't take your own thoughts too seriously, you'll be on your way to greater control of your life.

Insensitivity to Guests' Needs

Every guest has special needs. Some are more obvious than others. The handicapped or the elderly may need special care. Teenagers and families have their own problems and priorities.

Business guests require different service than romantic couples; groups celebrating special occasions want a more festive experience – so many possibilities you may feel overwhelmed. Relax. If you're undistracted and empathetic, you'll instinctively do what works. All it takes is a clear mind and a focus on pleasing your guests.

Going Straight for the Upsell

The lobster mac and cheese is way better than the regular one, huh? And that Cabernet is a steal at just eight times its retail value? It's blatantly obvious – and upsetting to everyone at the table – when servers treat them like fools and recommend only the most expensive dishes and wines on the menu. When people are having fun and feeling like they aren't being manipulated, they tend to spend more in the long run anyway.

Having to Ask for Water More than Once

If your house policy is not to serve water unless a guest asks for it, be aware of two things: 1) if one guest at the table wants water, just bring it to everyone, and 2) once they have indicated they want water, keep refilling the water glasses when they get below a half. Just to avoid misunderstanding, it's probably wise to mention your water policy on the menu.

Not Remembering Regulars

Some servers have a hard time discerning between customers, since they serve so many daily, but you should keep note of who is recurring and who isn't. Nothing is more saddening to a restaurant regular than realizing they haven't been remembered, despite weeks, months, or years of dutiful attendance.

Make the regular crowd feel special, even if you have to fake the fact that you have no idea what their name is. When in doubt, ask your manager or another server for the name. Your guests will be happier, their checks will be bigger and your tips will be better.

Doing Your Work at the Table

Never do anything at the table not for the benefit of the guests. Add up checks in the service stand, not on the table. Do you expect your guests to stop their conversation and just watch quietly while you take care of other business?

Spacing Out a Request

Poor memory is a symptom of lack of focus. If your thinking is scattered, just write things down. Otherwise you'll try to think of everything at once and end up forgetting it all. Give your brain a break. Efficiency comes from lack of distraction not from more activity. If your goal is to assure your guests have an enjoyable experience, keep your head clear. You're less likely to get behind, making it easy to handle changes and snags as they come up.

Endless Wait for the Check

At the end of the meal, getting the check should easy, yet some servers mess it up and ruin what was otherwise solid service.

> **TRUTH IS STRANGER THAN FICTION**
>
> Awhile ago I got the craving for a really great hot turkey sandwich. A local diner prided itself on real mashed potatoes and I figured if I'd find a world class hot turkey sandwich anywhere in town, this would surely be the place.
>
> I could already taste the thick slabs of freshly sliced turkey breast as I ordered, but when the sandwich arrived, it was made with some sort of shredded turkey-like product covered in a pale gravy that was more like library paste!
>
> The waitress came back a few minutes later to inquire about my meal. I told her the sandwich was not at all what I expected and I was very disappointed.
>
> "Yeah," she said. "A lot of people tell us that," and just walked away!

First, just because your shift is ending, don't insist a guest settle the check before their food arrives. You took the table, so tough it out. It's presumptuous to ask for the money (and your tip) before either has been earned. If you don't take credit cards or are cash-only, make sure you tell your table as soon as they sit down. It will make everything go smoother at the end.

When the table is ready to pay, be swift about it. The table obviously wants to head out (particularly if there are children with them), so don't prolong the process. Quicker exits mean more turns and more tips, so it's a win-win. And never balk at splitting the tab into separate checks. Anyone who's worked a POS system knows it's easy to do.

Poor Policies

Many service problems arise from well-intentioned but misguided company policies. It puts your staff in an awkward position when they have to defend policies that stand in the way of guest gratification. If they displease *you*, they could lose their jobs. If they displease their guests, it goes against all their instincts.

The only way out of this dilemma is to make pleasing guests the most important job in the restaurant. Period. Give·your staff the authority to do whatever is necessary to assure your guests have a memorable dining experience.

Not Bringing the Full One Before Removing the Empty One
This is such a simple touch, yet so often overlooked. If you take an empty glass/roll basket away before you return with the full one, for a period guests will feel deprived – there's an empty spot where that item used to be. The solution is just to reverse the order of the tasks. You'll do the same amount of work but guests will never be left without. It shows an awareness that creates another point of difference from your competition.

Not Promptly Resolving a Complaint (In Favor of the Guest!)
If you're serious about guest gratification, there is no negotiation when if comes to a guest complaint. The only approach that will work is to apologize for the situation and fix it immediately. Don't ask the guest what they want you to do – it puts them on the spot and makes them uncomfortable.

When you understand the nature and source of the problem, propose an overly generous solution that will make the guest happy. Remember you're not just solving a problem, you're making an investment in securing a regular patron.

Stacking Plates up the Arm to Carry Them to the Table
Many diner-style concepts and coffee shops use this operating style. The look may be traditional, but when the bottom of one plate sits on top of the food on another, the novelty quickly fades.

If you choose to use this approach, coach your service staff that sanitation considerations are as important as how many plates they can carry in one trip. It is preferable to make an additional trip rather than alienate guests because they feel you soiled their food.

"Do-It-Yourself" Doggie Bags
If you pack your guests' leftovers to take home, do it with the same care and attention you show everything else in the restaurant. I've seen servers simply leave a container or bag on the table and expect guests to do it themselves. Some guests may ask for it that way, but absent a specific request, this practice is for the convenience of the staff rather than that of the guest. Stamp out this short-sightedness before it puts you out of business. Don't ask your guests to handle their own leftovers.

Adding a Tip to the Credit Card Slip

A brewpub in Park City, Utah did this to me ... once. They never got a second chance. If a guest signs the credit card receipt, fails to indicate a tip and leaves the slip untotalled, that's the luck of the draw. Add a tip yourself and you've put your hand in their wallet without permission ... and likely lost them forever.

Even if the cardholder intended to leave a tip and just forgot to do so (like me!), they'll never forgive your presumptiveness. If you feel it was an honest oversight, have the house tip out the server. It will cost you far less than alienating a potential regular patron.

Slow Morning Coffee Service

Most Americans seem to need a cup of coffee or tea to start the day off right. If guests get their coffee promptly, they will wait mor patiently for the rest of the meal service.

How you address this depends on your operating style. If your sales staff can't keep up with it, perhaps the bussers could fill coffee cups. Insulated carafes on the table might take the pressure off. Whatever you do, find a way to get a hot cup of coffee (or tea) to your breakfast guests right away. You'll have happier guests.

Confusing Service Format

A team service format can be effective, provided you explain it to guests at the beginning of the meal. Without a clear idea of what is happening, several service staff at the table can be confusing and confusion leads to lower tips.

In a team service restaurant I had three staff members ask me the same question. I gave the same answer to all three and none of them filled my request! I didn't know who to be upset with or who to tip. If you use a team service format, be sure your guests understand how it works and have one person to look to if there's a problem.

No Fresh Fork for Entrée or Dessert

You don't set the table with dirty utensils, why would you hand a dirty fork back to a guest and ask them to reuse it? The easiest approach is to have enough forks in the place setting to begin with although some prefer the look of presenting a fresh fork with the salad or dessert.

In any event, don't ask the guest to reuse a soiled utensil. Some guests will ask for a fresh fork; others will just remember it wasn't a memorable meal and go elsewhere next time.

Slow (or No) Refills

Beverages are as essential to the meal as the food, more so if you're on a diet that calls for lots of liquids. If someone orders only a drink, you must be alert for refills. Don't think you can neglect a glass only because the tab isn't going to generate a huge tip. Let the cup stay empty and there may not be a tip at all. This is especially true during breakfast/brunch, because you know everyone at the table is craving caffeine.

Failure to Honor Menu Prices

You must honor whatever you've said on the menu. I don't agree with the practice, but some places charge less for an item at lunch than they do at dinner. If you give a guest the wrong menu by mistake, honor the prices. You can never win those arguments.

Not Advising the Guest of a Service Charge

If you impose a service charge in lieu of voluntary tipping, courtesy (and perhaps the law) requires you to note this on your menu and on your guest checks. I also recommend you have your service staff verbally inform your guests of the policy.

If a guest feels they were not properly notified, they may suspect a ploy to gain a double tip. It might work once, but when your guests figure out what happened (and they will), they'll feel cheated. You can't cheat a person and expect to keep their business.

No Fuss for Special Occasions

If you're going to help guests celebrate a birthday or anniversary, then celebrate! Decorate the table. Have candles or sparklers on the [preferably complimentary] cake. Sing a special song instead of falling back on the stale standards. Make the celebration tasteful and appropriate to the mood of your dining room, but celebrate ... unless, of course, the guest wants to stay low key. (Ask first!)

Three-Foot Peppermills

Perhaps oversized peppermills were unique back in the day, but now they're quaint ... and who wants to use something that arrived tucked into a waiter's sweaty armpit anyway?

Offering fresh ground pepper is still a nice touch, but think about presentation. How about small salt and pepper mills on the tables instead? If you must bring the monster, perhaps it could contain white pepper or some other uncommon variety. Re-think this practice and see if you can give it a fresh twist (pun intended!)

Glass Coffee Pots in Upscale Restaurants
In coffee shops and casually-themed restaurants, guests expect coffee from the standard glass pots. As the check average climbs, though, a more formal presentation is appropriate. Make your coffee service a point of difference and you can give your guests another reason to think of you any time they dine elsewhere.

Failure to Accommodate Special Requests
In his book *It's Not My Department,* author Peter Glen offers a simple approach to special requests. He suggests you find out what people want, find out how they want it ... then give it to them just that way! (Duh!) People with special needs will give their business to those restaurants who can (and will!) meet them.

Refusing to Heat a Baby's Food or Bottle
If guest service is your most important job, then service your guests. Warming baby food or formula is a simple task. There's no reason to treat a parent's request for this service as an imposition. If there are very young children at the table, offer this accommodation to the parents before they ask. They'll recognize your caring whether or not they need the service.

Unpriced Specials
Why would you think that just because an item isn't normally on the menu you no longer have to disclose the price? Guests are already suspicious that the special items are really just a clever way to clean out the walk-in and get rid of excess ingredients, but even when the specials are legit, patrons want to know the price.

Don't make them have to ask and look like cheapskates in front of their companions. Just work the price information into your spiel about how amazing the striped bass is today and have a small (priced!) daily special menu to leave on the table.

Coaching Concerns

While all the points in this chapter are legitimately management's responsibility and therefore coaching concerns, some are more clearly so than others. As a manager, your job could easily become finding and correcting faults. That makes you a cop. If you approach your job like a coach, the job becomes discovering and developing the strengths of your staff. The shift is subtle but it will make all the difference in helping your crew recognize and correct these annoyances.

Sketchy Menu Knowledge

Walking into a new restaurant can be intimidating, especially if it is a new concept or one serving an unfamiliar cuisine. Fortunately there's a server to guide guests' decisions and take them through the menu. At least, that *should* be true. Unfortunately, too often servers barely know anything about what is on the menu and endless excuses are just embarrassing.

When a guest asks how a dish tastes or what's in it, you must be able to provide an informed response. This means you know the ingredients, how it's prepared and the flavor profile. Servers should have personally tasted (and been tested) on everything the menu offers. This information has the most impact when it comes from personal experience rather than a memorized list.

Make it like staging a television cooking demonstration. Include managers, greeters, cocktail staff and bussers in the classes. You never know who a guest will ask. Money invested in these training meals for your staff will pay regular dividends.

Taking the Initiative to Refill Wine Glasses

If you refill wine glasses at the table from a bottle that one of the guests ordered, you're divvying up someone's else (expensive) property. Don't do it unless they ask you to. You don't know who's planning to finish what, who's driving, or who is picking up the check. It also looks like you're trying to hurry people into ordering another bottle.

Bait and Switch

When a particular wine is not available and the patron asks for another recommendation, they have a right to assume that if their first choice wine was under $30, your suggested alternative won't be one costing twice that amount. Under such circumstances, the guest also has the right to expect they will be informed of the price and allowed to make the final decision.

Full Service ... That Isn't

If you profess to be a full service restaurant, do the work required to actually deliver full service. Don't ask a guest to pass a beer to a fellow diner when you could walk around the table and deliver it yourself. In fact, don't ask guests to do any task you can't do for them. Booth service can sometimes require passing plates, but only when placing items yourself would be more awkward. Doing it right may take a little more effort on your part ... but that's why you're there, isn't it?

Long Waits for Service

Diners hate waiting (seemingly) forever for someone to take a drink order, bring menus or offer water. The lag time between being seated and getting started with the actual process of eating dinner could easily be stricken from the restaurant experience entirely. Menus should just be there when there is a decision to make. The server should at least acknowledge the table within sixty seconds and start service within three minutes.

Most guests will want some time to get acquainted with the drink list or the menu, but that isn't a twenty-minute activity. Everyone is more forgiving with a cocktail in hand, so cut to the chase and get things started promptly.

Time seems to go faster when guests have something to do, so get them something to nibble on quickly. Mexican restaurants have this figured out with chips and salsa arriving almost instantly. It could be a bread basket, a small *crudité* or an *amuse bouche*, but do what you can to avoid subjecting guests to long periods of simply sitting.

Canned Communications

Scripted communication is often worse than no communication at all. Guest enjoyment is created by the human dimension in service, not the mechanical content. You must communicate certain points to the guest at various times during the meal, but the real message is always in your tone of voice and the warm human connection you can establish with them.

After some basic skills training, it's usually more effective to specify the desired ends and leave the means to the discretion of the service staff. This lets them be themselves and respond more appropriately to what the guests want. Anything less is about as satisfying as making love through an interpreter!

Clumsy Handling of Credit Cards

When you deal with a guest's credit card, you have your hand in their wallet, a position of trust. Take particular care to avoid making the guest uneasy and be sure all staff knows and follows proper procedures for handling credit card purchases.

It is equally crucial to handle the card itself with respect. This means never leaving a patron's credit card unattended or handling it casually. A credit card is essentially a blank check on your guest's account. Make sure your behavior demonstrates that you take that responsibility – and their trust – seriously.

Not Serving Children or Elders First

Serve children first. They haven't developed social graces and will not wait their turn. Serve women next starting with the eldest. Finally, serve the men, older gentlemen first and the host last. The arrangement of the table or the size of the party may dictate a different order of service, but come as close as you can.

No Alternatives to Sold-Out Items

When you've sold out of an item, the situation is already awkward. You only make it worse if you don't suggest alternatives. How is the guest supposed to know what else they can order? Make a suggestion and you won't place them in an uncomfortable position.

Not Removing Extra Place Settings

Don't have anything on the table the guest doesn't need, including extra place settings. If you don't remove extra settings, guests may wonder what is going to happen with the place setting after they leave. Will it just stay there for the next diner? If that worry enters their mind, they may start to wonder about their own silverware.

Serving with the Elbow in the Guest's Face

Serving from the left and clearing from the right is the preferred standard, but if you serve from the left with your right hand or from the right with your left, it puts your elbow in the guest's face. For smoother service, just be sure to use your left hand when serving from the left and your right hand when serving from the right.

No Suggestions or Recommendations

Your mission is to help your guests have a good time. Part of that job is educating them about the unique and exciting choices your restaurant offers. If you don't tell them, how are they going to know? Even the most well-written menu is a poor substitute for an enthusiastic and knowledgeable personal suggestion.

Always offer two alternatives when making a recommendation to avoid appearing like you're pushing an item. If the guest wants something other than what you suggest, they'll ask about it. The important point is that they feel comfortable during the process.

Pushy Sales Techniques

Skillful suggestions can help guests have a more enjoyable evening, but an insensitive, memorized sales pitch will irritate your diners. The goal is to make people eager to buy, not to attempt to forcefully sell them something. The less distracted you are at the table, the more personal and effective your check-building efforts will be.

Clattering Dishes

Professionals don't call attention to themselves or detract from the guests' enjoyment of the meal. Clattering dishes are usually a sign of an over-eager busser who doesn't see their behavior as part of the overall dining experience. Reset tables as quickly as possible, but never at the expense of diner enjoyment. Show bussers what to do and coach them on why the way they do it makes a difference.

Filling a Doggie Bag or Box at the Table

Never scape food off a plate at the table ... it makes it seem like garbage. Unless guests object, take the plate to the kitchen, place the leftovers neatly in the container and bring a tidy package back to the table. Respect your food and your guests will do the same.

Napkins or Plates with the Logo Askew

Always place a customized item with the restaurant's logo facing the guest. Haphazard placement only shows a lack of concentration and inattention to detail. Guests may not always notice when you do it properly, but they'll always notice when you're sloppy.

No Prices for Oral Specials

Just because you recite the daily specials doesn't mean the price information isn't important. If you find it awkward to mention prices, complete the presentation by handing guests a small menu with the day's specials and their prices. This also will help them remember what you said when they make their dinner choices.

Inconsistent Service Methods

People are creatures of habit, and feel more comfortable when they know what to expect. Toward this end, always approach the table from the same position and always serve and clear from the same sides. Whether that is the classic "serve from the left, clear from the right" or not is less important to smooth service than consistency.

Not Warning of Hot Plates or Beverages

Refilling the coffee cup is part of good service, but make sure the guest is aware you've done it. If not, you take the chance they will burn their mouth on a cup of coffee that is suddenly much hotter than expected.

Ask permission before refilling the coffee, too, particularly if the guest uses cream and sugar. It is annoying to alter the balance of the cup when your guest has it adjusted just the way they like it.

Hot plates are a different issue because in a great restaurant, hot plates are the rule. If you can hold a plate of hot food without a towel, the plate isn't hot enough to keep the food at temperature. Serving hot food hot requires hot plates. Make sure you do it ... and make sure your guests know you've done it.

Not Moving With the Speed of the Room

Good service is almost invisible. Guests should only notice what is going on at their table and not be distracted by other movements around them. If you're moving fast in a slow-paced dining room, you will be a distraction. The same is true if you're moving slowly in a fast-paced room.

The speed at which you move from place to place is different from the speed at which you do your job. You can still be very quick and efficient in a slower-moving dining room. Your movements just take on a different quality.

The process is like the martial arts master whose power comes from a state of focused relaxation. If you can move with the speed of the room, you can give responsive service and your guests will hardly notice you are there.

Serving a Bowl Without an Underliner

Bowls hold liquids and liquids often spill. The only question is whether the spill will fall on the underliner or on the table! If it falls on the underliner (after it has been served), at least the table stop stays clean. If it falls on the table, it affects the guest's enjoyment of the meal and creates a cleaning problem. Give everyone a break and make underliners standard practice in your restaurant.

Dropping Plates vs. Presenting Them

You show your respect for the work of your kitchen staff by the way you handle their food. Train your staff to *present* the plates at the table. Place plates in front of the guest with respect, entrées closest to the diner. If there is a logo on the plate, be sure it faces the guest.

The problem comes when servers look away from the table toward their next activity before finishing what they're doing now. It is equivalent to a football receiver starting to run before he has complete possession of the ball. As in football, talk to your servers about looking the plate all the way onto the table.

The idea is to *present* the plate, not just deliver it. If you distribute the plates like you're dealing a hand of cards, expect your guests to be less enthusiastic about their meals.

Not Knowing the Brands at the Bar
How often can you say "I don't know" before you feel stupid? Basic service staff training must include a thorough knowledge of the bar operation. This includes knowing the brands you carry and the ingredients in your specialty drinks. If you have signature drinks (and I recommend you do), be sure your staff has tasted them and can describe them in an appetizing and accurate way.

Not Bringing All Necessary Serviceware
A bowl of soup without a soup spoon is useless. If you forget, the soup will be cooling while you find a spoon and return to the table. Meanwhile, all your guest can do is sit there staring at the bowl and feeling awkward. As with condiments, it can be helpful to bring the necessary serviceware before you serve the item. This way you can be sure guests can eat hot food while it's still hot.

Not Checking Back Within Two Bites
If there is a problem with the entrée or if the guest needs anything, they may not know that when you first serve the item. So, asking if they need anything else at the time of service is not the end of it. After two bites, the guests will know what they think of the food and what they may need to go with it. Give them a minute and then return to ask if everything is prepared the way they expected.

Having to Ask for Basic Condiments
Most concepts have salt and pepper on the table before seating the guests because these are items guests are likely to want throughout the early stages of the meal and it is impolite to make them have to ask. In most cases you can remove salt and pepper when you clear the entrées.

During the breakfast period, you'll want to have sugar on the table. At lunch and dinner you can create a small point of difference by bringing cream and sugar just before you serve the coffee. Don't waste time asking, just do it.

Clearing Before All Guests Are Finished
Many people eat slowly. It is embarrassing to them, and the others at the table, when they are the only ones left with a plate in front of them. I'm sure there are well-intentioned motives to remove a guest's plate as soon as they finish but be aware the practice places more pressure on those who are still eating. If a guest wants their plate removed, they'll let you know. Otherwise, it is always more considerate to wait and clear the entire table at once.

Not Warning About Potential Food Hazards
There may be some legal implications in this point but it is just common courtesy to advise your guests of potential hazards in your menu items. For example, "boneless" fish could still contain some bones. If there is a potential hazard, you are only being polite when you alert your guests to it.

Not Regularly Scanning Your Station
The situation on your station can change quickly. A rapid visual check will provide eye contact with any guest who is trying to get your attention and allow you to identify new parties that have been seated since you left. If a guest is trying to get your attention and feels ignored because you don't notice, they will become irritated. Irritated guests seldom tip well or become regular patrons.

Missing Utensils
Don't make a guest ask for a utensil that is obviously needed for the items they've ordered. The need can arise when an item requires a specific utensil (like a soup spoon) or when you remove soiled silverware at the time you clear each course. (I won't re-use a soiled fork and always ask for a fresh one.) Either replace missing utensils before serving the next course or bring the necessary utensil when you serve the next item. Don't make the guest have to ask.

Not Clearing One Course Before Serving the Next
You can't serve a meal gracefully if you're trying to set a plate down with one hand while you slide another out of the way with the other. Besides, nobody wants to look at soiled plates and fresh food in the same glance.

Once the table finishes a course, remove everything from that course. If they need a particular item later in the meal service, bring it back at the appropriate time. A clean table makes guests feel more comfortable with the meal service and the restaurant itself.

Not Servicing the Table After Presenting the Check
The meal isn't over when you place the change on the table and the need for service doesn't end until guests have left the building. They may need more coffee. They may decide to order after-dinner drinks. Anything could happen and your job is to stay alert so you can be there to handle it smoothly.

Sometime between the check presentation and when the guest gets up to leave, they decide how much of a tip to leave. If there are still guests at the table, you're still on stage. Stay in character.

Uncleared Tables

The most attractive decor in a dining room is butts on chairs, not dirty dishes on tables. The problem is more irritating if the staff is on a break while the condition persists. The excuse I often hear is that the rush just ended. If so, why isn't the dining room staff busy clearing tables? When the rush is over, the amateurs take a break. Pros get the place reloaded for the next rush, *then* take a break.

Refilling Water or Coffee after Each Sip

This annoyance happens when you've only told bussers to keep the water or coffee full. If they're eager to please, they will aggressively do exactly what you told them. Your task as their coach is to help them develop a sense of what makes a good dining experience and understand how their job functions fit into that.

Clearing Plates Without Permission

You are there to enhance the guest's experience, not intrude on it. It is only common respect not to take anything away from the guest without asking, particularly something as personal as their dinner plate. And don't reach for the plate as you are asking the question. Your eagerness and lack of sensitivity will cost you points.

That said, nobody likes to linger over soiled plates once they are through eating. As the last diner finishes, pause a few beats, make eye contact with the host for the OK, then quickly clear the table. The pause is important to prevent guests from feeling rushed.

Vanishing Waiters

Why can you never find a waiter when you want one? Most diners have had this frustration. The best defense is a good offense. Make a visual check of each table at your station every time you re-enter the dining room. Look for diners who are obviously looking for you. If you take a break while you still have occupied tables, be sure another server keeps an eye on your station.

If your shift is over and you must clock out while you still have occupied tables, don't just walk away. Thank your guests for their patronage, introduce the person who will see to their needs and reassure them the quality of their evening is in good hands.

The problem of disappearing waiters is particularly acute when the guest is trying to settle the check and be on their way. If you need an incentive, recall that this is when guests are deciding how much of a tip to leave. Don't blow it at the end!

Watching the Guest Complete the Credit Card Slip
The tip is a personal decision. If you give the impression you're looking over the guest's shoulder, you've invaded their privacy. The sensation of being spied upon is extremely uncomfortable and gives the impression you're trying to rush the guest or pressure them to leave you more money – not good thoughts to implant while they are deciding your tip.

All Dollar Bills as Change
If you appear to be angling for a tip, you may irritate your guests. Make it as easy as possible for them to leave a reasonable tip but don't overdo it. The exception to this rule is when you make change for a blind guest. In that case, ask if they want their change in singles. It will reassure them that they have the proper change.

Not Thanking Guests When They Leave
Gratitude is powerful. All things being equal, people go businesses that appreciate their patronage. Thanking guests as they leave is not just courtesy, it is an investment in their future loyalty. When guests feel you are sincerely grateful for their business, they feel better about giving it to you. Heart-felt gratitude is so uncommon that your guests will remember your appreciation and return for more.

Professional Problems

The next few items relate to the skill and knowledge of your service staff. Physical skills only develop with practice. Do not allow staff to serve your guests until they have been thoroughly trained and have mastered the basic knowledge and skills of their trade.

Dribbling Wine on the Table When Pouring
Proper wine service is smooth and unobtrusive. Dribbling wine is both annoying and unnecessary. Train your staff to roll the bottle slightly at the end of the pour to cause that last drop to stay on the rim of the bottle, not fall on the table top.

As a further note, skill in opening and pouring wine only comes with practice. Ask your wine supplier to help you find a supply of foil caps so your staff can practice foil cutting. An "Ah-So" wine opener will allow you to re-cork the bottles for re-tries.

Drill your crew until they are confident in their abilities to handle wine service smoothly. The more comfortable they are with the process, the more likely they are to suggest wine to your guests.

Asking Guests to Help with the Service
People don't come to your restaurant to serve themselves. If you need help, ask another staff member. Do whatever it takes to make the service as smooth as possible for your guests. After the shift, turn this into a learning opportunity. Sit down with the crew and discuss what led to the need for the guest to get involved. Then determine what action, if any, is needed to avoid future repetitions.

Touching a Wine Bottle to the Rim of the Glass
It is bad form to touch the wine glass with the bottle. The outside of the bottle is not necessarily clean and many guests are sensitive to what touches surfaces from which they eat or drink. This is a simple training problem that may be caused by the server being unaware of their actions or trying to avoid dripping wine on the table.

Incorrect Change
If you return the wrong amount of change, guests may think you're either incompetent or trying to cheat them. Neither conclusion will work to your benefit. Clearly state how much money the guest gives you and count the change twice when you take it out of the drawer.

If you have a cashier, be sure she counts the change again when she hands it to the guest. If counting back change at the table would be distracting, fan the bills slightly and place the change on top so the guest can quickly be see you've returned the correct amount. You can't be too careful when handling your guests' money.

Little Knowledge of Community Attractions
Newcomers to the area want good "inside advice" about where to go and what to do. It is helpful when all your staff can respond knowledgeably to these questions. Contact your local Chamber of Commerce or Visitors Bureau for information on events, attractions and activities. Update your crew at your daily pre-shift meeting. Remember the longer a visitor stays in town, the more opportunities they'll have to dine at your restaurant.

Spilling Food or Beverage
Sloppiness is the sign of a distracted server. Part of management's job is to help the service staff maintain their composure. If a staff member is getting buried "in the weeds," give them a hand and take some pressure off. Spilling food or drink is unprofessional and you can usually avoid it. If an accident occurs, just take it in stride. Apologize quickly and quietly, clean up any mess and continue the meal service. Don't get dramatic about the incident.

If you spill something on a guest, immediately make it right. Give them more than enough cash to cover the cost of cleaning, and something extra (like a dessert or after-dinner drink) to make up for the inconvenience. I also recommend a gift certificate for the next time they visit the restaurant. It is a generous gesture and improves the odds they will return to give you another chance to get it right.

Wet, Stained or Mis-Added Checks
Everything you place on the table should reflect the personal care and professionalism you want your guests to associate with your restaurant. Messy food checks are the mark of an uncaring amateur.

No Idea How to Handle Advertised Specials or Coupons
Special promotions are an effective way to create excitement and generate new business for the restaurant, but if people respond to an advertised offer and nobody knows what they're talking about, it creates an uncomfortable situation for everyone.

Since (hopefully) many people responding to your special offer will be first-timers, they won't be sure if you are incompetent or just confused. In either case, it's not a desirable first impression. Be sure to brief your staff thoroughly on the content, goals and procedures of your promotions *before* you advertise them to the public.

Losing or Damaging a Credit Card
When you handle a guest's credit card, you are toying with their money. If you damage the card, they won't have access to their funds until they can get a replacement card. That's hard enough for local residents, but if your guests are from out of the area, the problem even is more serious. Vacationers who lose the use of their credit card may not be able to continue their holiday.

You must make a management decision about how to handle this situation if it occurs. Work out your plan of action now, not in the emotion of the moment. You may offer to cash a check so they can continue their vacation until a new card arrives. Take responsibility for finding a solution that works for them.

Cafeteria Calamities

Just because an operation has a self service format doesn't eliminate the need to provide exceptional guest service. Remember that it *is* possible to be the restaurant of choice ... even when your patrons don't have another choice. All it takes is the same service orientation we have been discussing. Here are some details to avoid:

Pouring Old Product on Top of New

This is another bad habit developed for the convenience of the staff. It is dangerous – and repulsive to informed guests – because it is blatant cross-contamination. If the older product is tainted, it will contaminate the fresh product, so avoid it. Present items in small quantities. Attend your line constantly so you can *replace* containers as soon as they get low. Your line will look better, your guests will be happier and your food will be safer.

Inattentive Line Workers

All the attributes of good table service apply in a cafeteria; only the context changes. The game is still about personal connection. This means the staff must be mentally present and listen carefully to the guests be sure they understand and respect any special requests. It will also build business – and make the shift more enjoyable – when the staff can relate to those in line as individuals rather than simply the next to be served.

Awkward Replenishing of Buffets

I was at a Thanksgiving buffet at a major new hotel. Since I hate lines, I waited until the main surge had gone through the buffet line before going up for my meal.

I was the last person in line when an overzealous staff member cut in front of me to replenish and rearrange the buffet line. I asked if she could let me go through before she continued but she ignored me. I stood there with hot food on my plate for several minutes while this thoughtless individual finished her work and left. Unless someone decides to buy my next meal, I won't be back.

Unsupervised Buffets or Salad Bars

The major complaint against salad bars is that they're unsanitary. Some of the people you serve are very sensitive to this issue and some are unconscious.

Children are proven violators of salad bar etiquette. They will stick their fingers in the dressing to taste it or nibble at something then put it back. They will refill a dirty salad bowl and spread your salads all over the floor. (As you may have noticed, children come in all ages and sizes!)

Unless you supervise the salad bar closely, these practices will drive away many of your guests. You also run the risk of passing a food borne illness to the ones you don't scare off.

A successful salad bar is constantly supervised by a knowledgeable staff member. Display items in small quantities and allow them to run down before changing. Wipe up spills promptly. A great salad bar has striking presentation and that doesn't happen accidentally.

Not Changing Utensils When Changing Food Containers

Always bring clean serving utensils when you replace food containers. If you place a soiled spoon back into crock of fresh product, it's cross-contamination again. Your guests will appreciate the gesture.

It's also annoying to use a serving utensil that has food smeared on the handle from a previous patron. Replace soiled utensils with clean ones, don't just wipe them off – it's more professional and increases your guests' confidence in your operation.

Bonus Points

While true hospitality comes from how you *are* rather than what you *do*, it is also true that the actions which make sense to you are a direct result of how you are thinking in the moment. Once you develop a hospitality mind set, everything you do will come across as hospitable. Here are some practices that reflect that way of being in the world:

The Unexpected Extra

Everybody likes to get something for nothing. The unexpected extra is just some small gift to guests as a gesture of caring. In New Orleans culture, the word for this is *lagniappe* (pronounced LAN-yap) and means "something extra."

The unexpected extra can be anything. Some operators have institutionalized it: the donut holes for waiting male guests at Lou Mitchell's in Chicago (women get a small box of Milk Duds!) or the complimentary glass of sparkling wine to start the meal at Brix 25° in Gig Harbor, Washington. Others prefer to mix it up. At Gramercy Tavern in New York there's always a different take-home treat from the bakeshop when the check arrives.

The unexpected extra could be an offer to sample a new appetizer, a taste of new wine you just received or the recipe for your daily special. When I was a Navy foodservice officer in the Philippines, we had our cute female line attendants pass out hors d'oeuvres to the sailors waiting in line! The possibilities are endless.

The impact doesn't come from the gift, but from the gesture itself ... provided it is offered from a hospitality state of mind and not just another task. To set yourself apart from others, "Give 'em!"

Remember Likes and Dislikes

Everyone has personal preferences. For example, my wife has sensitive teeth. She prefers water with no ice. When we go to a new restaurant, though, they automatically fill the water glass with ice.

So we ask for a glass without ice. Servers often roll their eyes and walk away mumbling something about being picky. Eventually they bring it the way she wants it. Halfway through the meal they'll refill the glass ... with ice! Lately she's just stopped asking for no ice in a new restaurant. She just won't drink any water.

Places that know us bring it the way she likes it from the outset and it's *so* nice not to have to deal with that hassle! Servers who are truly present will ask if her teeth are also sensitive to heat (they are). When they bring her coffee, they bring a dish of ice cubes on the side to help her cool it down. Brilliant!

> ## WHOSE JOB IS IT?
>
> I had a favorite dry cleaner in Colorado Springs. They did good work at a fair price, but so did others. I patronized them because they always remembered how I wanted my shirts done.
>
> I was usually in a rush and liked that I could just drop my cleaning and run. They'd take care of everything else ... except when there was a newly-hired counter person on the job.
>
> When that happened, my normal dash for the door was abruptly halted when the new staffer demanded to know who I was and what I wanted them to do with this pile of clothes.
>
> I understand why that might happen, but it's not my job to train their staff. If they were really serious about my business, *they* would have found a way to educate new workers about their regular patrons' expectations.

Detroit's Rattlesnake Club kept a card on all their regular guests with everything they knew about them: family names, food and drink preferences, even trips they were planning.

When a regular made a reservation, the server got the card. Their challenge was to learn something new on each visit. By now I'm sure they've put that database on a computer, but it doesn't matter *how* they keep the data. The important thing is they want to know more about their guests ... and have a way to do it.

Make Knowledgeable Suggestions

People don't dine out to save money, they go to restaurants to have a good time and knowledgeable suggestions help them know about the wonderful choices they can make at your place.

"Suggestion" is not a dirty word if your intent is to help the guest have a more enjoyable experience rather than just to pump the check. They won't take you up on every suggestion. Still, you know what the restaurant has to offer. If you know what the guest wants, you can help your patrons find items that will delight them.

Remember Names

Do you have regular guests? Of course. Do you know their names? Probably. If I came to work for you, is there a *system* in place – a system – so I'd learn that information as well? Remember the theme song from the old TV show, Cheers? "Sometimes you want to go where everybody knows your name." It's true.

Personal connection is the key to building a following and nothing is more personal to someone than the sound of their own name. If you see the importance of this seemingly small point, you will develop a system to know not only the name of the host, but that of their mate, their kids, their dog and their boat! If it's important to them, it should be important to you. But for that to happen, you need an actual system, whether that be captioned photos on a bulletin board, a photo album or continual coaching.

To get on the regular staff at Shari's, a Northwest coffee shop chain, you must know the names of fifty regulars. If you can't learn fifty names, you don't work there. After that, for every hundred names you learn, you'll get your name on a plaque on the wall. There are some servers in this coffee shop who allegedly know 1400 names ... because they have a system that's has become part of their culture.

Coffee Cup Handle at 4:00

In standard American service, you place the coffee cup to the right of the diner with the handle in the 4:00 position. This positions the handle is just where it needs to be for the typical right-handed guest to pick up the cup easily. It is a small detail, but it shows your awareness of the guest's needs.

If you notice the guest is left-handed (and you should notice such things), imagine their surprise if you place the coffee cup on the left with the handle placed at 8:00!

Never Say Never

When people hear you say No, it can drop their mood (along with the check average and your tip!) Always tell a guest what you *can* do for them, never what you *can't* ... particularly if they seem to be in a touchy mood.

For example, if a patron asks for a brand of Scotch you don't carry, don't tell them you don't have it, tell them what brands they *can* choose from. Keep it positive.

If they order your Sea Bass special and it's gone (remember that you always *sell out*, never *run out!*), you could say something like, "I'm so sorry, we've sold out of that already. Because it comes in fresh, we can only make a limited number of orders and tonight it seems like everybody wanted it. If you really like Sea Bass, leave me your phone number. The next time we have it on the menu, I'll give a call and reserve some for you. In the meantime, let me suggest ..."

Handling things this way is more considerate of your guests' sense of well-being, increases personal connection, and it makes the shift a lot more fun for you as well!

Go the Extra Mile
Going the extra mile means doing more than the guest asks for ... or even expects. It's being in the moment with others (presence) and recognizing those moments when you could do something that would really WOW them.

These opportunities appear out of nowhere (and disappear just as quickly), so there are no guidelines on what to do or how to do it. But if your mind is clear and your heart is in the right place when you recognize a moment like this, you will instinctively know what to do ... and it will work. But you must grasp the opportunity of a lifetime during the lifetime of the opportunity!

Replace an Absent Guest's Napkin
This is a small touch but so uncommon that it can be impressive. When guests leave the table, they usually place their napkin on the table or on the seat of their chair. Just casually pick up the napkin and replace it with a fresh one. Wow! (By the way, this even works with paper napkins!)

Extra Napkins for Gentlemen with Beards or Moustaches
Those of us with facial hair have an additional problem when eating some foods. (When you finish an ice cream cone, it's gone. If you have a beard, an ice cream cone can last for hours!) Those of us who grow hair where we can (!) need one napkin for the lap and another for the face. Particularly if you serve a messy finger food item like barbecued ribs, bring an extra napkin or two and let them know it's for their moustache. Come to think of it, with finger foods, it's a good idea to just bring extra napkins for everyone!

Cafeteria Self-Service

When I took over the foodservice program for the U.S. Olympic Training Centers, I inherited a standard military-type cafeteria operation. The athletes were fed but not very excited. We made many changes, one of the first was to turn the spoons around. I made the entire operation self-service, allowing the athletes to make their own selections. They could take as much (or as little) as they wanted. Some very unexpected things happened:

The first change I noticed was that my cost per meal dropped almost 15%. When they could take whatever they wanted, the athletes actually took *less* food than we were giving them before!

That was cool enough, but the most pleasant surprise was the change in the relationship between my staff and the athletes. Freed from their serving duties, my crew's main job was to keep the line replenished and looking attractive. Their conversations with the athletes changed from task-oriented ("do you want peas?") to being more personal. Everybody had a more enjoyable time.

Offer Free Samples

Many less adventurous diners are reluctant to commit to a full entrée if they're not familiar with the primary ingredients. As with small children, the knee-jerk reaction to a strange new food offer can be, "I don't like it," even if they've never tried it.

There are three steps to introduce an unusual new item like ostrich or an uncommon species of fish: The first step is to offer your guests complimentary samples. "Free" is difficult to turn down, especially when the risk in only one bite and the offer is accompanied by a compelling story. People who enjoy good food love to feel like adventurers, and what better way to do that than to give them a chance to try something new and a bit out of the ordinary?

If the responses to the samples are positive, the second step is to introduce the item in one or more appetizer or small plate formats. This allows people to become familiar with it – or share a taste with others – without committing to purchasing an entrée-sized portion. It also provides some market research as to which versions sell best.

When a smaller portion has received general acceptance, you can safely introduce the item as an entrée special. From there you can determine if it deserves a more permanent place on your menu. Bear in mind some items will sell better as off-the-menu specials than they will as regular menu offerings.

Free Tastes of Wine

Many less adventurous diners are reluctant to commit to ordering a full bottle of an unfamiliar wine, particularly those at higher price points. An extensive by-the-glass program can help, but when you can do it, there's nothing as hospitable as offering a complimentary taste of a wine the guest had questions about.

You will pick up points whether they choose to order more or not ... and repeat patronage is ultimately the most profitable sale you can make.

Randy Rayburn, owner of Sunset Grill and several other restaurants in Nashville, is one of the best operators I know. He has several hundred wines on his list and if you want a glass of almost any of them, he will open the bottle and pour it for you.

When I asked him how he could make that policy work, he said, "First of all, I'm going to sell you a second glass. If I can't find a way to sell the remaining two glasses in that bottle, I'm in the wrong business!" (PS: Randy is *definitely* in the right business!)

8
Attitude Errors

Staff demeanor has an important role in guest gratification. The way your staff conducts themselves says a lot about your restaurant and your attention to detail. As always, all the issues noted are ultimately the responsibility of management. Many are traits to be alert for during your screening and hiring process. Some are training-related. All are important to your success.

Just as you can't prepare first class food with goods of inferior quality, you can't provide memorable service with mediocre staff. The good news is that people can change their attitudes if they see a bigger picture. The bad news is that you're not in the rehabilitation business. You must help your present staff to develop and grow, but you can be more selective with new hires.

The majority always rules. If most of your staff take pride in their work and are serious about expanding their professional skills, the performance level of everyone on the team will improve. If most of your crew feels the game is to do as little as possible and get away with as much as they can, new workers will follow their example.

The quickest way to take the temperature is to see who is quitting. Are you losing your good workers or your troublemakers? The real pros won't stay long in an organization that does not operate to their standards while slackers will be uncomfortable if their peers demand they produce at a high level. You can determine the direction your company will take by which attitude you allow to predominate.

Horrible Habits

Habits are unconscious behaviors. Your staff may not even be aware of what they're doing or its impact on your guests. Eliminating these actions increases the chances of having delighted diners ... and it is your responsibility as the coach to guide your team in that direction.

Eating or Drinking at Work Stations

Other than routine tasting by the cooks, eating at work stations is a serious violation of basic sanitation rules. Eating puts your fingers around your mouth, contaminates your hands and increases the risk of transmitting foodborne illness. Even if you wash your hands immediately after eating, you still place the restaurant and your guests in peril. The habit is a major distraction for the guests, particularly the ones who understand proper sanitation.

For example, my wife will never return to a restaurant where she's seen this behavior. Admittedly, she's a bit of a germaphobe, but I've heard the same comment from many other diners. Eating in work stations brings you unfavorable attention and diverts the guests' focus from their experience. When it's time to eat, sit down and enjoy your meal. You'll be doing yourself and your guests a favor.

Uncovered Heads in the Kitchen

All health departments require some form of hair restraint in the kitchen and in many jurisdictions, a hair net or hair spray is enough to keep stray hair from falling into food. For kitchen workers who are visible from the dining room, there's another consideration:

To feel comfortable, guests must be able to *see* that the cooks' hair is restrained. The only sure way they can do this is when the kitchen crew are wearing hats. The style of head covering will depend on the style of your restaurant, but make sure your cooks are wearing something the guests can see.

Chewing Gum

Chewing gum makes you look like you're eating something. Seeing staff eating on the job is repulsive to many diners. In some diner concepts, gum-chewing is part of the look for the service staff. Personally, it's a reason I don't patronize many of these operations. Regardless of the concept, there's no valid reason for servers, cooks or bartenders to be chewing gum. Your safest position is just to prohibit all staff from chewing gum on the job.

Standing Around Doing Nothing

Coming up in the biz, I was always told, "If there's time to lean, there's time to clean." Yes, there is always something to do in a restaurant. The place is constantly in motion and a person who's not moving becomes obvious. When you stand out this way, you become a distraction to your guests. The distraction is worse if your hands are in your pockets or, heaven forbid, you are sitting on a table. To be safe, always be in motion.

Poor Personal Sanitation Practices

Don't think the public doesn't know, doesn't care or doesn't see poor sanitation practices. The habits most often mentioned to me and in online comments are the following:

- Touching your hair and then touching food without washing your hands
- Handling cash and then handling food without washing your hands
- Paying undue attention to your face and not washing your hands
- Coughing or sneezing and not washing your hands
- Scratching various body parts and not washing your hands
- Clearing a table then handling clean dishes or food without washing your hands

You can see the importance of handwashing in preventing potential point loss. It is also sound sanitation practice. Have conveniently located hand sinks and make sure your staff is in the habit of using them. If these sinks are partially visible, guests can see you wash your hands and may feel more comfortable.

Sharing Guest Restrooms and Not Washing Hands

Effective handwashing is the single most important way to prevent the spread of foodborne illness. Guests are particularly sensitive to handwashing in the restrooms. Even if it wasn't required by the health department, it's only common sense.

My wife told me of a time when a cocktail server came into the ladies restroom, set a full tray of drinks on the floor while she used the facilities and left without washing her hands. Unbelievable!

When you share the guest restrooms, everybody watches you more closely. Be sure to wash your hands and be particularly thorough about it. Your conscientious cleaning will make your guests feel more confident.

Poor Personal Hygiene

You must be as appetizing as the food you serve. Guests will notice dirty or untrimmed fingernails. Dirty hands are always a major turn-off. Body odor or bad breath will drive away even the most loyal patron. Shower before coming to work each day and wash your hands immediately after you arrive at the restaurant.

The pre-shift line-up is an old idea but still a good one. If the guest contact staff has poor hygiene, there's a good chance the crew in the kitchen does too. Be sure your staff knows your standards. If they don't measure up, send them home to handle it. They will do what you *inspect* of them, not what you *expect* of them.

Speaking a Foreign Language in Front of the Guest
Unless staff is speaking the language of the country where the restaurant is located, guests find this behavior insulting, no matter what the actual content of the conversation. If your staff talks in another language, train them never to look at the guests while they are having a conversation. To do so makes the conversation appear to be about the diners. Don't risk offending your guests this way.

Using Poor Grammar When Addressing a Guest
When interviewing job applicants, pay attention to their speech, particularly if they would be in direct contact with your guests. Guests will form an impression and memory of your restaurant from the tone and grammar of your staff. The ability to do the job includes not only physical skills and knowledge but the ability to leave guests with a good impression.

Whistling or Singing with the Background Music
I hope your restaurant is a place where your crew feels cheerful enough to sing. Happy staff always make for a more pleasant dining experience. Unfortunately, singing or whistling rarely makes your guests feel happy. Vocalizing may work in some concepts, but it must be an overt part of the operating style. It is seldom a positive point elsewhere. Singing or whistling may just be unconscious habits but the result can be distracting to your guests. If you feel the urge to break into song, hum to yourself with a smile on your face.

Not Moving at the "Speed of the Room"
Good service is almost invisible. Guests should only notice what's going on at their table and not be distracted by other movement in the room. If you move quickly in a slow-paced dining room or slowly in a fast-paced restaurant, you're a distraction.

The speed at which you move is different from the speed at which you do your job. You can still be very quick and efficient in a slower-moving dining room. The quality of your movements is just different. It's similar to the martial arts expert whose power comes from a calm and relaxed state rather than frenetic movement. If you can move with the speed of the room, you can give responsive service and your guests will hardly notice you are there.

Pointing in the Dining Room ... Ever
Directing a guest by pointing is rude. It is always preferable to say "let me show you" and lead them where they want to go. Pointing the way to the restrooms, in particular, can embarrass your guest.

If you can't lead them there yourself, be sure you can give discrete directions that don't require waving your hands. Bear in mind the only guests who won't know the location of the restrooms are those who have never been in the restaurant before.

Train your staff to let the manager know of any suspected first-time guests so they can be personally welcomed to the restaurant. [Hint: If guests ask how you knew they were first-timers, don't tell them about the restroom trick!] In any case, don't let a pointing finger become a substitute for responsive guest service.

Unintelligible Speech

To feel comfortable, guests must easily understand what you say. Never address the table before you have the guests' attention. Speak at a moderate pace in a clear voice and pronounce your words carefully. Use complete sentences as much as possible.

Be aware of guests' reactions as you speak and be sensitive for signs that they don't understand what you are saying. If you see guests with furrowed brows or quizzical looks, stop and regroup. It is rude to press on if you've lost the people you are trying to serve.

Rattling Pocket Change

Keep your hands out of your pockets. It looks unprofessional and is even more annoying when accompanied by jangling coins. Male managers are most likely to have this nervous habit and it can drive your guests up the wall! If you can't keep your hands out of your pockets, at least keep your pockets empty.

Absent-Mindedly Clicking a Ball Point Pen

This is another unconscious nervous habit often seen when servers are waiting for guests to make their meal decisions. If you need something to do with your hands, juggle (or better yet, clean!)

Walking Past Items Dropped on the Floor

Any time a member of the staff ignores debris on the floor, it shows their lack of pride in the restaurant. Assuming you have repeatedly covered this point is a staff meeting, look for the cause of this attitude rather than addressing the behavior directly.

Poor behavior usually suggests a low level of personal security and a feeling of not being a part of the company. If so, all the lectures in the world won't solve the problem. If you can help your staff feel better about their role in the success of the restaurant, the problem behaviors are less likely to appear.

Interrupting Another Staff Member
Unless you have to evacuate the building in an emergency, never interrupt the flow of service at the table. This habit is inconsiderate to both the staff member and the guests. If you break in on another staff member while they're talking with a guest, you are saying your needs are more important than those of your diner. If that is actually the case, you don't understand this business.

Answering a Question with a Question
Guests ask questions because they want answers. If you expect them to enjoy themselves, give them those answers. You may need more information, but don't ask for it until you've given them some recommendations, reassured them you can solve their problem or explained that you need a little more clarification to be able to help them properly.

Irritating Appearances

How you look is important to your success and the prosperity of the restaurant. Your appearance delivers a message from across the dining room and, right or wrong, guests will draw conclusions about you and your professionalism from what they see.

Kitchen Staff Loitering in the Dining Room
Your restaurant is a place of business, not a social club. Don't let your kitchen staff hand around in the dining room while the service staff is working. There's a difference between loitering and taking a scheduled break. Designate an area for your staff to take their breaks so they will know what you expect.

If the dining room is the only place a worker can sit, staff on break will be in view of the guests. This makes them part of your dining room decor. Establish standards for staff appearance and behavior that will enhance your guests' impression of the restaurant rather than diminish it.

The gathering must be purposeful instead of random. It must be obvious that the workers are there for a legitimate reason. Their appearance must be appetizing. If the kitchen crew is wearing shredded Harley Davidson t-shirts with filthy aprons, your guests will get very nervous.

Soiled or Ill-Fitting Uniforms

If you invest in uniforms to provide a more professional look, get serious about how they are worn. Be sure uniforms are spotlessly clean and fit properly. Looking neat is good but looking *crisp* is better. You and your guests can tell the difference. Be sure shirt tails are tucked in and never let anyone wear a soiled tie.

Issue enough uniforms that your crew can have a clean one every day. Replace them before they start to look dull. An investment in attractive, well-constructed uniforms makes a bold statement about the way you do business. A professional public image makes your guests feel more confident in your skills. Oh, and don't forget to provide a uniform look for your managers.

Smoking in Uniform

Staff smoking in the restaurant is obviously not allowed, but watching a staff member puff on an cigarette, no matter where it happens, just looks like hell! Smoking is not a clean activity and anything that makes your guests feel your restaurant is less clean will hurt you. Seeing staff members smoking behind the restaurant works against your image as a professional organization.

If you still allow your staff to smoke while in uniform, the only safe place to have a cigarette in the restaurant is either in a designated smoking break room or in their cars. Your restaurant's uniform is part of your restaurant's image with the public. When you smoke while in uniform, smoking becomes part of that image also. It's not the impression you want to leave in the minds of your market.

Unkempt Hair

Foodservice workers' hair must be kept clean and off the shoulder. Longer hair must be tied back. Foodhandlers must keep long hair tucked inside their hats. Remember that neat hair also applies to facial hair. If you allow male staffers to sport beards or moustaches, they must be neatly trimmed and attractive. Unshaven faces may be fashionably trendy, but are rarely appealing to your guests.

No Staff Uniforms

In the 70's, we wanted people to be natural. We thought if we let the staff wear their own clothes, they would feel more comfortable and provide better service. It might have worked then, but today, allowing the staff to wear anything they want gives the restaurant a haphazard appearance. Without uniforms, it can be difficult for guests to tell your staff from other guests.

A less obvious advantage to uniforms is what they can do to help staff attitude. When people dress for work, their thinking changes. Like actors getting into costume before going on stage, your crew starts to "get into character." Their performance will likely be more professional when they look the part.

Filthy Footwear

Dirty running shoes caked with food spills will not help guests remember you more fondly. Footwear is an often overlooked part of creating a professional appearance.

For safety reasons, restaurant footwear must be grease-resistant to help avoid slipping accidents. Good traction also lets the staff safely move faster in the kitchen and dining room. To prevent fatigue and lower back pain, footwear should be comfortable and provide proper arch support. To enhance the professional image of your uniforms, be sure all footwear is clean, shined and of similar design.

The only sure way to do this is to specify the footwear you'll allow to be worn on the job, meaning you must also become involved in the purchase. You might require your staff to buy a particular style of shoe and repay them over time or buy the shoes yourself and deduct an amount from each paycheck until the cost is recovered.

If a worker stays a certain length of time, you could reimburse them for the full cost of the shoes. State laws may have a bearing on what you do or how you do it, but regardless, you can't re-issue footwear. Consult your legal advisor if you have questions. I can only advise you that attractive footwear is attractive to your guests. What you do with that information is up to you.

Poor Posture

Those who stand erect convey a more professional image and instill more confidence than those who slouch. During the screening and interviewing process, notice how job applicants carry themselves. When job skills and willingness to do the job are equal, the person with the best posture is likely to get the job.

Silly-looking Uniforms

The purpose of uniforms is to have the crew look sharp and more professional. Consult them before making the selection of what to wear. If you require them to wear uniforms they hate, they'll be self-conscious and look uncomfortable. Why would you do this to people you respect? Silly-looking uniforms accomplish the opposite of your intended result and just waste money.

Inability to Speak Basic English

Communication is the heart of service and personal connection. There are wonderful opportunities in this industry for people from all ethnic backgrounds, but they must have the ability to talk easily with our guests. If a guest must struggle to make themselves understood, they won't have a pleasant experience.

Distracting Accessories

All restaurant staff must look clean and professional. Remember your role is to enhance the dining experience of your guests, not to make a personal statement. Any time your appearance distracts your guests' attention from the reasons they went out to eat, their level of well-being goes down a little. As their level drops, they become more critical of their experience.

I'm not suggesting you don't have a right to your personal beliefs and affiliations, only to point out that making personal statements on the job is inappropriate and counter to the best interests of your guests and the restaurant. The most common distractions are the following accessories:

- Excessive or gaudy jewelry
- Brightly colored nail polish
- Wristwatches
- Union buttons
- Political buttons
- Religious symbols
- Heavy perfume or aftershave scent
- Ornate belts or belt buckles

Tattoos and Piercings

Tats and piercings are becoming more common, particularly among younger workers. Whether this is a plus or a minus depends on the restaurant's concept and the age of its clientele, but the bigger problem is not the body art, but the fact that most of it is intended to be seen by others. As such, visible tattoos necessarily distract the guests' attention from their dining experience.

Since there is nothing to gain and a lot to lose from visible ink and perforated body parts, the safest approach, at least in guest contact positions, is to limit piercings to one pair of modest earrings and require that all visible tattoos be covered. Staff members who feel these restrictions unfairly deny their right of personal expression are more concerned with themselves than they are with delivering a memorable guest experience.

Sitting on the Counters

My culinary professor always admonished us not to put anything on the counter we wouldn't eat! He made his point. Take a break only in appointed break areas, not on the tables. Sitting on the tables only reflects lack of coaching or a feeling of detachment from the restaurant operation. It is unprofessional and unsanitary.

Obvious Hangovers

People don't come to the restaurant to hear your problems. They are not interested in how you stayed out all night and drank too much. Your physical impairment only draws the focus of attention away from your guest. The secret to assuring happy guests is reducing distractions, so you can figure out the problem.

Bandages on the Hands

How safe would you feel if the person preparing or serving your food had a dirty bandage on their hand? Do you think your guests are any different? If a foodhandler in the kitchen has a bandaged wound, have them wear rubber examination gloves like medical professionals use. These are more sterile than plastic gloves and provide a secure grip when handling knives. Give staff with bandages on their hands a job out of the public eye and be sure the bandage is protected from food contact.

Sleeveless Tops

Tank tops may be the hot summer look in your area but it is usually a marginal choice of attire for restaurant staff. Many sleeveless tops are simply too revealing for foodservice operations. Nobody comes to the restaurant to look at your staff's underarms. The look may be sexy but it's not appetizing, particularly on male staffers. Another issue is that sleeveless tops often expose part of women's brassieres, another distraction, particularly for male guests. Bottom line: be sure uniform tops are built to maintain decorum.

Smelling like Cigarettes

People who smoke may not realize that everything they own smells like cigarettes, especially to non-smokers. Even the smell from a smoker's automobile can permeate clean uniforms on the drive to work. There's not much you can say about what your staff does after work. Still, be aware that non-smokers are very sensitive to the smell of smoke. The safest course is to have staff who smoke work only in the smoking section. If you don't have one of those, be aware that in the foodservice business, you can legally give hiring preference to non-smokers.

Dour Faces

If you are having a good time, notify your face! Guests will have a better time when the restaurant staff is enjoying themselves. It's important that guest contact staff have naturally pleasant facial expressions. People who smile easily make others feel better and usually see life in a more positive, friendly way. They are more likely to help your guests have a pleasant evening.

Unattractive Staff

You can't make personal appearance a valid job requirement. Still, restaurants are a visual experience. You spend lots of time and money to prepare beautiful meals in a striking environment. If your service staff doesn't look equally appetizing, you can lose much of the impact. I'm not suggesting every staff member must be a candidate for a magazine cover. Attractiveness involves more than a personal perception of physical beauty.

Weight, skin tone, posture and fluid motion figure into perceptions of attractiveness. Workers with naturally pleasant facial expressions and a ready smile appear more attractive than those with perpetual frowns. Remember that your staff is also part of the environment of your restaurant and will have an effect on your guests' experience.

Sick Foodhandlers

Guests have a legitimate concern for their health when they see sick foodhandlers preparing their meal. If you're too sick to work, you should be recovering at home. If you're well enough to work but shouldn't be handling food, do a job where you won't pose a hazard to your guests. There are always storerooms to clean, trash cans to wash and other essential tasks that can help the restaurant.

Attitude Atrocities

Attitudes are often just unconscious habits, but they have more impact with guests because they appear to be willful.

Excuses ... for Anything ... Anytime

Making excuses for the food, service, restaurant policies or even personal behavior makes you an amateur. If you're not proud of it, don't serve it. If you don't agree with a policy, work to get it changed. If you can live with it, live with it; if you can't, leave. A successful restaurant sets high standards and brings its staff up to meet them. When you hear your crew make excuses to your guests, it may mean they have higher standards than you do.

Profanity Within Earshot of the Guest

Profanity peppers modern speech and you must be constantly alert to avoid accidentally offending your guests. The safest practice is to refrain from using profanity anywhere in the restaurant, even in conversations with co-workers. Assume guests can hear *everything!* The staff will reflect the example of management. There can't be a double standard about profanity in the workplace.

Personal Conversations Loud Enough for Guests to Hear

Part of what makes the restaurant experience special is its removal from the routine affairs of the day. Conversations between staff members, particularly if they are personal (non-business) and loud enough for guests to hear, break the spell. Keep conversations in the dining room to a minimum. Use a quiet voice and limit the topics to those affecting guest service.

Kitchen staff also must be sensitive to their conversations. It's easy to forget how far voices can carry in some restaurants. In the heat of the rush, normal kitchen conversation can become shouts. Just because the guests are out of sight doesn't mean they can't hear what you say.

Whining or Complaining

Nobody likes a whiner. Make it a house rule that nobody is allowed to complain to anyone who can't solve the problem. Complaining to your co-workers is bad enough; whining to a guest is even worse. People don't go out to eat to hear your problems. Griping to them only ruins their opinion of the restaurant ... and of you.

Arguments or Displayed Anger

Few events destroy a pleasant mood as quickly and as thoroughly as the eruption of anger. You can't prevent arguments among guests in the restaurant but you are always accountable for your own demeanor and actions.

Because of the pressure of business, it is likely that a staff member will get angry from time to time. You must address it and it helps to understand that the more positive a person's mood, the less likely they are to have a dispute with anyone. Start with that.

The way to avoid anger (and the damage it can cause) is to maintain a positive environment. You do this for your guests by avoiding the momentous minutia in this book. You do this for your staff through continual training, consistent support and the authority to do their jobs in a way that works for them.

Flirting with the Guests

Making advances to your guests can create all kinds of problems. When you flirt with one guest, you ignore the others and they'll resent it. Your behavior is self-centered, unprofessional and may give your restaurant a reputation you don't want.

Worse, if you have an affair with a guest, they'll be uncomfortable about coming back. If your guests resent your intentions, they will never return. Flirting with guests is dangerous, particularly if either party is married. Be smart enough to pursue your social life away from the restaurant.

Confusing or Indirect Communications

People don't go to restaurants to hold long conversations with the restaurant's staff. They won't appreciate you trying to be too clever when you talk with them. You make their meal more pleasant if you just say what you have to say clearly, directly and with a smile in your voice and move on.

Pretentiousness

The most effective staff are friendly, accessible, understanding and professional. Arrogance, haughtiness and aloofness turn off most patrons. Staff members who display these traits could have a control issue that makes it difficult for diners to feel well-served. Remember it is the human connection, not the technical execution, that brings guest gratification. Watch for it and reward it.

Raised Voices in the Dining Room

Unless this is part of your operating style (and very few concepts can get away with it), keep the noise down. Loud voices disturb the guests' dining experience and make you look like an amateur.

"Stonewalling" Guests Who Ask to Speak with the Manager

The only real job in the restaurant is to make sure that guests get what they want. If they want to speak with the owner, they will only be happy when they speak to the owner. If a staff member tries to prevent that from happening, it only makes the guest more angry and determined.

Often, servers resist such requests because they fear the guest is about to complain about the service. Complaints are far less likely if guest gratification is the focus of the restaurant. Give staff members the authority to do whatever they feel is necessary to be sure your guests enjoy themselves and prepare to be pleasantly surprised at how well they do.

Lack of Support for Company Policies

Management's job is to be sure everyone on the staff understands the reasons for company policies, but I recommend you have as few policies as possible. Policies usually just provide a reason you can't do something the guest wants done and get impede guest service.

The more your team understands *why* you want something done a certain way, the easier it is for them to support the policy. When you see a conscientious worker having a problem with a policy, question the policy before you raise questions about the individual.

No Response to Guest Complaints

Most guests won't tell you their complaints. If they have a bad time in your restaurant, they'll just complain to their friends and never return. Statistically, when a guest cares enough to tell you about a problem, they're speaking for two dozen others who've had similar difficulties. Treat it as a unique opportunity to identify and correct a flaw in your operating system.

Never ignore a complaint. Usually guests don't expect you to solve their problem on the spot, they just want to know you are listening and interested in what they have to say.

Interestingly, surveys suggest that people are more loyal to a place if they have a problem that was handled well than if they never had a problem in the first place. I'm not suggesting you screw it up just so you can fix it, but it does show that handling complaints properly can create enthusiastic regular guests.

Ignoring or Not Thanking Guests as They Leave

Gratitude is powerful. People can't get enough of it, particularly when many events in their lives are so negative. People support businesses that appreciate their patronage. Thanking guests as they leave is not just courtesy, it's an investment in their future loyalty. When guests feel you are sincerely grateful for their business, they feel better about giving it to you. Sincere gratitude is so uncommon that peoples will remember your appreciation and return for more.

Bonus Points

Everybody likes pleasant surprises. These little unexpected touches are opportunities to improve your score and put your guests in a better mood. They help make up for any lapses in the operation and give people something to talk about to their friends.

High Staff Presence

There's something special about a person who is obviously thinking of nothing but your well-being. Your staff will follow your example. If you're distracted when you talk with them, they will be distracted when they talk to your guests. If you define the job of the manager as maintaining a positive climate in the restaurant, high staff presence will be more common.

Rapid Communication Among Staff

It always impresses me when I tell the waiter something and the manager arrives a few minutes later to follow up. It indicates a professional working environment with good teamwork.

Case in point: A number of years ago now, I was in Raleigh, NC on a project with my colleague Joel Cohen. We made reservations at the Angus Barn, one of my favorite restaurants for the two of us and his daughter, Rebecca. At the last minute, she couldn't join us. When we pulled up, the valet commented that Rebecca was absent and hoped she was OK. The greeter expressed disappointment that Rebecca wouldn't be dining that night. Impressive!

Smiling Eye Contact

Nothing warms the heart like smiling eye contact. Coach your staff in the importance of starting the relationship with every new guest by looking them directly in the eye and giving them a big smile.

One of my mentors, the late Mike Hurst, owned Fifteenth Street Fisheries in Ft. Lauderdale, FL. He'd tell his servers to go to the table and recommend the fish the guest most looked like! Huge smiles every time!

9
Vacant Verbiage

Language is powerful. The meaning of what you say is determined not only by the words you use, but by your tone of voice when you say them and the prior experiences of the person who hears them. It's critical that you not only say what you mean, but that you avoid any unintended interpretations.

You can help your staff accomplish this through regular coaching. Training doesn't mean scripting. Scripting each interaction produces robot-like communication that is usually interpreted as lack of caring. To be effective, training must help people understand the responses that can be elicited by particular words and phrases.

Without this awareness, you are likely to have well-intentioned but mindless conversations that do little to endear your restaurant to your guests. The easiest way to deal with these "dirty words" is to prohibit their use and challenge your staff to find more effective phrases. It makes for lively shift meetings!

System Slip-ups

When you hear these phrases spoken in your restaurant, it indicates a breakdown in one of your operating systems.

"Who Gets What?"
Establish a system so anyone can read the guest check and know where each meal belongs. This is particularly important if anyone other than the server ever brings food to the table. A simple system of table and seat numbering can make all the difference in how guests perceive your professionalism.

"That's Not Our Policy"
Design company policies to enhance guest gratification. If it doesn't work for your guests, change the policy. In any event, tell guests what you *can* do for them rather than what you *can't* and be alert for staff who are hiding behind policy rather than finding ways to help guests get what they want.

141

"It's Not My Station"; "It's Not My Job"; "I'm on My Break"
A response like this indicates a serious lack of focus on the needs of the guest. Creating and maintaining this focus is management's job. Immediately counsel any staff member who uses phrases like these and watch them closely. They could be a loose cannon!

"I Think This Is the Diet Soda"
This arises when the order has two or more similar-looking soft drinks, draft beers, scotches, etc. Work out a system with the bartender to distinguish between drinks that look similar. Never ask the guest to tell *you* what's in the glass.

"You'll Need this Later"
You don't set the table with dirty utensils. Why would you hand a dirty fork back to your guest during the meal and expect them to reuse it?

Negative Communication

Perhaps it is human nature, but it always seems easier to phrase things negatively. Unfortunately, negative expressions leave your guests feeling unserved. The phrasing and tone of many commonly-heard expressions are about as warm as an irate third-grade teacher berating an innocent eight year-old!

"We Don't Do That"; "We Can't..."
Explain what you *can* do and keep it personal. "I can...," is much more effective that "We can..." Positive communication is more pleasant, positive and rewarding.

"We Don't Have..."; "We've Run out Of..."
If you *run* out of something, it appears that you don't know how to run your business. On the other hand, if you *sell* out of something, guests perceive that you have highly desirable items. Any time you can't provide what the guest ordered, tell them at once and always suggest alternate choices.

"Why Didn't You..."; "You Should Have..."; "You Have To..."
Don't expect your guests to know your procedures. You're there for *their* comfort, not the other way around. If there's a problem, take care of the guest first and figure out what happened later. Your guests are intelligent adults – don't try to make anything appear to be their fault.

"You Made a Mistake"
A mistake by whose standards? Nobody likes to make a mistake. Better to take responsibility for the miscommunication, straighten it out to the guest's advantage and get on with the service.

"Is That All?"
This is too abrupt. How about "Is there anything else I can get you right now?" Keep your voice modulated and your tone soft. Guests will feel much more comfortable.

"Yes, I Know"
This makes the guest's comment sound insignificant. Better to just say, "thank you." Remember the only goal is to be sure the guest has an enjoyable experience in the restaurant.

"What Do You Want?"
Just *try* to say this phrase in a pleasant way! It can't be done. Better to ask "how can I help you?" or something similar. If you can develop the habit of addressing your guests in complete sentences rather than choppy phrases, your speech will be smoother and your level of guest service will increase.

"I'll Try"
At the risk of sounding rather like Yoda in the Star Wars movies, there is no "try" – either you'll do it or you won't do it. Most people recognize "try" says little or nothing. Take personal responsibility and tell them what you *will* do ... then do it with a smile.

"I Don't Know"
It's your *job* to know! If you get caught on a question where you don't know the answer, avoid the phrase "I don't know." Say something like, "Just a minute. I'll find out for you." Then be sure you *do* find out and promptly report your findings to the guest.

"I'm Sorry, But..."
If something goes wrong, apologize at once and suggest acceptable alternatives. Starting a sentence with this phrase puts your guests on alert that something unpleasant is about to happen. Rather than risk dropping their mood, find a more positive way to state your case. The appropriate phrasing will depend on the person involved and the degree of formality in your restaurant. A little humor can be of real benefit in these situations.

Mindless Communication

When people aren't trained to be aware of the impact of their words, they often speak without thinking. Stale words make for a stale dining experience. Take responsibility for your words and their impact.

"How's Everything?"; "Is Everything OK?"
Dennis Berkowitz, owner of Max's Diner and other creative San Francisco eateries, will give you a free round of drinks if anyone on his staff says this. Ask questions that are more thoughtful and helpful to your guests. Outlawing the phrase forces your staff to think before they open their mouths.

"Just One?"; "Are You Dining Alone?"
Some people are self-conscious about eating alone. It is uncaring to use words that might make them feel worse about it. "May I seat you now?" or "Are you ready to be seated?" will handle the situation more smoothly.

"I'll Be Right Back with Your _____"
This phrase is just mindless social noise. Only use phrases that *say* something to your guests. If you can't say something meaningful, you're probably wiser not to say anything at all! After all, if a server is truly *present* (not distracted) when they're at the table, comments are not always necessary.

"My Name Is _____ and I'll Be Your Waiter this Evening"
Who cares? This phrase has become a restaurant cliché. Unless you are prepared for an annoyed response of "My name is _____ and I'll be your guest this evening," think of another opening line. How about just a big smile, a warm welcome to the restaurant and some enthusiastic insider suggestions of what your place is known for?

Truth is, when you first get to the table I don't know you well enough to *care* who you are. I just want a drink and a chance to relax. So unless you're trying to get adopted, take care of business first. If you don't have a name tag and want to let guests know your name, leave it at the end. By then we may have established enough rapport that I will want to remember it.

"Okay"; "Yeah"
These slang expressions can sound flip or impolite. Be aware of your words and find something else to say. Phrases like "Certainly, sir" or "That is correct" sound much better and leave your guests feeling you were polite and responsive to their needs.

"I'll Give You a Few Minutes"

How wonderfully generous of you! First of all, it's not your time to give. Secondly, if people are having difficulty making a decision, it's time for recommendations, not retreat. Third, the phrase is trite and only shows you're not paying attention to your guests' needs.

"Have You Eaten Here Before?"

Ask the question this way and it is likely to make guests shudder, because it usually leads to a tedious explanation about how the restaurant works, what's so original about how you prepare your food, etc. I like to be able to identify first time guests, but it must be done a bit more subtly ... and by the greeter rather than the server.

A very slick way for greeters to flag the rest of the staff about a first time guest is the red napkin idea. As the greeter is walking guests she doesn't recognize to the table, she tries to determine if they are new to the restaurant.

If this is their first visit, when she seats the party, the greeter puts down a red cocktail napkin (instead of the regular cocktail napkin). This signals the server, manager and anyone else on the staff who may come by the table that this is a first-timer and to be sure to go the extra mile to make sure their experience is flawless.

"Do You Know How the Restaurant Works?"

This is another cringe-worthy question from a server, for all the reasons mentioned above. If there really *is* something unusual about your service system, returning guests already know about it, hence the value of the red napkin trick.

Even first-timers may have checked out your menu and website (where all your unique features are explained ... aren't they?) Your menu should also explain everything a guest should know without requiring the server to make an extensive verbal presentation.

I can think of one restaurant in particular where the server looked sad when I stopped her midway through her rambling explanation so I could order a drink!

"Enjoy"; "Enjoy Your Meals"

These phrases are also worn and don't add anything of value to the guests' experience. You will improve your level of communication if you develop the habit of speaking in complete sentences rather than choppy phrases. Put this idea to your service staff and get their suggestions. You may find their insights and creativity surprising.

"Guess What?"

What a juvenile comment! Don't play games with your guests - it's not the reason they came to the restaurant. If you have something to say, state it clearly, get your answer and move on.

"Have a Nice Day"

There has to be something more original and personal you can use than this clichéd phrase. Your guests hear the same thing in K-Mart! Find a different way to show each party how much you appreciate their patronage. As you approach the table, pause, clear your head of other thoughts and say what comes to your mind. You may not even remember what you said, but when it comes from your heart, the impact will be memorable.

"Who Gets the Check?"

Does it make a difference to you? The question only serves to satisfy your curiosity and distract the diners. It is often impossible to tell who will pay the check. You risk insulting your female guests if you automatically give the check to the male diner. Place the check in the center of the table, thank the guests for coming and continue to service the table until they are out the door.

"I'll Take this Whenever You're Ready"

This is another filler phrase of unnecessary conversation. Most guests will assume the server will settle the check, but if there's any question about whether to pay at the table or go to a cashier, print it on your guest checks. Even if you have a cashier, if a guest places the check and payment on the table, take it up for them. Give the guest the service they want or risk losing them forever.

"Good Choice"

Reinforcing a guest's decision is a good thing (nobody wants to make a mistake), but telling someone they made a "good choice" implies that other selections aren't. Rather than make a value judgement, tell guests something unique about the dish ("The salmon came in fresh this morning." "We grow the dill in our own garden.") or speak to the popularity of the item ("We're getting rave reviews on that tonight.")

"Your Order Is on the Way"

The only reason you'd say this is that you want to say *something* but don't really have anything to say. The comment has no meaning and only distracts the guest. Save your words (and interruptions) for something relevant that will enhance the dining experience.

"Mathers, Party of Two"
Anytime you make the guest feel processed rather than served, you lose points. This phrase is another restaurant cliché that really irritates some diners. The most personal approach, of course, is to have a greeter go to the Mathers party personally and escort them to their table. If calling them on a speaker is the only solution, change your wording. "I have a great table ready for you, Mr. Mathers," or words to that effect are more cordial.

"How Was Everything?"
This question usually comes after the meal as the guests are leaving. If you ask "how was everything," the answer is invariably "Fine." If your reason for asking is to get a truthful answer, change the wording. Ask if everything was done the way they liked it.

When they give you an answer, ask how you could do a better job for them next time or what it would take for things to be absolutely perfect, then shut up and listen. You'll be amazed at the suggestions you'll receive. Remember that nobody will say a word if they don't think you really want to hear what they have to say.

"Do You Need Anything Else?"
If you ask this when the entrée is served, the guest has no way of knowing the answer. Give them a minute (two bites) with the food and ask the question when they can answer it.

"Everything's Good Here"
When asked for a recommendation, please don't say "it's all good." That response is like fingernails on the blackboard. The statement should be true, of course, but it's not particularly helpful as a recommendation. Your greatest sales aids are your enthusiasm and sincerity. Have knowledge and insight into your own menu and speak from your own experience rather than reading from a list.

What's fresh today? What's looking particularly good tonight? What are your other guests are raving about? On my travels, I'll often ask servers, "What's the best thing on the menu?" or "What is the restaurant is famous for?" I'm appalled at how often they don't have a ready answer to the question.

Sometimes I'll be asked what I'm in the mood for. (That wasn't my question ... and if I knew what I wanted I would just have ordered it.) Other times I'll be "bracketed" with a line like, "Well, if you feel like pasta, we have ____, or if you like beef, we have ____, or ..." This is also not particularly helpful.

Apparently they are scared to have an opinion. Why? If you go on about the steaks and I want a piece of fish, I'll ask you about the seafood. The best answer I can remember to my question about what was the best thing on the menu was one server who paused for a second, then said, "I'll give you my top three." Perfect!

"Are You Still Working on That?"

Dining isn't work. It is – or at least, it *should* be – a wonderfully relaxing experience. It's disrespectful to make it sound like some sort of task to be completed. When you show respect for your food, your guests will have a better time.

"Are You Done?"; "Are You Finished With That?"

If your guest's plate is clean, you already know the answer, so the question itself is silly. If their plate still has food on it, they might just be a slow eater or taking a break before finishing their meal. In either case, they may interpret your question as attempting to rush them, particularly if others at the table have finished their meals.

Your job is to "read the table" and enhance their dining experience by not only knowing what to do, but how (and when) to do it. If you're more concerned with turning the table and hustling guests on their way, those you serve tonight may never return.

The safest move is to clear a plate when the guest has obviously indicated they have finished by moving the plate to the side or to the edge of the table. In that case, simply seek to make eye contact for a silent OK and just remove the plate. When in doubt, just ask if you can remove their plate.

When everyone at the table has stopped eating, you might say, "I'm glad to see you've enjoyed your meals. Would you like me to remove your plates?" It sounds much better, is more polite, and won't make guests feel they are being rushed to make a decision.

"Like" as Every Other Word

I realize this word has become an unconscious part of teen-speak, but to anyone older than twenty, it makes the speaker sound stupid. It's just a filler – a way to stall for time when speaking. Peppering one's sentences with "like" is the equivalent of saying "um" or "ah" three times in every sentence.

Like it or not, the way you speak creates an impression on other people. A person with a good vocabulary is generally perceived to be more intelligent than someone who has a poor vocabulary.

"No Problem"

Somehow this phrase has become a replacement for saying "You're welcome" or "Certainly." It may be appropriate if what you've done or have been asked to do would, in fact, be considered a problem ... but it's turned into an annoying response to something that's just a normal part of the job, particularly with guests over thirty!

Self-Centered Communication

The sad reality is that the world doesn't revolve around you. Although you always see things from your own perspective, you must always remain sensitive to the guest's point of view.

"I Need..."

Who cares what you need? Find a way to phrase it in the guest's favor. If you're tempted to say "I need to know what dressing you want on your salad," try wording that's more sensitive. How about, "We have six house-made dressings for your salad. Your choices are ..." Do you hear the difference?

"We Have..."

Not bad, but it sounds nicer to say "You can have ..." Phrasing it in this way makes your comments sound more like you're providing a service than giving a lecture. Your guests feel better-served and you don't lose any points.

"We're Running a Little Behind Tonight"

Your guests just *hate* to hear you say this! First of all, if a guest calls on the phone and asks if you're busy, they are trying to find out if they'll have to wait very long for a table. Don't tell them you have a line out the door! You might offer to put them on the waiting list and suggest they arrive in 45 minutes. Whatever you do, sell them on the idea that you can show them a wonderful time. If you let them get away, they may never be back.

"This Is My First Day"

Everybody has to start sometime. It is reasonable to expect that the first few days on a new job will be a little rocky. Still, this phrase is usually an excuse for some lapse in performance. Guests expect a good time and responsive service. It's not their problem if you are a rookie. In fact, they may feel less comfortable if they think management is asking them to break in the new crew. Be a pro and don't hide behind excuses – it can become a habit.

"You Need To..."

This is self-centered because it attempts to shift responsibility from the server to the guest. The only thing your guests really need to do is enjoy themselves and pay the check before they leave. Anything that interferes with either is self-defeating.

Just as you should never tell a guest what you *can't* do for them, you should never tell a guest to do something that you can handle for them. If you must do something like this, make it a request rather than an order, choose your words carefully and give them the context first. "To comply with state liquor laws, we have to ask that you not take open containers outside the building."

"Do You Want Change?"

When a guest pays in cash, it's arrogant to assume that any excess is your tip. If a guest gives you a $50 bill to pay for a $33 check, don't assume the extra $17 is yours or ask if they want change. To do so all but guarantees an irritated guest, a smaller tip when the smoke clears and probably a flaming review on Yelp as well!

Tips may represent the bulk of a servers compensation, but they are still a voluntary transaction. It is presumptuous to assume the guest wouldn't want their change. Whether you get the tip they plan to leave now or in five minutes shouldn't matter.

"I'll Get Your Waiter"

When a guest has a request, they want action, not a referral. A response like this just shows you are too lazy to handle the matter yourself. A good policy to adopt is that the person who originally gets the request *owns* it and is responsible for seeing the guests's needs are met.

The phenomenon of shirking responsibility can be a major drawbacks of a tip-based system where no one actually cares about a guest unless they're going to get a tip out of it.

In the best restaurants, the staff is a cohesive team for hospitality excellence, all focused on assuring you have the best time possible. In others, you're treated like a minor nuisance by anyone not directly involved in the extraction of money from your wallet.

Does a guest really need to wait for "their waiter" to get the cutlery that "their waiter" failed to bring in the first place? Can't anyone just bring a fork to the table with a smile and an apology? The "it's not my job" mentality is a real turn-off, and it calls the restaurant's commitment to happy guests into question.

Make sure your policy is clear and all your servers are on board with it so nobody will get overly territorial about who makes their guests happy. If the restaurant doesn't care, guests don't have to care either. They just won't give you a second chance to get it right.

"I'll Get the Manager"
If a guest has a problem, saying you'll get the manager usually just makes it worse. Guests want their issues resolved quickly with minimal hassle. I believe servers should have the authority to do whatever they need to do at the table, at the time, to make a guest happy. After the fact, they can de-brief the boss.

The faster a complaint can be resolved (in favor of the guest), the better. If additional assistance is needed to resolve the issue, let the guest know who you need to involve and why ... and assure them things will be resolved in short order.

Rude Communication

Often, you use phrases that are offensive to your guests without even realizing you're doing it.

"Are You the Roast Beef?"
No, they're your guests! Treat them as people or you'll lose them. Perhaps you're used to thinking of your diners in terms of what they ordered, but I promise *they* don't think of themselves that way.

"Follow Me"
There's no way to say this without sounding abrupt. At the least, precede it with "please." It's smoother to say you have a wonderful table ready and lead them to it. They know to follow you.

"Can't You See I'm Busy?"; "I Only Have Two Hands!"; "I'm Only Human!"
These phrases are a sure indication of an over-stressed staff member or one who needs a refresher in guest gratification. Get them off the floor and have someone else cover their station. They'll only drive guests away until they regain their composure. Better to have guests upset for something you *didn't* do than for something you *did*.

"Are You the Mathers Party of Two?"
"Mathers party of two" is restaurant jargon; not even good English! Keep your conversation simple and personal. "Mr. Mathers, I can take you to your table now" is much more respectful.

"How Are You Guys Doing Tonight?"

This is mindless at best and rude at worst, particularly when addressing a couple or a group of women where everyone is obviously not "guys." For many people, simply being asked how they are doing by someone they've never met is annoying. The easiest way around this is to avoid the entire phrase. Welcome them to the restaurant and get on with it!

"Folks"; "Guys"; "See Ya"

Slang expressions are impossible to say without a disrespectful tone. Be aware of this and avoid them. It will take some awareness and desire to break old habits. Eliminating these phrases from your vocabulary instantly elevates the quality of your guest service. You will also make your restaurant more memorable to your guests.

"What Do You *Want?*"

The message is always in your tone of voice, never in the words. If you watch a foreign language film, can't you always tell if someone is upset? Compassionate? Caring? Your own communication is no different. If you're inadvertently abrupt with a guest, recognize it, own it, apologize and try again with more humility.

"You Must Have Been Hungry"

It's never appropriate to comment on how much (or how little) a guest ate, even when meant in a light-hearted way. When you say something like this, it demeans the guest (you sound like their mother!) ... and that's never a good way to build repeat patronage.

"Smell the Cork"

In wine service, this sounds like you're issuing an order. At best, that can be annoying. At worst, it can come across as condescending or disrespectful. The wine ritual does include presenting the cork to the host, but just place it on the table in front of them without comment. They may choose to smell it and they may not. What difference does it make to you?

Ineffective Communication

Some phrases just don't work. Their continued use only reflects lack of training. The problem with these phrases is that they do not enhance the dining experience and are too easy to just say "no" to. In all cases, you're better off to make one or two specific suggestions. Here are a few suggestions that may help:

"Would You like a Drink?"; "How about a Cocktail?"

How about "May I suggest something refreshing from the bar? Our special tonight is _____ or perhaps you'd like a cool _____?" You get the idea.

"Tell Me When to Stop"

The "tell me when to stop" game is playing with fire, especially when servers want to get it over with, their minds are on the next thing they have to do and their reaction time is four heaping scoops of cheese or an ounce of pepper too slow. By the time they're done, guests can be left to excavate their actual dinner from underneath a massive pile of stale peppercorns and Parmesan. Either slow down this whole process and take it more seriously ... or just let guests do it themselves.

"What Do You Want to Eat?"

This may be carrying the idea of straightforward communication to an extreme. Bear in mind that people don't go to restaurants just because they are hungry. There are many ways to satisfy hunger that have nothing to do with dining out. Be respectful and don't back them into a corner.

Perhaps you could ask if they have had time to make a choice yet? This phrasing gives them a way to say no gracefully. This way, if they say no, it's because they haven't had *time* to make a choice, not because they haven't been *able* to make a choice.

If they are uncertain, suggest two items you think they would like. If there is no ready response, quietly excuse yourself and check back in a few minutes or when they have put their menus down.

"Would You Like Another?"

When this question is asked in regard to a soft drink, it is often code for "no free refills," but don't assume that a delay in re-ordering is because guests are being cheap. (If they are, so what?) Still, if guests wants two Cokes, they will order a second one with confidence. Most diners are aware that not every restaurant is awesome enough to kick in a free refill on the house.

"Do You Want Appetizers?"

Very few people go out with appetizers on their minds, so this question could easily be annoying. Try something like "While we're preparing your dinner, perhaps you'd like to share an order of _____ or _____."

"Do You Want Another Drink?"

It seldom helps to remind guests how much they've consumed, whether it is food or alcohol. You want to sell the second drink, of course, but choose your words carefully. When the level of a drink drops below half, you might ask if you can "freshen it up" for them. Often just eye contact with someone in the group and a circular motion with your finger will get you the nod for another round.

"Would You like Dessert?"

This is another automatic "no." There are many ways to build dessert sales. "Have you ever tried our famous _____?" will always open a discussion ... with no risk of rejection. Whether they say yes or no, you have an opening. Remember most people who won't select a dessert for themselves will usually share one, so one dessert for every two diners is not an unreasonable sales target.

"Really Amazing"

Never use this phrase to describe one of your menu items. It's a slang expression that really tells the guest nothing meaningful. If a dish *is*, in fact, really amazing, tell the guests *why* you're so excited about it. Is it an unexpected combination of flavors? Is it addictive? Is it so memorable it's been written up in the media? Your words will be more believable when you talk in specifics.

"Nice"; "Good"

Both are non-descriptive words. They're weak, say nothing and sound trite. Your descriptions always have more impact when they come from your personal experience of the item.

Unnecessary Communication

Guests don't come to the restaurant to have lengthy conversations with the staff. These phrases are just unnecessary and do nothing to enhance the guests' dining experience. Don't even ask, just bring it!

"Do you want cream with your coffee?"
"Would you like more _____?"

Truth Is Stranger than Fiction

My favorite comment came in a small California coffee shop one morning. The waitress placed a glass of tomato juice in front of me and said, "Taste this and see if it's OK. It smells funny to me!"

Bonus Points

Everybody likes pleasant surprises. These little unexpected touches are opportunities to improve your score and put your guests in a better mood. They help make up for any lapses in the operation and give people reasons to recommend your restaurant to their friends.

Using Guest's Name Frequently

Nothing is more pleasant to someone than the sound of their own name. Make it a game to find out the names of your guests and use them whenever appropriate during the meal. The greeter is in a perfect position to get the guest's name, either from the reservation list or just by asking them as they are seated.

Unless they have asked you to use their first name, address guests only by their last name preceded by Mr. or Ms. If permission is granted to be more personal, it is given on a person-by-person basis. Permission for one is not permission for all.

Speaking in Complete Sentences

The dining trend in the country is away from the formal dining experience and toward more casual restaurants. Unfortunately, this trend has also been reflected in our use of the language.

The Nassau Inn in Princeton, New Jersey has ongoing training to encourage its staff to use full sentences, rather than curt phrases, when speaking to guests. Their goal is to re-establish a style of gracious hospitality and they believe proper language and polite manners better convey their desire to be friendly and helpful.

Speaking in complete sentences is more respectful and doesn't have to be stuffy. It will, however, force you to engage your brain before operating your mouth, improve your presence and be a strong indicator of your professionalism and caring. It will also help set your restaurant apart from the competition.

10
Culinary Catastrophes

Opening the subject of food with restaurant people is taking a tiger by the tail. There are so many small points to make about different dishes. The nuances of preparation, seasoning and presentation are the subject of countless books far more technical and scholarly than this one. Culinary details establish the character of a restaurant's kitchen and its reputation for fine cuisine. The more upscale the restaurant, the more food-related details figure into its success.

I won't even try to tackle the full spectrum of this subject. These decisions and judgements are properly between the skills of the chef and the palate of the guest. My focus here is on the more common annoyances of restaurant food preparation and presentation.

Poor Procedures

Regardless of your concept or menu, when it comes to food, there are some things you just should not do. I see these basic culinary truths violated every day. If awareness is the first step toward solving a problem, perhaps the points in this section will help.

Hot Food That's Not Hot or Cold Food at Room Temperature
Hot food hot and cold food cold. If there is a cardinal culinary rule in the foodservice business, this is it. Still, restaurant cooks regularly put hot food on cool plates or portion cold food onto plates hot from the dish machine.

If you can prepare food at the proper temperature, how do you get it to the guest that way? It's simple physics: if the plate is hotter than the food, it will raise or help hold the food's temperature. If it is colder, it will cool the food.

To serve cold food cold, you must chill the food to start with. Cold plates are simply a matter of refrigeration. Other than pre-portioned frozen desserts, don't store cold food plates in a freezer. Frozen plates are *too* cold and can freeze moist foods. You might want to bring a chilled fork when you serve a cold plate. A crisp, cool salad is simple, elegant and memorable.

157

Mike Hurst of Fort Lauderdale's 15th Street Fisheries used to tell his guests that 38° was the perfect temperature for a salad as he served a cool bowl of chilled greens. The statement created a point of difference for his restaurant whenever his guests got a warm salad at another establishment.

Serving hot food hot is a little more involved. To be perceived as truly hot, the food must be served at close to 190°F. Food cooked to order is usually at least that hot, but items held on a steam table are not. Stir frequently to be sure those items are up to temperature, preferably at least 165°.

Plates hot enough to keep food from cooling on the way to the table are too hot to hold in a bare hand. If you're serious about hot food, heat plates in the oven to around 250°F. Your staff must use a towel to hold 250° plates, but guests will get hot food. I also suggest you take out your heat lamps – they don't keep waiting food hot, just let it cool more slowly. Without heat lamps, there's a real urgency when hot food is up in the kitchen.

Cold Bread or Stale Rolls

There's nothing like fresh, hot bread and people can get stale rolls at home. Dining out needs to be more special. If you can bake bread or rolls on the premises and serve them piping hot, you'll have a big edge over your competition.

To make sure bread is hot and fresh, you have several options. Bake it in small batches throughout the meal and bring it to the table hot from the oven, keep it in a humidity-controlled warming drawer, or re-heating rolls in an injection steamer or a countertop pizza oven. The most effective method depends on the product and the physical limitations of your operation. Since every restaurant provides bread, make it a major point of difference for your establishment.

Incomplete Orders

You must get it right the first time or you'll throw off the timing of the entire meal. In fast-paced operations, an expediter can assemble and check orders. Incomplete orders will cost you points with your guests and create additional work for your service staff.

Hair or Foreign Objects in the Food

This is a difficult mistake to recover from. The only good solution is to not let it happen in the first place. Insist all food handlers wear hair restraints. Train everyone in the kitchen on proper techniques for storing, handling and preparing food. No detail is too picky when it comes to assuring the integrity of your food.

Making Guests Sick

There are many documented cases of successful restaurants put out of business by an outbreak of food-borne illness. If you fail to provide basic sanitation training to every member of your staff *before* you allow them to start work, you're just gambling with your future. Serious operators approach sanitation with as much passion as they give to food quality or guest gratification.

Devote a portion of every staff meeting to sanitation awareness. Make sure you have enough hand sinks and train your staff to use them frequently and correctly. Install hand sanitizers as a second step in personal hygiene. In short, get serious about sanitation.

Half-Melted Ice Cream

Maintaining ice cream at the proper temperature is a challenge. If it's too hard, it is difficult to scoop and hard to eat. If it's too soft, it will melt too quickly. Keep your ice cream cabinet properly adjusted and don't portion ice cream until you need it for service.

Pouring Old Product on Top of New Product

This practice is a bad habit developed for the convenience of the staff. It is repulsive to informed guests because it provides an opportunity for cross-contamination. If the older product is tainted, it will contaminate the fresh new product. Avoid it. Offer buffet items in small quantities. Attend your line constantly so you can replace empty containers at once. Your line will look better, your guests will be happier and your food will be safer.

Frozen Desserts Too Hard to Get a Spoon into

Nobody enjoys struggling with their food. If you pre-portion frozen desserts, especially for a banquet, be sure they are not too hard to eat. Take them out of the freezer long enough before service that they can soften to an edible consistency.

Improperly Prepared or Improperly Seasoned Food

The items on your menu create an expectation for your guests. If what you give them bears little resemblance to the item they expected, you will disappoint them. Serving your Steak Tartare medium rare is not likely to delight the patron who ordered it.

The determination of just what "properly prepared" or "properly seasoned" means is still subjective. It depends on the diner's tastes and expectations, the prevailing customs in your market area and the training of your chefs. To avoid problems, though, make sure that what you offer is what your guests expect to receive.

Not Changing Utensils When Changing Food Containers

Always bring clean serving utensils when replacing containers of food. Placing a soiled spoon into fresh product provides another opportunity for cross-contamination. It's also annoying to have to use a serving utensil that has food smeared on the handle from a previous patron. Replace soiled utensils, don't just wipe them off and put them back. It looks more professional and gives your guests more confidence in your operation.

"Tossed" Salads That Aren't

The restaurant critic for the San Francisco Chronicle educated me about this many years ago. Unfortunately, he did it in print! I had a tossed salad listed on the menu. When he ordered it, he received mixed greens with dressing on top. In his review of the restaurant, he pointed out that a tossed salad requires the dressing be tossed in the salad, not just dumped on top. He was right, of course.

True tossed salads use less dressing and create a better balance between the dressing and the greens. If you don't actually toss the salad, call it a mixed green salad and be safe. If you care enough to present a true tossed salad, though, you can create a point of difference ... and cut down on the amount of salad dressing you use.

Ordering the Item *Description* and Getting Something Else

Menu copy and verbal presentations must accurately describe the item you're offering. You will irritate your guests if the item on their plate doesn't contain the ingredients they expect. It's disappointing to order a crepe "filled with shrimp, crab and scallops" only to find it contains a single shrimp.

Guests also get upset if the item contains unexpected ingredients. Many people have food allergies, so be sure your menu, your servers and your cooks are all on the same page. The only sure way to do this is to follow standardized recipes for every item on your menu. Don't let your kitchen crew get creative with standard items.

Flavor Transfer in Fried Foods

When you can't taste the difference between the french fries from the fried fish, it's time to change the oil in the fryer. Flavor transfer comes from loose particles of one food item suspended in the oil and attaching themselves to another product. If you do a volume of different products, your safest approach is to have a separate fryer for each. If you can't do that, shake off excess breading before you put items in the fryer, regularly skim loose particles out of the oil, and filter your frying oil daily.

Inconsistency

Repeat guests develop favorite dishes, items they know and love that bring them back again. But if the taste or portion size of that favorite dish changes from visit to visit – particularly on a signature item of your establishment – they'll be disappointed and lose trust. Without trust, they'll never become loyal regulars.

Given fluctuations of workload and staffing, it's tough to prepare a dish exactly the same way every time, but you must at least come reasonably close. This can't be done without standard recipes for every item on your menu, strict portion control, rigorous training and continual tasting of the finished products. Do the work!

Pathetic Presentation

People eat with their eyes. If your plate presentations are exciting and interesting, the meal has more promise. If the plate looks depressing, the diner will be more apprehensive.

Boring Salad Bars or Buffets

Buffets and cafeterias enjoy one big advantage over table service restaurants: patrons can see the food before they make a selection. The possibilities for striking display and presentation are far more powerful than the best-written menu. Sadly, too few institutional operators have fully exploited the potential of presentation. Caterers have done a little better but still have only scratched the surface.

Poorly Garnished (Or Ungarnished) Plates

Earlier, I shared how I made plate garnishing a point of difference in my first restaurant. Fortunately, the industry is more conscious of garnishing now than in the 70s. Still, there are opportunities to make your plates more memorable to your guests. Plate garnishing is another way to separate a plate of restaurant food from the same meal served at home.

Messy Presentations

Unless they are part of your concept, avoid menu presentations that are messy for the guest to eat. It's irritating to be wearing good clothes while trying to eat a sandwich that's dripping down your arms. Hand-held sandwiches should not spill their ingredients or dribble sauce on the guest. You create the same problem when you put hard-to-cut items on a small plate loaded with vegetables and rice. Don't overcrowd your plates. Individual food items lose their identity and the meal is messy for your guests to eat.

Unappetizing Plate Presentations

Plates from a restaurant kitchen should have a positive impact when presented to the guest. Tell your kitchen staff that achieving this reaction is the goal. Coach them with some suggestions to get them headed in the right direction and then stand back! You'll be delighted at what they suggest. Plate presentation includes color, shape, arrangement of the food, a complementary garnish and a spotlessly clean plate.

Non-Food Items Served on Top of Food Items

Don't serve a plate of food with portion packs or ramekins stacked on top of the entrée. While the contents may be edible, the container is not. A good rule is never to put anything on the plate the guest can't eat. This also includes placing food checks on top of the plates when the orders are ready for pickup.

Salad Bowl Full of Water

A bowl full of water means the kitchen crew didn't drain the greens before making the salad. The good news, I suppose, is that at least they washed the greens! A bowl full of water makes the last few bites of the salad an irritation instead of a pleasure for your guest. Greens stored in water will soften and deteriorate quickly. A more effective solution is to spin the excess water off the greens after washing and refrigerate them until you need them for preparation.

Side Dishes Served on the Entrée Plate

It sounds obvious, but side dishes are, by definition, dishes that you serve on the side. That is where they belong. Like ramekins, the dishes themselves aren't edible so keep them off the plate. Separate dishes on the table encourage sharing and help expose others at the table to a wider range of your menu offerings.

Foil on Baked Potatoes

How did we ever start serving potatoes wrapped in metal? By now, most cooks don't even think about it ... but your guests do. Never put anything on the plate that people can't eat. If you choose to cook the potatoes in foil, remove the metal before you serve the plate.

Over-Sized Portions

A table of four ordering four entrées rarely wants 50 pounds of food to arrive at the table. If you've got huge portions, give people a written or verbal heads-up that meals are large and shareable. Better to do that than to have them upset by thinking they've been tricked into over-ordering.

Enormous Desserts

There is a WOW factor when an oversized dessert is presented, but the real impact of the dish comes in the first two bites – those are always the best. After that it's just work. Most diners want a little something sweet at the end of their meals but are put off by the need to take on excessive calories or add another ten bucks to the check just to scratch that particular itch.

The plus side of desserts, aside from the incremental income, is that few people prepare adventurous desserts at home, making them a special part of dining out. But the price of the desserts must be in proportion to the price of the entrées to be considered reasonable.

If your average food check is less than $15 per person, at least 75% of your desserts (and appetizers, for that matter) should be priced at 33-35% of your average entrée prices. If your average food check per person exceeds $20, desserts should be between 25-33% of the average entrée price.

Butter Floating in Melted Ice Water

Presenting butter on a bed of ice is an idea from the 1950's. Don't go there. Before the ice melts, the butter is too hard to spread. After the ice melts, the butter is soaking wet.

Mono-Colored Meals

When planning plate presentations, think in color. You probably won't get a spontaneous positive comment from a plate of french fries, breaded veal cutlet and refried beans! Use vegetables and bright garnishes to give the plate more visual impact. When you plan a presentation, consider how it will look, not just what's on it.

Tails on Shrimp

Particularly in a dish that should be eaten with a fork, leaving the tails on shrimp isn't very guest-friendly. The guest must get their fingers messy by picking up a sauce-soaked shrimp to eat it or trying to pull that succulent meat out of the tail.

The option is to give up on that last bit of goodness entirely (food you paid for!) and attempt to cut off the tail with a knife and fork – virtually impossible when the shrimp sits atop a pile of pasta!

If you decide to give your guests a break by serving tail-less shrimp, explain to diners what you've done and why you've done it. That will help create a point of difference when they encounter shrimp tails (and messy fingers) at a competitor's restaurant!

Bread Cut Only Halfway

As a diner, do you really want the others at the table handling the food you eat? That's the situation you put guests in when the bread isn't cut all the way through into individual slices. Granted, it may take a few seconds longer to be sure the bread is cut guest-friendly, but your patrons are worth your attention to that detail.

Dried-out Food on the Buffet

Cafeterias and buffets provide a unique opportunity for food presentation, but the longer food sits at temperature, the more it dries out around the edges. To keep the line looking appetizing, present hot food in smaller quantities and continually monitor their condition. Stir foods to keep them moist and distribute heat more evenly. Sauces on the steam table or in a chafing dish will thicken after 30 minutes. Be sure to add liquid to replace the moisture loss.

Pitiful Products

People don't go out to eat just because they're hungry, but if they're not hungry, they probably won't be in your restaurant. This is still the foodservice business. Whatever the other elements of restaurant success, your food has to taste terrific.

Dried-out Food or Condiments

Particularly in dry climates, food items can get crusty around the edges if exposed to the air for very long. This drying makes the food look unappetizing and disturbs your guests. Stay ahead of the problem by keeping the tops on condiment containers. Cover portioned foods in plastic wrap until you need them for service. You can stay ahead of this problem if you watch for it.

Over- or Under-cooked Meat

This is particularly annoying the second time it happens to the same guest. Part of the problem may be due to a difference of opinion about what a medium rare steak should look like, but if you can't get it right, they'll just take their business to your someone who can.

The difference between medium rare and medium may be open to individual interpretation, but there's no excuse for a steak ordered rare to be delivered well done. Even when the discrepancy is more subtle, you cannot win a debate with a guest who thinks you have over-cooked their order. Don't go there. Just smile and get them something to nibble on while you re-cook their order.

If you find there are recurring differences of opinions with your guests, establish a rigorous training program with your grill staff and have guests order using a more objective criteria:

Blue Rare: seared on the outside, completely red throughout
Rare: seared outside and still red 75% through the center
Medium Rare: seared outside with 50% red center
Medium: seared outside, 25% pink showing inside
Medium Well: a slight hint of pink
Well Done: broiled until 100% brown

Food Swimming in Grease, Butter, Gravy or Sauce

Most people don't think this is an attractive presentation. Excessive grease or butter will likely make them think your food isn't healthy for them. Too much sauce or gravy can overpower the dish. The goal is to make a balanced presentation where a guest is only aware of how tasty your food is, not the individual elements of the plate.

Mushy Vegetables

Unless you prepare vegetables to order, they're likely to be over-cooked. This doesn't happen intentionally, of course, but if you try to keep them hot on the steam table, they will get mushy. Most vegetables should have a fresh crunch to them. Cafeterias have a particularly hard time since the heat of the line continues to cook products while they await service. The solution it to put vegetables on the line a little undercooked. Use smaller pans and prepare to meet the demands of the line.

Unseasoned or Overly-Seasoned Dishes

A bit of salt and pepper prior to cooking will enhance the flavor of most any dish. Fail to do that and your food will come out bland and tasteless. Saying you prefer to let the guest season it to their taste is just a cop-out.

Under-seasoning is fairly easy to correct, but a heavy hand with the spices is a harder problem to fix. To a point, too much salt can often be offset with a little sugar. Over-spicing is a particularly critical point as guests get older. If an item is spicy, be sure to warn the guest when they order. Don't surprise them with seasonings they don't expect or can't handle. Excessive seasoning leads to dishes that are unbalanced and reflect poorly on the restaurant.

If you profess to be a professional cook, then cook in a professional manner ... and be sure to taste as you go. Mistakes will happen, but a pro will catch (and fix!) them before the food leaves the kitchen.

Tough, Brown, Spotted or Wilted Lettuce

Because you present salad greens in their natural state, you can't disguise a poor quality product. To protect your professional reputation, use only top quality produce. If you can't get (or can't afford) the quality you need, make a substitution. If you don't compromise your standards, you'll gain the loyalty of your guests.

Soggy or Greasy French Fries

French fries are the most popular menu item in America because most people don't have deep fat fryers at home. McDonald's built an empire with exceptional french fries and you can too ... provided you take them seriously. Fries that are under-cooked, greasy or hard as rocks can be enough to send an otherwise satisfied guest down the road. Most of your competitors are likely to offer frozen french fries. If you opt for a fresh-cut product and are picky about quality, you can gain a market advantage.

Boring Bread

Bread presents another excellent opportunity to create a point of difference in the market. To become famous, never feature the same old bread or rolls as your competitors. Consistent with your concept, see what you can do that is special.

Perhaps you can bake bread during the early morning hours when the kitchen is empty and reheat the bread to order in a pizza oven the next evening. Bake biscuits, muffins or quick breads in small batches throughout the meal and bring them to the table hot from the oven. How about fresh bread sticks, foccaccia or hot garlic cheese bread?

Lambert's Café in Sikeston, Missouri is famous for their "throwed rolls" with sorghum. I don't know if the roll itself is unique, but the delivery system is certainly memorable.

Fishy Fish

There are definite signs that fish is fresh – it has a mild scent and firm moist flesh. Don't accept (or serve) fish with a strong, fishy odor. Whole fish should have bright, bulging eyes and bright red or pink gills. Frozen fish should meet the fresh-smell test and have taut packaging with no evidence of ice or blood.

Fresh fish is best when used immediately, but you can store it for up to two days in the coldest part of the refrigerator, so buy only a few day's needs at a time. It's better to be sold out one night than to feel financially pressured to offer guests a poor product.

Surprise Sauces

Guests can be disturbed when sauces appear where none were expected (or desired), like on a broiled fish. This is another example of the importance of meeting your guests' expectations. If menu items come with a sauce, be sure to mention it on the menu and when the guest orders. As a matter of policy, you might want to serve sauces on the side to give guests an option. Your diners may request this of you anyway.

Unimaginative Salads with Bottled Dressings

Every restaurant has a salad. If you can create a point of difference with your salad, you have a point of difference in the market. Offer a salad guests can't make at home, not iceberg lettuce, cherry tomatoes, sliced cucumber and Thousand Island dressing out of a jar. Use several different mixed greens, add interesting garnishes, develop signature salad dressings. Be a real restaurant.

Old, Over-ripe or Under-ripe Fruit

Fresh fruit offers an exceptional opportunity to introduce color to the table. If you select your produce carefully, you can gain points from an attractive fruit plate or fruit salad. If you use a product that is less than perfect, you risk disappointing your guests. You are wiser not to put an item out at all than to do it poorly.

"Can Opener" Cuisine

In the quest to simplify operations, you can easily start to substitute prepared convenience foods for your own recipes. It is tempting to move in this direction when culinary talent becomes too expensive or too hard to find.

True, you can purchase many items that are superior to those you can make yourself. The danger is that, over time, you can end up buying more products than you make yourself. In the extreme, you could end up not offering anything unique when your competitors (and perhaps your guests) could duplicate your shopping list and through that, your menu.

Add convenience products with caution. Periodically, re-examine your production program to be sure you're still a restaurant and not just an assembly line.

A Heavy Hand with the Paprika

Many guests dislike restaurants that get carried away with the paprika. A light touch of paprika is a garnish; a heavy dose is a spice. Be sure your line staff knows and respects the difference.

Moldy Bread

Treat your bread with care and never take it for granted. Make (or buy) your bread in small quantities so it will never be around long enough to become moldy. Train your staff to look for the signs of mold every time they handle bread. Your guests deserve at least that much attention.

Excessive Gristle or Fat

There are some wonderful dishes you can prepare with cheaper cuts of meat. You get in trouble when you try to make a poor cut work where you really need a more expensive one. Remember that the important point is whether your guests have an enjoyable experience, *not* what sort of food cost you are can maintain. If you serve your guests tough or fatty meat, they will remember it long after they have forgotten your restaurant.

Too Much Dressing on the Salad

Why do so many restaurants want to drown the salad in dressing? The notion of "more is better" is simply not true. Dressings should complement the salad, not overpower it. The tastiest salads are tossed with the dressing, literally a "tossed salad." You use less dressing, create a point of difference in the market and serve a tastier salad.

Undercooked Eggs

Just the *texture* of undercooked eggs is disturbing to some people. With the current concern about salmonella and raw eggs, the problem is more acute. To be safe, many operators now use pasteurized eggs for everything but fried eggs at breakfast.

Things That *Should* Be Crisp That Aren't; Things That Shouldn't Be Crisp That *Are!*

Your guests expect certain foods to have certain textures. If the texture is different, it diminishes their dining experience. Crispness is a marketable texture. If you doubt that, look at the number of products that make claims of crispness. People know the difference between crisp and soggy. Don't disappoint them.

Fresh Fish or Seafood That Isn't

It is always a treat when you can offer your guests fresh fish. If your fish has ever been frozen, though, don't lie to your guests just because it sounds better. "Fresh fish" that isn't really fresh is the verbal equivalent of flowery copy on the menu.

Bread That Can't Hold up to the Sandwich

The messier the filling, the more substantial the bun needed to hold up to it. Nobody likes soggy sandwiches or disintegrating buns. Test the bread choices thoroughly before you decide which to use for various sandwiches. Train service staff to watch for problems at the table and have your dish crew monitor food left on plates coming back from the dining room. If you notice a problem, fix it.

Dried-out Desserts

The problem with cutting desserts in advance is that they can easily dry out. A moist cake is a true delight of the baker's art but cakes are particularly susceptible to drying. If possible, don't cut a piece of cake until needed for service. Cover exposed surfaces with plastic wrap to keep them from drying out. It's more work but it's the price you pay to serve a quality dessert.

Powdered Mashed Potatoes

The bane of institutional feeding is making an appearance in some family restaurants. Instant mashed potatoes can work in some cases, but don't try to save money with inexpensive products. If you must use instant potatoes, get the highest quality product you can find. Better yet, use real mashed potatoes. They'll cost less, taste better and can be another point of difference.

Unimaginative Vegetables

Vegetables should reflect the same creativity as your entrées. When they don't, it detracts from the meal. For example, I was in a restaurant recently and ordered Veal Piccata. The plate arrived with a creative garnish, a lovely piece of hand-crafted veal ... and clump of cubed carrots out of the freezer that looked like they came off a school lunch line! Don't undermine your culinary talent by failing to pay attention to everything you put on the plate.

Sand in the Spinach

Fresh spinach is a wonderful product, but it can be sandy if it's not properly cleaned. If you use fresh bulk spinach, break the leaves apart and rinse them thoroughly in a sink full of fresh water. If you buy spinach in bunches, cut off the stems before you wash the leaves. You may lose a little spinach this way, but you'll eliminate most of the sand (and the labor) that makes fresh spinach a problem. Spin the excess water from the leaves and store them under refrigeration until just before service.

Poor Quality Ice Cream

People eat bargain ice cream at home. They want something special when they go out. (If they eat premium ice cream at home, they can tell the difference!) For ice cream to be a satisfying, restaurant-quality dessert, it must be a premium product.

Lumpy Soups or Gravies

As more convenience food products enter the restaurant market, house-made products can be a point of difference for your establishment. If you're going to make it from scratch, make it properly. You don't need lumps to prove the item is an original.

Prosaic Policies

You can create culinary problems by management decree. Fortunately, you can solve them the same way. Here are a few policy-related irritants to consider.

Re-Serving Food

A restaurant should never re-use unwrapped foods like rolls. When you remove a partially-filled basket of bread from the table, guests wonder what happens to the leftover rolls.

A friend told of dining with a Federal health official. Suspecting the restaurant was recycling bread, the inspector slit the side of a roll and inserted his business card before the waiter removed the roll basket. As their coffee arrived, they heard a shriek from the other side of the dining room. Another guest had found the card!

To provide responsive service and maintain cost control, serve rolls in small quantities. Explain to the guest you'll bring more fresh, hot rolls whenever they want more. This way, the guest gets a better product, the service becomes more personal and the restaurant doesn't waste food.

Inconsistent Portion Sizes

Standardized recipes specify portion sizes as well as ingredients. If your portions are inconsistent from one meal to the next, guests become less trusting. It's even more annoying when portion sizes differ among guests at the same table.

Human nature being what it is, guests with the smallest portions will feel cheated. Inconsistent portion sizes also make cost control impossible. Portion control is the key to managing your food cost and avoiding unhappy guests.

Unpleasant Surprises

If your restaurant charges for extra dressing, salsa, maple syrup, refills and such, let the guest know the cost up front to avoid sticker shock when you present the check. "Nickle and dime" policies, like failing to clearly advise patrons of these costs in advance, exist solely for the benefit of the house, not to serve the best interests of your guests. As such they are fraught with peril.

You and your guests will be better served by pricing menu items at a level where you can offer these occasional extras without the need for an additional charge. Don't risk that "gotcha" feeling. Why waste time solving a problem you can simply eliminate?

Repetitive Sauces

Every item on your menu should have several uses but variety is the spice of life. Vary the sauces you offer to protect your menu from an image of sameness. This is particularly important in hotels where a group may be meeting for several days. Review the group's entire menu to be sure you're not repeating similar tastes.

Surprise Substitutions

If you can't give guests exactly what they expect, let them know and give them alternative choices. An unrequested substitution, no matter how good the product, will irritate your patrons.

Butter So Hard it Rips the Bread

Rock-hard butter is impossible to spread without destroying the bread. Figure out a way to present butter at a consistency that won't detract from the guest's enjoyment of the meal.

Food Spilled on the Rim or Bottom of Plates

Always wipe away food spills before plates leave the kitchen. Spills can recur when the server stacks plates up their arm. Food on the bottom of a plate means the plate was sitting on someone's meal.

Menu Items That Are Difficult to Eat

Watch out for ingredients in soups or stews that are too big to eat in one bite and too difficult to cut in the bowl. These presentations are awkward for your guests and detract from their enjoyment of the restaurant. Older diners are particularly uncomfortable when they have to wrestle with their meals. If you offer a chunky beef stew, serving it in a shallow bowl instead of a deep dish will make it easier for your guests to eat.

Daily Specials That Aren't Very Special

Specials are a good way to provide variety for your regular guests and give the kitchen staff a creative outlet. They're also an excellent vehicle for testing potential new menu items, covering more cost points and giving guests something to talk about. If your daily special is always (and only) a way to use leftovers, you're missing an opportunity.

Pushing Bad Food

You can't build a stellar reputation with a substandard products. You may be able to save a few bucks tonight by trying to disguise the meat that's starting to turn or the fish you've had in the walk-in four days, but if you lose a guest's trust and loyalty in the process, that saving comes at a very high price. Specials are not the way to get rid of leftovers or products past their prime. My father always advised me never to make a bet I couldn't afford to lose. It was good advice then; it's good advice now.

Excessive Portion Sizes

It seems many operators' idea of good service is to "give them more than they can eat and keep the coffee cup full." Large portions can be a marketing advantage for some restaurants, but the trend now is toward lighter meals, with more diners are eating less but eating better. The popularity of small plates and grazing menus in many cities attests to the attraction of smaller portions at smaller prices.

Capitalize on this trend by offering half portions at 60-75% of the full menu price. This will make you more attractive to older diners who simply don't eat as much food. People who are just being more careful about what they eat will also appreciate smaller portions. If these patrons can't eat great food the way they want by dining out, they'll just stay home.

Inconsistent Taste

People are creatures of habit. If you want one of their habits to be dining in your restaurant, you must earn their trust ... and that won't happen if diners can't rely on the consistency of your food.

When the lasagna is delicious one day and disastrous the next, people will stop ordering it ... and won't risk the embarrassment of recommending your establishment to their friends. To achieve consistent product taste, have firm purchasing standards, develop standardized recipes for all menu items and insist your production crew follow the recipes precisely.

Remains of an Unordered Item on the Plate

I was in a local restaurant recently and ordered the daily special. The restaurant offered the item with mashed potatoes, but I asked the server to substitute french fries instead.

As I finished my meal, I noticed mashed potatoes stuck to the plate under the spot where the french fries had been! I suspect the kitchen first put mashed potatoes on the plate instead of french fries and removed them when they caught the error. At least I *hope* that was what happened. I'd hate to think the plate had mashed potatoes on it before plating even started!

Bonus Points

Everybody likes pleasant surprises. These little unexpected touches are opportunities to improve your score and put your guests in a better mood. They help make up for any lapses in the operation and give people something to talk about to their friends.

Housemade Desserts

Baking is a lost art at home. Exceptional signature desserts baked fresh on the premises are a major point of difference in the market. If you can't bake your own desserts, personalize a purchased product with a signature sauce, fresh fruit or something unusual. Don't just cut the cheesecake and put it on a plate.

Interesting Jams, Jellies or Preserves

Most restaurants simply purchase jams, jellies and preserves. If you make the product yourself, it brings a homey touch to your restaurant. You'll enhance your image as a quality operation and gain a unique position in the market.

After Dinner Treat

People love pleasant surprises. How about a chocolate covered strawberry, a tartlet or a fresh cookie with the check? In Australia and New Zealand, it is common to receive a fresh chocolate with the coffee. Angus Barn in Raleigh, NC has a barrel of picture-perfect apples at the door. See what you can come up with. Anybody can buy mints.

Housemade Croutons

Poor quality croutons out of a box can kill an otherwise memorable salad. Croutons are easy to use that stale bread and can be a point of difference in your salad presentation.

Exceptional, Piping Hot Bread

Oh, the magic of fresh, hot bread! It is *so* worth the effort to create a superior bread product and presentation. Go the extra mile and every time your patrons eat in a competing restaurant, they'll think of you when the bread basket arrives.

Signature Items

Success in today's market takes more than just doing a good job. You must be famous for something. ("I go there because ...") The idea is to develop items your guests can't find anywhere else in town, do them better than anyone else possibly could, and use them to build your reputation.

Garnished Food Pans on the Buffet

Legendary restaurants maximize the visual appeal of every food presentation. If you operate a cafeterias or buffet, you can't garnish plates, but you *can* dress up the food display by garnishing the pans of hot food. Do an imaginative job of garnishing and you can lose your institutional image.

Go the Extra Mile

Picture this: A guest's four year-old daughter is upset. The little girl wants a peanut butter and jelly sandwich but there isn't one on the menu. Instead of simply turning down the request, the waitress asks the kitchen what they can do.

The chef comes out in his whites to talk with the child. They put their heads together and have a serious discussion about various brands of peanut butter, the merits of chunky vs. creamy and the best kinds of jam or jelly to put on the sandwich. They discuss the tastiest bread to use, debate crusts vs. crustless and determine how the sandwich should be cut. It's a collaborative effort.

Armed with the proper inside information, the chef sends someone to the grocery store for any needed items. The little girl is thrilled to get her perfect PB&J, the parents are grateful (and stunned!) The chef, the waitress and the runner are all heroes.

Mini Desserts

We talked earlier about the problem created by over-sized (and over-priced) desserts. Why not make it easy for guests to satisfy their sweet tooth without requiring them to make a major financial decision? Orlando's Seasons 52, a Darden Restaurants concept, was among the first to address this issue ... and they did it right.

They designed nine spectacular mini desserts, each small enough to be served in a large shot glass. Servers bring a specially-designed rack containing all nine to the table, explain the various choices and let guests select their favorites.

This instant gratification saves time, gives guests what they want and helps control over-indulging ... but don't underestimate the care and attention that has been put into the preparation of each mini dessert.

At only $2.50 each, it's no wonder more that 75-90% of their diners give their taste buds a little treat at the conclusion of the meal! Some tables take two, others take all nine, but just imagine the conversation on the way home!

Better yet, if you can make these little gems weigh in at around 100 calories, you can even eliminate the guilt factor. If you're not selling dessert to 75-90% of your diners right now – and you know you aren't – this is an experiment well worth trying!

11
Beverage Blunders

$\mathbf{T}$his chapter covers beverages of all types, not merely the alcoholic variety. Many restaurants are as popular for their bar operations as they are for their dining. You may not sell a meal to everyone who walks in the door, but you'll surely serve them a beverage. You might as well do it properly.

Procedural Paralysis

Often, the way you choose to do things is a clue to the source of your problems. Sometimes, *not* making a conscious decision on how you want to handle something has the same effect.

Hot Drinks in Cold Cups or Cold Drinks in Hot Glasses
Containers that are colder than the liquid will cool the drink and those that are hotter will warm it. The result can be a lukewarm Irish Coffee or a drink with melted ice. Either situation will irritate your guests.

Unrefrigerated, Spoiled or Scummy Cream
Some diners prefer non-dairy creamer for dietary reasons and some operators use it just because it's easier to handle. There's nothing wrong with taking the easy way out, but if you use real cream, half and half or milk, you must handle it properly.

To avoid problems, keep real cream chilled and bring it to the table in small portions. Don't leave a pitcher of dairy creamer on the table and never add fresh cream to a partially full pitcher. Discard unused cream when clearing the table. Portion packs are even safer, but just don't have the visual appeal of a small cream pitcher, particularly in upscale restaurants.

Foreign Objects in the Beverages
If you prepare drinks properly, they'll have real "Wow" impact on your guests. Just be aware of what your guests see when they look at their drinks more closely. Foreign objects in the glass can come from dirty glasses, impurities in the ice or poor ice handling.

As a start, be sure glasses are clean. Store glasses upside down to prevent dust and dirt from getting inside. Install filters on the water lines to the ice maker. Keep ice bins and chutes clean. If you opt to buy ice, be especially careful when emptying ice bags into the bin. Dirty bags can contaminate the ice supply. Use only clean buckets and scoops for ice transfers and keep them properly stored so they will stay clean between uses.

Improperly Chilled Beer or Wine
Improper chilling can mean a product that's too warm or too cold. For example, room temperature beer works in Great Britain, but it doesn't meet the expectations of American beer drinkers. A crisp white wine is less enjoyable at room temperature.

People drink beer and (some) wine chilled because they taste more refreshing that way. If the beverage isn't cool enough, it lacks the invigoration your diners want. On the other hand, if a beverage is *too* cold, it can lose its taste and character.

Beer chilled below 40°F will tend to be flat and cloudy. The nearer it is to 45°F, the better it will taste. White wines have more bouquet and flavor at 45°F than at 35°F. White wine in a refrigerator you use to store food will typically be too cold for maximum enjoyment.

Unpriced Drink Menus
Beverage menus can be an effective merchandising tool, but like any other menu, they are incomplete unless they also include the price of each item. Unpriced menus can make guests nervous. Why is the price a secret? Will I get a larger bill than I can afford? In the face of such uncertainty, the normal reaction is not to take a chance and just order something "safe."

Glassware Gaffes

The proper glassware makes a major difference in the impact of your beverage service.

Oversized Wine Glasses on a Tiny Table
Oversized wine glasses can give your wine service more class, but only if they're the proper scale for the table. This may not be a concern in the bar, but in the dining room, a small four-top can quickly become overcrowded when you put down plates, water glasses, wine glasses and the other ancillary elements of your table top. Consider this when you select glassware.

Undersized Glassware

Small drinks are less impressive than large drinks, especially at high prices. Value is determined by a variety of factors but a large, attractive glass filled reasonably full is usually more appealing than a small glass filled to the brim.

Lemon Slices Too Thin to Squeeze

Fresh lemon enhances the flavor of iced tea. I appreciate the visual appeal of a thin slice of lemon hanging on the rim of a frosty glass of fresh-brewed tea, but what can you do with that thin slice of lemon? You can't squeeze it and dropping it in the glass doesn't add much lemon taste. Serve iced tea with a lemon wedge. At least your guests can do something with it! If you want a garnish on the glass, try a sprig of fresh mint.

Improper Glassware

Using the right glass is the key to presentation and cost control in the bar, particularly so with wine service. The more expensive the wine, the more elegant the appropriate glassware. It would be a crime to serve Chateau Margaux '81 in a water glass! Certain types of glasses are traditional for certain drinks. Varying too far from what your guests expect will disappoint them, even if you serve an otherwise excellent cocktail.

Soiled or Scratched Glassware

You can't present a drink attractively in a dirty glass. Also watch for glasses that have become scratched. Sparkling glassware accents the excitement of the tabletop. If glassware has been scratched or chipped, it not only looks terrible but can be a safety and sanitation issue as well. Glassware styles change over the years. When it's time to order more glasses, look at what you're using and decide if it still reflects well on your restaurant. If not, make a change. It's a simple way to inject some new life into a tired bar program.

Drinks Without a Stirrer or Straw

Include a straw or a stir stick in every drink. Many women prefer to drink from a straw. A stir stick also gives the guest something to do with their hands.

Refreshment Relapses

Guests will not enjoy their drinks, alcoholic or otherwise, it you serve a poor quality product. The list of potential drink errors is endless. Here are a few of the more common mistakes to avoid.

Lukewarm Coffee

Always serve coffee at 190°F, especially at banquets. Lukewarm coffee isn't hot enough to be enjoyable, cools too quickly and just irritates your guests, particularly coffee lovers.

Dried-out or Slimy Fruit Garnish

Fruit dries out after cutting, particularly citrus fruits like oranges and lemons. Storing cut fruit in its own juices can help maintain freshness longer. However, if bar fruit stays in liquid too long, it will take on a slimy feel. If you pre-cut too many, you risk increased bacterial counts, so pre-cut only the garnish you'll need to get through the rush and cut to order after that.

Flat Soft Drinks

Flat or metallic tasting club soda ruins drinks and cost bars money. Tonic water from the gun doesn't have the sharp carbonation of the bottled product. Since the mixer makes up half to three-quarters of a highball, it's just smart to serve good mixers. Soft drinks need sharp carbonation to be truly satisfying. If you have a problem, check with your supplier and have your system adjusted to correct it. Be sure to keep a spare cylinder of carbon dioxide on hand.

"12-Hour" Coffee

You really *can* smell coffee burning from across the room. Non-aromatic or burnt coffee will send your guests packing. For a truly memorable cup of coffee, start with the highest quality beans you can afford. Grind the beans just before brewing. Brew in small batches throughout the day and never hold coffee on heat longer than 45 minutes. Air pots will give you more holding time

The difference between premium coffee and economy coffee is day and night, and it only costs a few cents more per cup. Memorable restaurants serve memorable coffee. You can make your coffee a point of difference in the market ... *if* you get serious about it.

Tepid Tea Water

If the water isn't hot enough, it can't brew a proper cup of tea and the tea drinker will be disappointed. Since it's counter-productive to let down a paying guest, get serious about tea. Pre-warm the pot to keep it from cooling the tea water. Fill the pot with fresh boiling water and bring it to the table immediately.

Great restaurants also serve great tea, so offer a quality selection. Like premium coffee, the difference is only pennies a cup ... and your reputation is worth it.

AND WHAT YOU CAN DO ABOUT IT

Draft Beer That's All Foam

When draft beer is excessively foamy, it makes more work for the bartender and slows service. This condition can arise when the keg is agitated or too warm (above 45°F), gas pressure in the system is too high or the draft lines are dirty.

Improper pouring can also cause wild beer. If you hold the glass too far from the faucet or if the faucet is not fully open when pouring, the beer will foam. Draft beer can be a profitable beverage, but only if you handle it properly. If you don't get serious about pouring quality draft beer, you'll only annoy your bar patrons.

Overly Strong (Or Weak) Coffee or Iced Tea

Whatever you do, make it memorable. There's a proper balance between coffee and water necessary to brew a consistently excellent pot of coffee. Brewing great coffee takes clean water at the proper temperature and the right amount of coffee of the proper grind.

The water flow rate must keep water in contact with the grounds for the right amount of time. If you try to save a few cents by using less coffee, the grounds are over-extracted and your brew can be bitter. Your coffee supplier can help you find the right balance.

Iced tea is often a brewing problem, too. Weak iced tea tastes like stale water. Brew iced tea slightly stronger than hot tea to allow for dilution as the ice melts. In his various restaurants in the San Francisco Bay area, owner Dennis Berkowitz prepares iced tea by pouring a pot of strong, hot tea into a big glass of ice at the table. How's that for creating a point of difference on a common item?

Strong Chemical Taste in the Water

An off taste suggests a problem with the municipal water supply. If so, consider filters or softeners to treat the water and remove the impurities that create the taste. Some upscale restaurants are even bringing a bottle of mineral water to the table instead of using water from the tap. If this idea fits with your concept, it can be a wonderful way to create another point of difference. The most potent points of difference are the ones you can create with items every other restaurant serves. Water is a perfect candidate!

Partially-Filled Beer Glasses

Fill those pint glasses completely, with a proper head of foam that comes all the way to the top. Beer drinkers would rather have a bit slosh onto their hands than be left with a feeling you are somehow trying to cheat them by not serving all the beer they paid for.

Grounds in the Coffee Cup

Be careful when grinding coffee and filling coffee filters. Loose grounds that fall between the filter and the basket can find their way to the bottom of the pot and into the cup. Train your staff to avoid emptying the pot at the table. If you leave a little coffee in the bottom of the pot, any loose grounds tend to stay in the pot.

Throw out the remaining coffee and rinse the pot before refilling it. You may lose a little product this way but avoid the chance of irritating a diner with a mouth full of coffee grounds.

Instant Coffee

Your guests may drink instant coffee at home or on camping trips, but real restaurants brew real coffee. Fifteen years ago you could get away with using instant decaffeinated coffee, but no more. Decaf drinkers deserve the same quality beverage as regular coffee drinkers. Handling two brews takes a little more work, but happy guests are worth it.

Beer with No Head

Beer drinkers want to see the proper 1"-1½" head of foam on their glass. More of a head than that makes guests feel they're getting less than full measure. Little or no head and the beer not only looks flat but has no eye appeal and little aroma.

To get the proper head on draft beer, the keg must be properly pressurized, the lines kept clean and the beer kept cold from the keg to the tap. In addition, the glass must be dry and "beer clean," – oil-free and washed with the correct non-detergent cleaning agent. A detergent residue on the glass prevents the beer from developing a head. How the beer is poured is also a factor, determined by the size and shape of the glass.

Pay attention to the details. The neat collar of foam on a glass of beer makes the beer taste better, provides more profit and gives you a more attractive presentation. The important point, though, is that your guests are happier when the glass looks inviting.

No Beer List

The increasing variety and popularity of craft beers dictates these beverages should be treated with the same respect you give to your selection of wines. In addition to showing more respect for your beers, a priced beer menu can help avoid the repeated recitation of the brands you carry. That saves time (and annoyance) for the server and speeds service to the guest.

Pathetic Pours

I hate a skimpy glass of wine when I'm paying double digits for it. Pointing to my sad glass, I've asked, "Isn't that kind of stingy?" The waiter or waitress invariably answers, "It's five ounces!" as if quoting a city ordinance. Or, the ever-popular, "It only looks small because it's in a large glass."

It's not that I expect a brimming tumbler of expensive wine, I merely want one that offers fair value for the money and isn't a transparent attempt to force me into ordering another $15 glass! Granted, some guests expect a wine glass to be filled to the top, even in oversized stemware, but their ignorance is the exception rather than the rule.

Should the fill level be an issue ... and even if it isn't ... an elegant solution is to present wine by the glass in a 6-ounce carafe so guests can see they are receiving full measure. Pour a small amount into the glass and let the guest handle the rest. It is a much nicer service for wine by the glass, makes the guest feel like they're getting more, and most patrons will appreciate the extra attention to detail.

Poor Quality Coffee

There's nothing worse than to have a fantastic meal followed with a decadent dessert ... and then be served a cup of watery swill mislabeled as "coffee." This isn't rocket science. Coffee is often the last impression guests have of your place, and they know a good cup from a bad cup. Don't try to save a few pennies by buying poor quality coffee and calling it gourmet.

Inconsistency

Repeat guests develop favorite drinks, tastes they know and love that bring them back again. But if the taste of that favorite cocktail changes from visit to visit – particularly if it is a signature drink of your establishment, they'll be disappointed and lose trust. Without trust, they'll never become loyal regulars.

Given the fluctuations of workload and staffing, I know it's tough to prepare a drink exactly the same way every time, but you must at least come reasonably close.

This isn't going to happen without standard recipes for every drink in your repertoire, a rigorous training regimen and continual coaching, but the effort is worth it. Every bartender I've ever met has their own recipe for what they swear is "the world's best Bloody Mary," but they all must make it *your* way, not *theirs*.

Pathetic Policies

Many beverage problems are caused by a management decision to do (or not do) things a certain way. Changing the policy can solve the problem without much other effort.

Drinking with Nothing to Nibble on

Many people like something to munch on while they're drinking. Snacks make sitting in the lounge more of a social event than an alcoholic one. You could have simple bar snacks, an elaborate hors d'oeuvre spread or an appetizer menu in the bar, but at least have *something* interesting to nibble on. It will make your guests more comfortable and increase your beverage sales.

Charging for Second Pot of Tea Water

This is a insane! I've even been in restaurants where they wanted to charge for another tea bag – a classic case of being "penny wise and pound foolish." The cost of a tea bag or a pot of hot water isn't worth losing the patronage of a potential regular guest. Take care of your guests and the profits will take care of themselves.

Allowing Someone to Buy a Woman a Drink Without Her Permission

If you let this happen, it puts the woman in an awkward situation. In my San Francisco restaurant we had a policy that nobody could buy a woman a drink without her permission. We also trained the staff to be alert for any woman who looked uncomfortable with a gentleman's advances.

When anyone on the crew spotted what looked like an issue, we would approach the scene, ask the woman if she was having a problem and defuse the situation if necessary. By making our bar feel safe for unaccompanied women, we attracted ladies who wanted to be social but didn't want to be harassed. Our bar scene never got out of control because the men knew we wouldn't tolerate any inconsiderate behavior.

No Fresh Glass with a Fresh Drink

When guests are drinking beer or wine, bring a fresh glass when you bring a fresh bottle. Whether they accept the glass or not, this touch is a mark of attentive service. Don't forget to replace any damp or damaged cocktail napkins on the table when you bring fresh drinks.

Substituting a Lower Grade of Liquor

I suppose this still happens in sleazy taverns but I hope it never happens in a serious restaurant. Brand substitution is illegal cheating and it will come back to haunt you. The practice comes from an idea that the guest is too stupid (or too drunk) to notice the switch. Either notion is dangerous.

If you believe your guests are stupid, they won't get the respect they deserve and will go elsewhere. If you're serving people who have had too much to drink, you're also flirting with disaster. Not only is it illegal to serve an obviously intoxicated patron, but you can create major liability for your establishment if that person has an accident after leaving your place.

No Alcohol-free Options

With the increasing awareness of drinking and driving, many patrons are looking for alcohol-free options. Most of your guests go out to be social, not to get drunk. There are a lot cheaper (and safer) ways to get drunk than to do it in a restaurant.

Americans are drinking less alcohol than in the past but they *are* drinking higher quality liquor than before. If you offer interesting alcohol-free drinks, you'll allow guests to stay longer and spend more. Remember that drinking is primarily social. You can charge nearly as much for alcohol-free signature drinks as you can for your regular well drinks and end up with happier guests and healthier profit margins. What a civilized idea!

Sorrowful Service

Beverage service follows the same rules as serving food at the table. A well-trained staff providing unobtrusive service is the measure of a legendary establishment. As always, the coach makes the difference.

Coffee in the Saucer

This is just sloppy service. What is the guest supposed to do with a saucer full of coffee? They can't drink it and pouring it back into the cup is unappetizing. One way around this is to pour coffee into the cup at the table instead of trying to carry the cup already filled. Be careful not to splash hot coffee on your guests when pouring. It's also nice to place a soft coaster or cocktail napkin in the saucer to absorb small spills and act as a silencer.

Water, Iced Tea or Coffee Not Promptly Refilled

Americans expect free refills on coffee, water and iced tea. Be attentive but not overzealous. Refilling glasses after each sip is annoying and intrudes on guests' enjoyment of their meal. Many restaurants place a carafe of iced tea, ice water or coffee on the table to give guests the option of pouring their own refills.

Holding Glasses by the Bowl or Rim

Never let your crew handle a glass by the bowl or rim. It not only leaves fingerprints, but it's like sticking your fingers in the guest's mouth! Many diners will send back glasses if you handle them this way. You don't need the aggravation ... and neither do your guests. Handle glassware only by the stem or the lower third.

Pouring *Anything* from a Stained Container

You wouldn't serve food on a dirty plate. Why would you pour from a dirty container? Serving pitchers for water or iced tea must be as spotless as the glass you are filling.

Awkward, Improper or Inept Wine Service

Proper wine service is smooth and unobtrusive, a skill that only comes with regular practice. Your wine supplier can help you find a supply of foil caps so your staff can practice foil cutting and an "Ah-So" wine opener will allow you to re-cork the bottles between exercises. Drill your crew until smooth wine service seems natural. Train them to roll the bottle slightly at the end of the pour to avoid dribbling wine on the table. The more comfortable they are with the process, the more likely they are to suggest wine to your guests.

Empty Snack Bowls

Snack bowls are like water glasses. People expect you to refill them regularly. If people are eating your snacks, they're also drinking. Avoid large communal snack bowls. People get nervous about sharing finger food, particularly with strangers.

Popping a Champagne Cork

Champagne is a civilized beverage that deserves civilized handling. Only amateurs or college fraternities loudly pop a champagne cork or shoot it across the room. The gaffe is particularly rude when the guest is paying big bucks for the bottle. You can serve champagne properly without dampening the spirit of celebration at the table. Hold the cork and twist the bottle to release the pressure slowly, then fill the glass in two pours. It's more professional and far safer.

Cold Drinks Without a Coaster or Napkin

Cold drinks sweat and get the counter or tabletop wet. Without something to absorb this moisture, condensation will drip on the guest when they lift the glass to drink. Diners will appreciate your awareness of this problem if you bring a coaster or cocktail napkin to absorb condensation.

Napkins or coasters with your logo will continually remind your guests of your restaurant's name and reinforce your image every time they pick up or set down their glasses.

Pouring Regular Coffee into a Cup of Decaf

This error is particularly annoying. It usually requires the service staff to replace the coffee cup and inconveniences the guest. To avoid the problem, have a way to tell which kind of coffee your guests are drinking. This is particularly true if someone other than the regular server pours coffee. Use different color cups or different underliners to identify who's drinking what.

Serving the Wrong Drink

Getting orders confused embarrasses everyone. The guest doesn't know what to do with the drink, the service staff looks inept and the guest who originally ordered the drink doesn't get served.

A further problem is what to do when you realize the mistake. You can't pick up a drink off one table and serve it to another. If a drink mix-up happens, acknowledge the mistake to both parties and apologize for the error. Leave the drink as a complimentary gift to the incorrect party or remove it promptly. Bring a complimentary replacement to the person whose order you misdirected.

If you try to talk your way out of the error or avoid responsibility for correcting the mistake, you'll only irritate both parties. The cost of a few drinks is far less than the cost of losing two groups of potential regulars ... and it flags a breakdown in your system so you can fix it.

Scooping Ice with a Glass

Using a glass to scoop ice is both unsanitary and dangerous. From the public health perspective, scooping ice with the glass puts your hands in the ice and makes your guests uneasy. There's also a real danger the glass could break in the ice. (You can count on that happening in the middle of the rush!) If the glass breaks, you must *immediately* empty the ice bin, clean it thoroughly and refill it with fresh ice before service can continue. But wait, there's more!

If a glass chips and you don't notice it, you could serve a piece of glass in a drink, causing serious injury to your guests. Don't make a bet you can't afford to lose. Always use a proper scoop to fill a glass with ice. Your guests will appreciate your professionalism.

Not Getting the Order Right the First Time
Guests are happier when they are eating and drinking. Don't make them wait while you shuttle between the bar and the table trying to get their drink order straight. Know your drinks and how they might be served. Ask the right questions when you take the order. Do they want it up or on the rocks? Do they want salt on the rim of their margarita? Be a pro. Get it right the first time.

Overfilling Coffee Cups
More is not always better. Remember that many people like their coffee with a lot of milk or cream. Leave enough room for guests to adjust their coffee to taste.

Iced Beverages That Are All Ice and No Beverage
Unless you make iced tea by pouring hot tea into a glass of ice, don't fill soft drink or iced tea glasses to the top with ice cubes. Guests will end up with significantly less of the product they're paying for. Two good sips and the glass is empty. It also creates more work for the service staff who must provide refills sooner. Find a proper balance of ice and beverage.

Depleted Array of Bar Snacks
If you offer a food buffet in the bar during happy hour, approach it as professionally as you do the rest of your food operation. Plan memorable menus. Decorate the buffet table attractively. Be sure to skirt the buffet table – it makes the presentation more impressive.

Keep the buffet clean and neat. Replenish items promptly right up to the end of happy hour. The bar buffet is a sneak preview of the culinary skill guests can expect when they have dinner. Do it right and you may entice bar guests to stay for a meal.

Refilling Coffee Cups Without Permission
This is especially annoying for guests who take cream and sugar in their coffee. Just when they get it blended the way they want it, some well-intentioned server destroys the balance! If you leave carafes on the table, you can avoid the problem. If not, train your staff to pause with the pot by the guest's cup, make eye contact and wait for permission to proceed.

Wet or Sticky Bar Top
I know your Mom taught you not to put your elbows on the table, but everybody still does it. If their elbows (or their wallet, notebook or newspaper) *stick* to the bar top, watch out! How are they going to clean themselves up? What are they thinking about you while they're doing it?

Overfilling Glasses
Unless it's a small juice glass, never fill glasses any closer than half inch from the rim. This gap provides a frame for the surface of the beverage. It lessens the chance of a spill while carrying the glass and makes it easier for the guest to drink without spilling. Spills ruin the presentation of a great drink and diminish your guest's enjoyment of their evening.

Not Serving Everything at the Table from a Tray
At home, people carry plates and glasses to the table in their hands. If you want to make dining out a more pleasant experience than dining at home (and I hope you do), this is a good place to start. To your guests, trays look clean and professional while hand-carrying looks dirty and amateurish. How do you want to be remembered?

Cocktail Napkin with the Logo Askew
Always place a cocktail napkin or coaster with the restaurant's logo facing the guest. Haphazard placement only shows your lack of concentration and inattention to detail. Human nature being what it is, your guests will notice a crooked placement. They may *not* notice if you do it properly.

Not Knowing the Brands Carried at the Bar
How often can you say "I don't know" before you feel stupid? Basic service training must include the brands you carry at the bar and the ingredients in your specialty drinks. If you have signature drinks (and I recommend you do), be sure your staff has tasted them all and can describe them in appetizing and accurate ways.

Disappearing Servers
When guests' frustration reaches the point where they get up and get their own drinks, you're losing serious points. It's false economy not to schedule enough servers to handle the demand.

Not Serving Wine Promptly
On the infamous evening that originally led to this book, I was out to dinner with my father and stepmother. The restaurant was *not* having a good night (and neither were we!)

When the server asked for a cocktail order at the beginning of the meal, we ordered a bottle of wine instead. The wine didn't arrive until well after the entrées were served! We knew we wouldn't finish a bottle before we finished dinner so we sent the bottle back.

Had the wine arrived promptly, we would have undoubtedly been ready for a second bottle when the meal arrived. When you serve the first bottle promptly, you increase your chances of selling a second one. If you don't serve the wine until after you serve the entrées, you'll just create resentment ... and lose a sale.

Overzealous Pouring

If you refill wine glasses from a bottle on the table, you're divvying up someone else's (expensive) property. Don't do it. You don't know who's planning to finish what, who's driving, or who is picking up the check. It also looks like you're trying to hurry people into ordering another bottle.

After pouring a bit into everyone's glass, ask the host,"Would you like me to pour or would you prefer to do it yourself?" and let the them decide.

Overzealous pouring of water can also be intrusive. I remember one meal where the busser apparently had been told to keep the water glasses full, so he raced around an otherwise tranquil dining room topping off the glass virtually after each sip! Talk about distracting!

It's fine to top off all the water glasses at the table, but do it when one of the diners' glass is down to about half. Once the ice in the glass has melted, just bring a fresh glass of ice water and take the other away.

Bartender Boo-Boos

Bartenders are subject to most of the observations and suggestions in the chapter on service. They also have some unique opportunities to alienate guests. Be sensitive to the following mixology mistakes.

Making Guests Wait While Washing Glasses

Only undistracted, focused attention will cause your guests to feel well-served. By trying to do two things at once, no matter how good your intentions, you tell guests their needs are not the most important thing happening at the moment. I've seen more than one party walk out when faced with this mindless behavior.

If you're involved in something else when a guest arrives, at least acknowledge their presence with eye contact and a smile. Let them know you're aware they are waiting, stop what you're doing and take care of business.

Handling the Garnishes

Think about it. The bartender is moving like a blur, handling cash and credit cards, knocking out cocktails for servers and bar patrons, all the while repeatedly reaching into the caddy for garnishes *with unwashed hands*. Yuck!

I appreciate the need for speed, but guests find these lapses in sanitation unnerving. Toothpicks and tongs can eliminate the issue for items like olives and cherries, but lemon twists ... not so much. The only good answer is for bartenders to visibly wash their hands after handling money and before handling anything that will touch the guest's mouth. (If the bar is too busy for one bartender to do that, you need two bartenders on that shift!)

No Knowledge of Basic/Classic Drinks

There are certainly some requests that may force a bartender to look up the recipe for an obscure drink, but there's no excuse not to know how to make common or classic cocktails. If you are clueless about a Margarita, look befuddled when I ask for a Manhattan or a Stinger – or worse, just make something up that isn't even close – it screams "amateur." I lose all trust in the integrity of your bar and the house is out the cost of your ignorant experiment.

Cell Phone Use/Texting on the Job

There's no case you can make that whatever you are doing on your phone is somehow improving the experience for the guests seated in your station or waiting for a drink you should be preparing. The world will continue to turn just fine without you for a few hours. If there's an emergency, just have your family call the restaurant.

What you do on breaks or after your shift is your own business, but when you're on stage, stay in character. If it is not already a firm policy in your restaurant, be a pro and just say no to cell phone use when you're on the clock.

Inconsistent Taste

Guests rely on the consistency of your products. If the margaritas taste different from day to day, people will stop ordering them. To achieve consistent product taste, develop standardized recipes for all drinks and insist your bar staff follow the recipes precisely.

Commenting on Prior Impairments

No matter how well you know the patron, never mention their prior antics. If someone has behaved poorly, they know it. Have the good taste not to embarrass them by bringing it up, even jokingly. No matter how well you think you know them, when you're on the job you must be a professional, not a buddy.

Altering Classic Cocktails

I'm all for creative expression behind the bar, but you should never mess around with classic names and recipes, no matter your egotistical belief that your new combination tastes better than the original. When you get creative without alerting the guest ahead of time, you risk disappointing the patron who expects to receive something quite different from what you serve them.

With classic cocktails like a Manhattan, Stinger, Rusty Nail or a Negroni, the name alone evokes a specific taste the guest knows and loves. Even the Martini, more recently corrupted to apply to anything served in a martini glass, has a classical composition. Mess with that at your own peril. If you want to offer your own variation on the traditional recipe, that should be reflected in the name you call the hybrid drink. Ignore this warning at the risk of wasted drinks and unhappy guests.

Sloppy or Inept Moves

The appeal of drinks prepared by a bartender over those from a service bar is the ability to watch the performance. Bartenders are part of the entertainment in the lounge. Practice makes perfect and a little choreography helps. Work with your bartenders to develop their style. The flair antics of the bartenders in the movie "Cocktail" are a bit over the line, but a few good moves can't hurt.

Short-Changing the Guest

Never try to cheat or short-change a guest. No matter how much they've had to drink, the guest will eventually figure it out. Other guests at the bar also may catch on to what is happening. Your establishment will get a reputation from which you may never recover. Screen your staff well, train them thoroughly and coach them consistently. Make sure guest gratification is always Job One.

Wet Change

Yuck! If you hand the guest wet money or place change on a wet bar, your point total drops quickly. Some lesser life forms do this to encourage the patron to leave the money as a tip. Perhaps the inconsiderate bartender is the one who should leave!

Inconsistent Drink Sizes

Consistency is the mark of a professional. If a bartender gives his friends a larger pour, he's not really making any friends. Those patrons who are *not* receiving special treatment will feel slighted. Those favored with the heavy hand will not have a good time, either. Most people drink to be sociable, not to get drunk. After being knocked on their tails a few times, people are likely to decide to patronize another establishment.

Wiping the Bar with a Smelly or Stained Rag

Using a dirty rag gives guests the impression that you're soiling the bar rather than cleaning it. Since guests sit at the bar while you are wiping it, pay attention to the cleanliness of your cleaning cloths. Don't use them for anything other than wiping the bar top.

For example, never clean a floor spill with the same cloth you then use to wipe the bar top. Replace cleaning cloths when they get soaked or look dirty. Remember that wiping the bar with a wet rag makes it unpleasant to the touch. If you use a wet cloth on the bar, be sure to follow up with a clean, dry one to remove the dampness.

Polishing Glasses with a Towel

Polishing glasses looks good in 1930s movies, but the practice is unsanitary and can bother some guests. If bartenders are polishing glasses, it could mean the glasses weren't clean enough after the washing process. Train staff on the proper way to wash glasses and follow up to assure they have it right. Sparkling glassware is important. How you get it to sparkle is equally significant.

Not Remembering Regulars

Bartenders should keep note of who is a recurring guest and who isn't. Nothing's more saddening to a regular patron than not being remembered despite months, or years of dutiful attendance. Make the regular crowd feel special, even if you have to fake the fact that you don't know their name. When in doubt, ask your manager or another bartender for the name. Your guests will be happier, stay longer ... and tip better.

Eating or Drinking While Dealing with Guests

Always remain in character when you're on stage. This means not visibly engaging in any activities that aren't in direct service to your guests. When you break that rule by allowing guests to see you eating or drinking at your work station, it makes them feel you have other priorities than seeing to their well-being. Not good.

You will eat and drink during your shift, of course, and the only acceptable way to handle this is to take your breaks away from your work station and out of sight of paying guests. Never drink while a guest is watching and never eat standing up. If you take your meal in the dining room, do it seated at a table away from the main traffic flow and conduct yourself as if you were a guest.

Not Removing Full Ashtrays When Clearing a Table

Your entire lounge may be a smoking area, but not all guests are smokers. While waiting for a table in a national chain restaurant, my wife and I (non-smokers) were seated at a table in the bar. The staff cleared everything off the table except the overflowing ashtray from the previous party.

Even if we *were* smokers, it would still have been disgusting. Perhaps it was just an oversight, but the cocktail crew didn't notice the problem. My suspicion is that nobody ever made them aware that such carelessness has an impact on their guest's experience.

Not Washing Hands Frequently

Guests notice when you don't wash your hands, particularly when they see you handling garnishes after handling cash without using the hand sink. (They know that money is the dirtiest thing you're likely to handle all shift.) Make frequent handwashing a visible habit and patrons will rest easier. It can also be a point of difference when they notice poor sanitation practices in your competitors!

Handling Beer Bottles by the Mouth

Putting your fingers on something the guest will ultimately put in their mouths is a serious lapse. Handle beer bottles the same way you handle glassware – only by the lower third.

Bonus Points

Everybody likes pleasant surprises. These little unexpected touches are opportunities to improve your score and put your guests in a better mood. They help make up for any lapses in the operation and give people something to talk about to their friends.

Separate Coaster for the Bottle and the Glass

Coasters or cocktail napkins keep the tabletop dry. Beer bottles sweat as much as glasses do. Your guests will appreciate your awareness that a wet table is an unpleasant experience.

Hors D'oeuvre with Each Drink

A small munchie with each drink is a very European touch. If it fits with your concept, the hors d'oeuvre approach can showcase your kitchen and increase your bar sales. If you use the hors d'oeuvres to allow guests to sample items from your menu, you also can build your dinner sales. At the least, you'll create a point of difference and build your reputation.

Free Tastes of Wine

Many less adventurous diners are reluctant to commit to ordering a full bottle of an unfamiliar wine, particularly those at higher price points. An extensive by-the-glass program can help, but when you can do it, there's nothing as hospitable as offering a complimentary taste of a wine the guest had questions about. You will pick up points whether they choose to order more or not ... and repeat patronage is ultimately the most profitable sale you can make.

Randy Rayburn, owner of Sunset Grill and several other restaurants in Nashville, is one of the best operators I know. He has several hundred wines on his list and if you want a glass of almost any of them, he'll open the bottle and pour it for you.

When I asked him how he could make that policy work, he said, "First of all, I'm going to sell you a second glass. If I can't find a way to find buyers for the remaining two glasses in that bottle, I'm in the wrong business!"

Chilled Mugs and Glasses

Beverages stay colder in cold glasses. While the practice of chilled mugs for beer is not particularly unique, those who like their beer cold always appreciate the service. Many establishments chill wine glasses for white wine sold in the bar. You have nothing to lose by making the gesture ... and may just gain a regular patron.

Inventive Garnishes

There are some cocktails where guest expectations will dictate a particular garnish. In other cases, you have more options. Why not experiment a little and see if you can find a fresh way to present some of your old favorites?

Exceptional Snacks

If your establishment only serves alcohol, guests won't expect too much creativity. If you're a full service restaurant, though, you can use your bar snacks to display your culinary prowess and entice drinkers to stay for dinner. Go beyond what people expect.

Back in the day, Paoli's in San Francisco built one of the strongest happy hours in the City by offering a free buffet that put most hotel brunches to shame. They gave away a lot of food (probably clearing out the odds and ends in the walk-in) ... but they also sold a lot of cocktails! How many cocktail franks and cheese cubes can people eat ... and what does offering them say about your culinary skill?

Unusual Glassware
Visual appeal is an important part of beverage presentation. and unusual glassware is an easy way to create a point of difference for your bar operation. Pat O'Brien's, the legendary New Orleans bar, merchandises their world famous Hurricane by using a distinctive glass that becomes a souvenir of the restaurant.

Designated Driver Program
An important part of the sale of alcohol is to promote sensible consumption. If the industry fails to promote responsible drinking voluntarily, you can be sure some bureaucrat will dictate how we have to run our businesses.

Large groups of people create energy and excitement in the bar. If you can help them have a good time and get home safely, they will be alive to patronize you again. Support responsible drinking by providing an incentive for groups to have a designated driver. Call a cab for any guest who may not be in a condition to drive home safely and have the house pick up the cost of the ride. Remember just one alcohol-related accident can put you out of business.

Crested Glassware
Very few establishments seem willing to spend the money for personalized glassware, creating an open field for those who see the power of it. Custom crested glassware makes a memorable impact on the public. It adds variety and distinction to your beverage service. It also can be an effective advertising vehicle if you use it as a giveaway. Since some guests are going to steal your glasses anyway, you might as well get the promotional value when they use them to serve friends in their apartment!

Bottled Mixers
Bottled mixers have a sharper carbonation than post mix soft drinks from a gun. This is particularly true of tonic water. Since most of your competitors use guns, you could make another distinction for your bar by featuring bottled mixers. If you train your staff to tell guests the reason behind this special touch, your patrons will have something to talk about to their friends.

Signature Drinks

Success in today's market takes more than just pouring a good drink. Every bar in town can put out Chivas Regal on the rocks. To become a legend and draw business, be famous for something. Find an item you can do better than anyone else in town and push it. Better yet, invent a drink your staff can honestly recommend when talking to your guests. Pat O'Brien's success with their Hurricane in New Orleans attests to the power of a signature drink.

Fresh-Squeezed Juices

In an era of reconstituted juices, you can create another point of difference by using fresh juices at the bar. It takes more work to make a Screwdriver with fresh oranges, of course, but imagine how distinctive the drink will be to the Screwdriver fan!

It isn't practical to make *all* your juices to order. For example, it's almost impossible to make an acceptable tomato juice on premises. Still, the exceptional freshness and merchandising value from squeezing juices to order can put your bar on the map.

Individual Coffee Carafes

One way to be sure guests don't have to wait for coffee is to give them a personal coffee pot. There are attractive carafes of all sizes and styles on the market at very reasonable prices. If you present them properly and keep them clean, carafes are a welcome touch, particularly in the morning.

Extensive Selection of Wines by the Glass

As the public becomes more aware of the dangers of drinking and driving, they are consuming smaller amounts of higher quality beverages. People who would have previously ordered a bottle of wine are showing more interest in premium wines by the glass.

You can easily take advantage of this trend. Some restaurants even offer individual glasses of most selections on their wine list. Wine lovers and would-be wine lovers will appreciate the opportunity to expand their wine experiences without having to buy a full bottle.

Oversized Wine Glasses

There's something elegant about a big wine glass. When I had my first restaurant in San Francisco in the late 70s, white wine was the drink of choice. All my competitors were serving nine ounces of wine in a ten-ounce glass. When we opened, we served ten ounces of wine in a 17-ounce glass and promptly gained the patronage of most of the women in the Financial District!

They loved the look and feel of the glass. We also found we were less likely to spill the glasses while carrying drinks to the table through a crowded bar. Better yet, we sold ten ounces of wine for 25% more than our competitors were getting for nine ... and had better word-of-mouth and happier guests in the process!

Premium Well

Guests get nervous about brands of liquor they've never heard of. Why incur the expense of having a bottle of every liquor in the world on hand when the majority hardly sell at all? A premium well may offer the solution to both problems.

For example, instead of stocking seven medium-grade scotches, you might have Chivas Regal in the well with Glenlivet as a top shelf upgrade. There are very few regular Dewar's drinkers who will refuse Chivas Regal. A premium well simplifies inventories and provides a point of difference for your establishment ... and in most markets, you can charge more for the premium pour.

Start a Mug Club

If you sell draft beer, start a mug club. Members of your mug club buy a personalized beer mug that is kept for them behind the bar. Whenever they come in, they drink from their own mugs and receive a special deal. For example, if you sell a 12-oz draft for two dollars, the mugs for club members might be 14-16 ounces for the same price.

This idea isn't limited to beer. You could adapt the same idea to breakfast by offering a great-looking personalized coffee mug and a deal to make it interesting to members of your coffee club.

> **CASEY'S MUG CLUB**
>
> Jim Casey implemented a mug club at his Casey's East Restaurant in Troy, New York. It cost $15 to join the club (which paid for the mug and your first beer) after which members could get a refill for 25% less than a non-member would pay for an equal-sized pour.
>
> When he first started the idea, Jim figured that one or two dozen people might take him up on it. Mug club membership rose to over 100 in three months and kept growing.
>
> Jim said the camaraderie among the members helped keep his bar full and his regulars became a lot more regular after the program went into effect.

You could also establish a wine club where members receive an over-sized crystal wine glass with their initials etched on it, the better to (frequently) explore the finer wines from your cellar ... or just show off for their friends!

Regardless of their form, the premise behind mug clubs and their kind are similar:

1. The mug, glass or cup stays on display at the restaurant so the guests have to return to the property to use it.
2. The appearance of the vessel is distinctive, obvious to the other guests in the room when it is being used, making the user (member) feel privileged.
3. The container is personalized with the name of the member and the restaurant's logo to tie the two more closely together.
4. Club members receives a deal – usually either a lower price, more product at the same price, or access to entirely different products, like a special wine list only available to wine club members.

Get Serious About Tea

Everyone who eats at your restaurant expects a good cup of coffee, and it's difficult to wow them, because, of course, your competition is working to do the same thing.

But of course, not everyone wants a cup of coffee. Some want a cup of tea, or a cup of herbal tea, and those folks are used to being ignored, or handed an old Lipton tea bag, or something boring.

What if you had thirty varieties of tea for them to choose from?

12
Cleaning Calamities

Surveys by the National Restaurant Association and others suggest that cleanliness is one of the most important consumer considerations in choosing a restaurant. In one survey, guests even ranked cleanliness ahead of price, food quality, location, speed of service, meal sizes, courtesy and menu variety. If that's an accurate measure of preference, how much time and training do you give to cleaning compared with those other areas? You clean the place every day, yet how much thought do you actually give to it? Most people just assume they know how to clean. You may make the same assumption of your staff.

Don't confuse *clean* with *sterile*. Sterile is a germ-free condition that not even hospitals can maintain consistently. Sterile has a harsh look and takes tremendous physical and mental energy to achieve. If your goal is to make your restaurant sterile, you'll have a life of frustration.

Clean, on the other hand, is more a state of mind. Clean is the absence of dirt and clutter. Clean is pleasing to the eye. If you have clean as a state of mind, anything that doesn't look clean jumps out at you and you just take care of it without a problem.

Tableside Transgressions

A guest doesn't have to go looking for cleaning problems. Often they can just sit at the table and the problems will come to them.

Streaked Glasses
Hard water or improper warewashing is usually the root cause of streaked and spotted glassware. Your detergent supplier may suggest a water softener or a rinse agent that can solve the problem. If cost is a concern, bear in mind you can't present a streaked or spotted glass. Re-washing costs time, supplies and hot water. It's always less expensive to do it right the first time.

Dirty Sugar Containers
When was the last time you emptied the sugar containers and ran them through the dish machine? Make this a regular weekly duty.

Dirty or Spotted Flatware

Unclean flatware will bring the mood down quickly. Flatware must come to the table straight from the dish machine. Using a towel to polish off the spots is poor sanitation. Spotting is caused by a poorly adjusted machine, hard water or incorrect drying. Your detergent supplier can adjust your dish machine but you have to train your staff in the proper way to clean flatware.

When used flatware comes back from the dining room, soak it until you're ready to wash it. This loosens food particles and makes cleaning easier. Spread the flatware on a flat dish rack and pass it through the dish machine. Then sort it into perforated silverware cylinders, *handle down,* and pass it through the dish machine a second time. Don't handle it again after the second washing.

Placing the handles down allows water to drain away from the eating surfaces. If there is a water spot, it will be on the tip of the handle, not the middle of the knife blade. This method will usually solve most of your soiled flatware problems.

Carry eating utensils to the point of service in the cylinders and dump it directly into the silverware bins. If you dispense flatware directly from the cylinders, place a clean, empty cylinder over the full one and invert the pieces so they sit handles up.

Salt and Pepper Shakers Sticky, Greasy or Half Empty

Make wiping the shakers a regular part of the table setup process. This is also the time to check to be sure the tops are on tight, particularly if you have playful younger guests! At least once a week, wash the shakers in the dish machine. Let them drain and thoroughly dry overnight before refilling.

Stained Coffee Cups

Tea and coffee will stain the inside of cups. This is particularly unpleasant if the cups are of a light-colored china. Train your dish crew to check for stains inside cups every time they handle them. Soak stained cups in a solution containing bleach, a vinegar/water solution or coffee pot de-stainer. Wash and re-check them before placing them back in service. Your guests are worth the effort.

Soiled China

Nobody wants to eat off a dirty plate. It's critical that china come out of the dish machine clean and sanitary, so keep the dish machine clean. This means draining the tank, removing and cleaning the filter screens and washing out the machine before every rush period and at the end of the day.

Any food still on the plate when it enters the machine goes into the wash water. Proper scrapping and pre-rinsing will keep the water cleaner for a longer time. Scrape all excess food off the plates when they come into the dishroom. Either put them directly into the rack or stack them for later washing. Spraying down the edge of a stack of plates will flood the plate surfaces and help loosen food particles.

Load dish racks evenly, leaving space for water circulation between the plates and rinse the plates with the pre-rinse hose before putting them in the dish machine.

Glass Coffee Pot with Stained Bowl
The accumulation of coffee residue builds up inside coffee pots and makes the pot look dirty when you pour coffee at the table. Guests will notice and become uncomfortable. To prevent buildup, wash the bowls every day using soap and a bottle brush. Once a week, soak them in coffee pot de-stainer or a vinegar/water solution.

Menus or Placemats That Are Ripped, Stained or Smudged
Menus with creases, stains or beverage rings look unappetizing. Those that are greasy, dog-eared or sticky get the meal off to a bad start. The condition of your menus can cause many patrons to draw conclusions about the cleanliness of your kitchen. If that conclusion is unfavorable, everything you do will be more suspect. Inspect all menus before the meal and discard all those that aren't perfect.

Dining Room Disasters

As your guests look around your dining room, what they see will either make them feel more comfortable or more nervous about their upcoming meal. Cleaning problems are sanitation/safety worries and serious visual irritants. Chapter 5 discusses other unsightly scenes that can annoy your guests.

Wiping Tables with a Greasy or Dirty Rag
How can you expect to make anything clean with a dirty rag? Pay particular attention to the cleanliness of your cleaning cloths and keep them in sanitizing solution between uses. When they become visibly soiled, replace them. Overnight soaking in a mild bleach solution will usually restore the whiteness to cleaning cloths. Train your staff to measure the proper amount of bleach – too much of it in the soaking solution will deteriorate the fabric.

Flies in the Dining Room

Flies are a major annoyance and if you can keep them out in the first place, your problems will be less. Install an air curtain over the outside kitchen door and screen all open doors and windows.

Check with your health department before using any insecticide sprays. Many are not approved for food preparation areas (a major violation) and can be toxic if they're misused. To reduce flies around the property, keep the back of the restaurant and the dumpster area clean. Wash dumpsters and trash cans regularly and use a disposer to minimize wet garbage behind the building.

Chairs or Booths That Are Dirty, Stained or Have Crumbs

Nobody wants to sit on a dirty seat. If *all* your seating is soiled, people won't want to sit in your restaurant at all! Train your staff to clean and wipe seats thoroughly when clearing the table. At the end of the day, spray plastic or vinyl upholstery with de-greaser and wipe it clean. Vacuum fabric upholstery daily and schedule regular shampooing to avoid soil buildup.

Wiping Seats and Tabletops with the Same Cloth

Almost every diner I've talked with mentioned that this practice annoyed them. To be sure your guests are aware you're doing it right, just use two different color cleaning cloths. Clean the seats with the yellow cloth and the tabletops with the white cloth.

Smudgy Windows, Doors or Display Cases

You must stay ahead of fingerprints. The easiest way I've found to do that is to clean the glass thoroughly, then apply a coat of silicone (not wax) auto polish. It will dry clear and for days you can just wipe fingerprints off this surface with a dry paper towel. It's sure faster and easier than Windex and paper towels each time!

Use a squeegee to clean windows and other large glass areas. It will be much faster that the spray bottle and towel method and less likely to leave streaks. [Hint: go left to right on one side of the glass and top to bottom on the other. It will make it easier to know which side any streaks are on.]

"Fur" Around the Air Supply Outlets

First, be sure your heating system has clean filters. Clean or replace them every month. Vacuum the supply outlets at least once a week to stay ahead of dust and grease accumulations. Clean air supply grills with de-greaser every month. Replace discolored ceiling tiles around the air vents – they call attention to the problem.

Dust or Crumbs Around the Baseboards

Upright vacuum cleaners can't clean right up to the wall, so debris along the baseboards shows cleaning efforts are only superficial. Use a straight broom to sweep these small pieces out where the vacuum cleaner can pick them up. Once a week, use a canister vac with a radiator nozzle (the long, thin attachment) to clean this area thoroughly. It will make a big difference over time.

Dead Bugs on the Windowsills

I suppose it's better than finding live bugs, but it's not an attractive sight for your guests. Vacuum or wipe windowsills every morning to remove any insects that may have perished during the night.

Cobwebs in the Corners

It's almost impossible to keep spiders out of the building. You can spray around the foundation and try to seal every crack in the walls, but you'll have the problem anyway. If you clean out cobwebs while they're still fresh, the job will be quick and easy. If you let them sit, they collect grease and become obvious to your guests.

Remove cobwebs with a lightly oiled dust mop or a damp towel on the end of a broom. A cobweb will stick to a damp surface and can be neatly removed. If you knock it loose with a dry broom, it will just float onto something else.

Dirty Carpets or Floors

You can count on gravity to pull every bit of dirt and debris onto the floor and your guests will notice a dirty floor every time. You must vacuum carpets and wet mop hard floors at least daily, more often when dining room use is heavy. Many restaurants do their heavy cleaning at night. This idea makes sense but there's a danger:

The typical dining room lighting level is too dim for proper cleaning. Your crew can do what appears to be a thorough cleaning job at midnight but the harsh light of day will show the cleaners missed many areas of the restaurant. If you're going to clean at night, install cleaning lights. These fixtures contain 300-watt bulbs that flood the room with brilliant light. That's far too intense for dining, of course, but it will show every bit of dirt on the floor.

Cleaning or Mopping next to Guests' Seats

Except for emergency cleanups, avoid routine maintenance near seated diners. Your activity will disturb and annoy your guests because it suggests your guests are not very important. Some may even think you're trying to rush them out of the restaurant.

Dirty Table Bases

Table bases are often neglected, probably because cleaning them requires that someone crawl under the table. Still, diners kick the table bases all day and you must clean them regularly. Check them at the end of each day and clean them with all-purpose cleaner at least weekly, more often in inclement weather. While you're under the table, remove chewing gum and wipe down the chair legs.

Tarnished Brass

Brass can provide sparkling highlights in the room, but if you allow it to tarnish, you'll only call attention to your lack of maintenance. If you're installing new brass railings, be sure to specify the type coated with an epoxy that prevents oxidation and keeps the brass from tarnishing. If you have uncoated brass, use a polish designed specifically for brass at least weekly. Keep brass looking sharp and your dining room will look the same.

Scuffed Baseboards

Baseboards are the impact point for all the abuse in the building. Because they form a frame for your floor, their appearance can really undo an otherwise tidy dining room. Check your vacuum cleaner to be sure the bumper is clean and functional.

Clean baseboards with all-purpose cleaner in a spray bottle and a white nylon-backed sponge. Avoid harsh chemicals – they can damage the baseboard and stain the carpet. When you re-carpet, you can save a lot of baseboard maintenance by coving the carpet up the wall instead of installing conventional baseboards.

Careless Spraying of Cleaning Solutions

This is particularly disturbing when it happens on a table next to where guests are eating. People appreciate clean tables but they resent careless spraying of strong cleaning solutions. Sensitize your staff to use spray bottles with restraint and respect.

Hazy Mirrors

People always tend to look in mirrors, so they'll notice when your mirrors aren't clean. Haze from smoke, dust or grease in the air destroys the brilliant sparkle that mirrors can bring to the dining environment. Clean your mirrors every day.

Mirrors aren't just another piece of glass. The silvering on the back will turn black if it gets soaked with water or cleaning liquids. Clean mirrors with an alcohol-based glass cleaner in a spray bottle, never with ammonia or heavy-duty cleaners.

Too Much Ammonia in Cleaning Solutions

There are few smells more overpowering than ammonia. The odor of ammonia will destroy a guest's dining experience. If you use an ammonia-based solution to clean floors, coach your staff carefully about the proper amount to use and only clean when the room is empty. Better yet, find another cleaner that is less aromatic.

Disturbing Details

Cleaning is a business of details. Trying to cover them all would be a complete volume, clearly beyond the scope of this book. For now, here are a few more points that can cause your guests to go away mad.

Dirty or Disorderly Kitchens

Yes, guests can see into the kitchen. If you don't have an exhibition cooking area, they will get a view through the pickup window. Even if you have an enclosed kitchen, natural curiosity will cause guests to sneak a peek when the kitchen door opens. Remember that clean is a state of mind. The visual condition of the kitchen will reflect the value you place on cleanliness throughout the place.

Dirty, Smelly or Un-stocked Restrooms

Most restaurant guests will visit your restrooms. If that experience is unnerving, it will color their impression of your operation. Train *all* staff in the proper techniques of restroom cleaning. This will help keep restroom cleaning from being "somebody else's job."

In case you're wondering, all coaching staff should be qualified to clean restrooms and lend a hand when needed. If management avoids restroom care, what attitude do you think the rest of the staff will have? The condition of your restrooms is so important I devote the next chapter entirely to the subject.

Rancid Smell from the Back of the Restaurant

If you have any smell at all wafting over the parking lot, it should be aromas from the kitchen that draw people in, not fumes from the trash that drives them away. A dirty dumpster or a build-up of grease behind the restaurant is most always the culprit.

Local health codes usually require your waste service to remove, wash and replace the container periodically. Insist that they do. Periodic application of a good de-greaser around your back door and renewed emphasis on exterior cleanliness can keep this problem from negatively affecting your business.

Dirty Door Handles
The dirtiest item in your restaurant may be your door handles. Everyone who enters or leaves puts their hands on the door hardware. Children with sticky fingers complicate the problem. Restroom doors are prime areas for spreading diseases. Clean every door handle and knob several times a day. Spray them with a disinfectant cleaner and wipe dry with a clean cloth.

Dirty Telephones
Doorknobs may be the dirtiest item in the restaurant, but the telephone has to be a close second. Who knows how many dirty ears, hands and mouths have been in touch with your telephones? Cell phones have mitigated this problem to some extent, but guests often borrow your phones and your staff uses them all the time. Be sure to wipe your telephones every day with a diluted disinfectant solution sprayed on a soft cloth to avoid spreading germs.

Back of the Restaurant Dirty or Disorderly
Your guests may have a good look at the area behind the restaurant from the parking lot. Some (poor) restaurant designs even require guests to drive past the back door to reach the parking lot. Train your staff that no place on the property is out of sight to your patrons. The neatness of outside area always reflects your attitude toward cleaning the inside.

Pest Strips or Fly Paper
Check with your health department before using pest strips or fly paper for insect control. Most jurisdictions prohibit their use in food preparation areas, but even if they're permissible, their appearance disturbs your guests. Other methods of insect control are always preferable to hanging these eyesores in your dining room.

Any Signs of Insect or Rodent Infestation
Diners aren't encouraged by signs of infestation, especially if they actually see pests. There's something about the sight of a cockroach that ruins even the most brilliant meal. Every foodservice operation has a potential infestation problem, so contract with a reputable exterminator to spray your property regularly. If you wait until you notice a problem, it'll be too late.

Follow a professional's advice on steps to reduce potential breeding areas and how to make your building less inviting to insects and rodents. A clean building is more reassuring to your guests ... and more enjoyable for your staff.

Messy Back Bar
Think of your bar as an exhibition kitchen for beverages and look at it with a fresh pair of eyes every month. Does it look inviting, professional and businesslike? Is the appearance of the back bar pleasing to the eye? Is it cluttered with guest checks, snacks, menus or personal items? Are the bottles clean? Do all the lights work? Is the mirror clean? Is it cluttered with promotional pieces? The back bar is the focal point of your lounge. Be sure it reflects well on you.

Dirt on the Outside Doors
Wind, weather and blowing dust continually ravage your building. It just gets dirty. The front doors are particularly important since your guests come so close to them. Clean your front doors at least once a week. If weather permits, scrub them with soapy water and hose them down. Clean the door hardware inside and out.

Stained Grout in Tile Walls or Floors
Ceramic tile is impervious to most common cleaning chemicals, but the cement in grout is more porous and fragile. Avoid harsh acids that can eat away the grout. Commercial grout cleaning compounds followed by a mild bleach solution will normally clean grout without much effort. Occasionally, you may need to scrub with a nylon brush.

Bonus Points

Sparkling Dining Rooms and Restrooms
Everybody likes pleasant surprises. Your guests expect your restaurant to be clean, but when you surpass *clean* and make your restaurant *sparkle* ... now *that* is impressive! Not only will you improve your score but it will enhance trust and put your guests in a better mood. Sparkling facilities can help make up for any lapses in the operation and give you a reputation for spotlessness. You could do worse than being known as the cleanest place in town!

13
Restroom Repulsions

Most guests will use the restroom sometime during their visit to your restaurant and many draw a conclusion about the cleanliness of the kitchen from the cleanliness of your restrooms ("washrooms" to my Canadian friends!) Using a public restroom is a very personal experience. If that experience is unpleasant, the uncomfortable memory and cause guests to think twice about returning.

Monitor the condition of your restrooms closely. Have different staff members repeatedly visit each restroom during the rush. Note if the facilities are adequate and where the congestion occurs. See what maintenance problems come up. If you have problems, fix them.

Design Deficiencies

Many restroom irritations are inherent in the design. The fortunate part of this unfortunate situation is that once the deficiency is corrected, you don't need to be concerned by it any longer. Don't you wish all your problems were that easy to solve?

Tiny Restrooms
If you can, make an extra effort in the ladies room – women will particularly appreciate the extra space. Remember there's also a certain social dimension to the ladies room that men will never understand. Get the suggestions and reaction of several women before finalizing any plans for the ladies facilities.

Restrooms That Provide a View to the Fixtures
This means that when the door is opened, people in the hallway have a view of the urinals or stall doors. Most codes don't allow this condition in new construction, but you may have an older operation where the problem exists.

Often, changing the direction of the door swing can help. In other situations, you may have to make a single occupancy restroom with a locked door. Whatever the case, the privacy and security of your guests is important enough to fix the problem without delay. Embarrassment brings a person's mood down quickly.

Electric Hand Dryers

Hand drying methods are purely a question of preference. I understand the arguments of cleanliness and reduced maintenance made for electric dryers, but my unofficial surveys have yet to come up with anyone who prefers hot air to paper towels. If you have electric hand dryers installed, you might want to put in paper towels as an alternative ... or vice versa.

Poor Lighting

Illumination in the restrooms must be bright enough for comfort but not so intense that it's harsh, particularly in restaurants with dimly-lit dining rooms. As a special touch, think about installing makeup-style lighting around the mirrors in the ladies room.

Spring-Loaded Faucets

This is one of those annoying items installed for the convenience of the operator and not for the convenience of the guest. If you install spring-loaded faucets, they must allow water to run long enough for normal handwashing. Occasional restroom surveys can reveal if your faucets are an irritant ... or just glance at people's faces while they're washing their hands.

Poor Ventilation

Make sure there are enough air changes to keep the room fresh. Even if you have windows in the restroom, you won't want to leave a window open, nor can you count on that to make up for the lack of proper mechanical ventilation. While I'm on the subject, be sure your ventilation fans are as quiet as possible.

No Mirror

Strange as it sounds, awhile ago I was in a hotel men's room that had no mirrors! The women I know would clobber the restaurant owner if that happened in the ladies room!

No Place to Hang a Coat or Bag

Bear in mind the floor of a public restroom is not an inviting place to place anything. If the stalls don't have hooks, install them.

Quarterly Questions

Every so often, take a fresh look at the physical condition of the restrooms. The room deteriorates so gradually that you're unlikely to notice the small points. Your guests notice, though, and it affects the way they feel about the rest of your restaurant.

Chipped Paint on the Stall Enclosures
Using an electrostatic paint process, you can easily rehabilitate your stall dividers. Because the process pulls the paint onto the metal by magnetism, you can paint the dividers without removing them. No paint will adhere to anything else in the room. Repainting is an easy way to change the look and feel of the restroom for a small cost.

Soiled or Faded Paint on the Walls
When the walls start to look less than sparkling, it's time to act. The first solution is to give the walls a good washing. If that doesn't give the freshness you want, several coats of a good quality gloss enamel will brighten the room.

Torn, Spotted or Faded Wallcoverings
If they're easily cleanable, wallcoverings can give a classy look to the restroom. They are less durable than tile or paint, though, so watch carefully for damage. Your best move is to tile up five feet and install the wall covering material above that.

Daily Duties

At least once a day, check the integrity of the restrooms. The problems noted can't remain uncorrected or you risk offending your guests.

Leaking Soap Dispensers
Perhaps it's just a question of tightening a connection. Maybe there's a crack somewhere. Whatever the reason, correct it at once. It's an irritant for your guests and creates a cleaning problem.

Graffiti
Unless you have clientele who creates classy graffiti, it's better to remove these scribblings at once. In the graffiti mentality, one good word deserves another, so once it starts, graffiti can rapidly get out of control. If you attract people who write on the walls, renovate the restrooms with materials that don't provide a writing surface.

Sink Drains That Don't
It doesn't take much to clog a drain and it's a real irritant to guests when it happens. Check the flow at least once a day and be sure your maintenance closet includes a plunger, drain opener and the tools needed to remove the sink trap. Clear any blockages at once or accept a parade of angry guests and an extensive cleanup problem.

Cracked, Chipped or De-silvered Mirrors
It is a bad look and doesn't reflect well on your concern for details (puns intended!) The problem with an imperfect mirror is that it's the one place you can count on people to look! Just fix it.

Loose Fixtures
Loose soap and towel dispensers are the most common problem although your porcelain fixtures also can loosen over time. Check the stability of fixtures and dispensers as part of your regular daily inspections. If there's a problem, repair it at once before it becomes dangerous. It will not improve with age.

Broken Tiles on the Floors or Walls
Broken tiles are unsightly and pose a cleaning problem. Examine the physical integrity of the tiles daily and repair cracked tiles promptly. If you re-tile, keep some extras for future replacements.

Stall Doors That Don't Latch
Privacy and security are big issues for your guests. Wrestling with a stall door is embarrassing and embarrassment isn't the memory you want someone to have after visiting your restaurant.

Cracked Toilet Seats
The health department doesn't allow it. Your guests hate it. The company that sells you the replacement seat will love it. Make someone happy.

Broken or Missing Lights
Check the restrooms every day for burned-out lights or missing light covers. The physical integrity of the facilities creates an impression on your guests. Make sure that impression is positive.

Hourly Imperatives

The condition of your restrooms can change rapidly. At least every hour (more frequently during peak times), inspect the restrooms and correct any of the following situations.

Dripping Bars of Soap
Avoid bar soap at all costs. I have yet to see anyone truly excited about picking up a drippy bar of soap! If you don't already have wall-mounted soap dispensers, at least have a pump container of liquid soap on the counter.

Dispensers Crusted with Dried Soap
Crusted soap shows the dispenser has not been cleaned or wiped off for days! Some dispensers are easier to clean than others. When making your choice, consider how easy they'll be to keep clean.

Stale Smell
Lack of cleaning or improper air circulation will cause a stale smell in the air. Whatever the reason, you don't want guests equating your restrooms with those in most gas stations. Find the cause of the odor and correct it.

Overflowing Trash Containers
You have to stay on top of this. The quick fix is always just to push the paper down in the container, but be cautious about using your hand to compress a bin of used paper towels. There has been more than one report of someone puncturing their hand with a discarded needle. I won't elaborate on the potential dangers of that. Line all trash containers and keep replacement liners readily available.

Dripping Faucets
Washers wear out, and once the drip starts, it will only gets worse. If you delay the simple repair, dripping water can permanently discolor the sink.

Damp or Soiled Cotton Roll Towels
This is a less common form of hand drying but I still see it now and then. If you wait until a towel roll is gone before you replace it, you will continually be facing the problem of towels that are too damp or dirty to dry guests' hands. Check the rolls regularly and make sure you have enough capacity to get you through the rush.

Counter Tops Dripping with Water
You can't stop people from splashing. When you renovate your restrooms, keep the water problem in mind when you design the sinks. Some faucets splash less than others. A deep sink will create less splash than a shallow one. One piece counters and sinks allow water to drain more easily.

Stopped-up Fixtures
Clogged fixtures must be immediately cleared. So what if nobody likes to do it? How do you think your guests feel having to work around this problem? Besides, you know it will always happens in the middle of the rush! A blocked fixture won't fix itself, so have a plunger and a bowl snake readily available and take care of stoppages immediately.

Overpowering Perfume or Antiseptic Smell

The restroom should smell clean, not like a hospital or a bordello! A mild scent is desirable, but check your cleaning products out first. If you use an automatic aerosol unit, make sure the dispenser emits only the proper amount of spray for the size of the room.

No Toilet Tissue or Paper Towels

The only good answer is to replace or refill before the rush and periodically throughout the day. You can also install oversized rolls of toilet tissue that hold the equivalent of 10-12 regular rolls. They are worth considering in a high volume operation.

No Hand Soap

People who notice are the ones most likely to make a fuss. Plan for peak periods and stay on top of soap supplies. It's a good idea to keep an emergency stock of pump dispensers on hand just in case.

Cigarette Butts in the Urinals

Because restrooms are open to all patrons, many local ordinances require they be non-smoking. Even if you aren't required to do so, it's just a courtesy to your non-smoking patrons to make this designation. Smoking in a confined space like a restroom renders the room inhabitable for non-smokers.

If you don't have this restriction, you must clean out smoking debris at least hourly. Ashes on the sinks or fixtures are irritating to all patrons and cigarette butts on the floors or in the urinals make the room look and feel dirty. Your best defense is a good offense (no smoking in the restrooms). Eliminating the mess before it starts is easier than cleaning it up!

No Toilet Seat Protectors

Personal protection in public restrooms is important, especially for women. Paper toilet seat protectors are a small touch that can make your guests feel more confident when they use your facilities. The investment is small. If you don't yet have seat protectors, get them. Check the dispensers hourly and keep them replenished.

Bonus Points

Everybody likes pleasant surprises. These little unexpected touches are opportunities to improve your score and put your guests in a better mood. They help make up for any lapses in the operation and give people reasons to recommend your restaurant to their friends.

Facial Tissue
What if a guest needs to blow their nose, wipe off some makeup or do other little odd jobs? In most places, the choice is only paper towels or toilet paper – not really a stirring choice! Follow the example of most hotels and install a dispenser of tissues. Facial tissue is a small, inexpensive touch that creates another point of difference from your competition.

Panic Button
You can't count on your guests to tell you when a toilet is backed up or there's some other unsightly disaster, perhaps not wanting to give the impression (or admit) they were the ones that did it. A restroom "panic button" is simply a switch that turns on a flashing light somewhere out of sight in the restaurant.

A small sign says something like, "The cleanliness of the restrooms is important to us and we check them every hour to be sure. But accidents happen. If you ever see the restroom needs attention, flick this switch and we'll take care of it immediately." Then just make sure someone responds at once when the light comes on.

Amenities
Although restroom amenities are probably more relevant in upscale operations, anyone can add a few pleasant surprises. Unexpected touches like hand lotion, dispensed paper cups or complimentary packets of pain reliever will reflect your concern. Consider a selection of aftershave lotions in the men's room.

Amenities like a magnifying makeup mirror, a couch or flowers in the ladies room can make a big impression. A little effort in this direction and you will pick up the points even with people who don't take advantage of the amenities.

Separate Table for Diaper Changing
If a parent has to change their child's diaper, the counter at the sink is *not* an appropriate location. (I've seen it done on a dining room table!) A changing table can be easily wall-mounted to save space. Many operators I know mount it on a wall in the handicapped stall so diapers can be changed out of sight. Those who use it (and those who don't) will appreciate and remember your thoughtfulness.

If you install a changing table, remember to put one in the men's room as well. Include a separate, covered waste container for the soiled diapers. For a real point bonus, have some spare disposable diapers in different sizes on hand.

Full Length Mirrors

If you have the wall space, a full length mirror in each restroom is a nice touch. Most people want to check their appearance before returning to the dining room or lounge. If they can see themselves fully, there's less chance they might be embarrassed by a detail they couldn't see in the mirror over the sink.

Style

People expect restrooms to be utilitarian, but style is an unexpected surprise! Give the same attention to decorating your restrooms as you do to decorating your restaurant and watch the compliments you'll get!

Fresh Flowers

Fresh flowers in the ladies room might not be appropriate in a coffee shop. Still, a small vase of dried flowers on the counter could work. Interesting pictures on the walls or interesting light fixtures help avoid the institutional feel. If it makes your guests feel more comfortable it is worth considering.

Go Over the Top

Restrooms also can make a statement. Consider the Madonna Inn in San Luis Obispo, California where they actually give tours of the men's room! Could it be something about the nine-foot waterfall over natural rocks instead of more traditional urinals?

To give equal time to the ladies, my wife and I were staying at the Drake Hotel in Chicago for the NRA Show several years ago. We met some friends in the lobby and my wife was told, "You've *got* to see the ladies room," so off they went for a tour.

I'm told the stalls in the ladies room at the Drake were private rooms – full length door, toilet, sink ... your room. Whatever the details, it was unique enough that women felt compelled to tell each other about it. You could certainly do worse than a reputation for the greatest ladies room in town!

Ice in the Urinals

Have you heard about the 300-lb. blocks of ice in the oversized urinals at P.J. Clarke's in New York City? This was the sanitation method in the days before chemicals. The ice would melt slowly and keep things washed away and the cold would inhibit the growth of bacteria. The practice is over 100 years old and gives PJ's a clear point of difference in the market.

There's a variation on that idea that some operators use today – they simply keep the urinals filled with ice cubes. As one operator told me, it allows him to disinfect without chemicals, saving that cost and being more environmentally friendly. He also said that he knows about how long the ice will last so it is easy to see how long it's been since someone checked on the restrooms ... plus everyone always comments on it!

(If you give this idea a try, I suggest you have a totally separate and visually distinctive container to bring ice into the mens room. No need to make guests wonder if that's also used for ice at the bar!)

Over-Fixturing

Nothing succeeds like excess. If the code says three fixtures are required, put in four (particularly in the ladies room). The same with sinks and urinals. Stalls must be at least 30" wide? Make them 36" or 42". These small additions will help shift the public perception of your facilities from utilitarian to remarkable ... and if you take that much care in the restrooms, you surely must be going above and beyond in the kitchen!

Space

In most restaurant planning, restrooms use as little square footage as possible, just enough to meet minimum code requirements and no more. This is probably because most operators regard the facilities as non revenue-producing space and instead argue for more tables to maximize sales potential.

If you're fortunate enough to be able to design your restaurant from the ground up, I hope you will grasp the big picture and understand the talking power of some of the examples I've just shared.

Allocating a little extra space to allow your restrooms to really make a statement is like pre-paid advertising. If you have the courage to make a modest investment and go beyond the norm in terms of space and design, you can generate a positive word-of-mouth buzz for years.

(Really go over the top like Madonna Inn and the buzz lasts forever!)

14
Family
Fiascos

Families with children can be a profitable source of business for many operators, not just those billed as "family restaurants." As with other market segments, the trick in developing family business lies with understanding what they want and taking care of the details.

When dealing with families, it helps to understand that adults and children view dining in two different ways. For adults, meals are a social experience. Adults come to restaurants for conversation and to enjoy the company of their companions.

Children's are either eating, sleeping or playing, so for them, meals are just a biological necessity ("I'm hungry, feed me. I'm full, now what?") To serve families effectively, you must address both needs – Allow the children to be children while the adults are being adult.

Remember, too, that taking several children out to a restaurant can be like trying to nail Jell-O to the wall! Anything you can do to make it more painless for the adults, especially a single parent, the more you will endear yourself to them. Even if you don't actively market to families with children, families will come to your establishment. To serve them well, there are some basic problems to avoid.

Seating Shortcomings

Service to families starts the minute they walk in the door. Give the children something to do while you get the table ready – something to play with or even a packet of crackers to throw around. (That's what they do with them!) If you can't seat children immediately, they will find something else to play with, most likely be your restaurant! Give everyone a break and seat the family as soon as you can.

No High Chairs or Booster Seats

Even a restaurant that doesn't encourage children must have some provision to handle them. High chairs and booster seats are the minimum requirement. It's difficult to improvise children's seating safely. Make the investment.

221

Not Pre-Positioning Children's Seating

Give parents a break and don't make them ride herd on their young ones at the table while the busser prowls around in the back looking for the booster seats! If you must delay the family anywhere, delay them in the lobby, not in the middle of the dining room.

Dirty High Chairs or Booster Seats

People are more sensitive to cleanliness when it affects their kids. They know youngsters will put their hands (and mouths) anywhere. Be sure you don't give them any reason to worry.

Broken or Rickety High Chairs

Unstable seating is extremely dangerous for children. Even if *you* know the high chair won't collapse, the parents will ruin their whole meal waiting nervously for their little heir to hit the floor!

Waiting in Line

Many "family restaurants" have a service system where guests wait in line for their food before going to the table. On one hand, this may help keep the check average is within the family budget, but it also means a single mother with three young children in tow will have her hands full trying to keep control of her brood during the wait. Find a way to keep the wait from being a struggle for families or risk losing them to a more compassionate competitor.

No Place For the Stroller

When you are attracting a lot of family business, allocate some space for a stroller "parking lot" and be sure the staff knows where it is. Families will appreciate having less crowding at their table and your other guests will appreciate your maintaining the general order and neatness of the dining room.

Unsafe Placement of High Chair

Give some thought to where you place a high chair or booster seat. If possible, avoid seating children next to traffic lanes where a careless diner or harried server might bump them.

Seating Families at a Table with a Tip on it

Earlier we talked about why you should never seat a party at a table with a tip on it. It's bad form under any circumstances, but far more critical with children because the little ones will grab the money and put it in their mouths! Make sure the table is completely cleared and properly set before you seat the family.

Tableside Turmoil

When a family is finally seated, how well you relate to the children and understand their needs sets the tone for the rest of their meal. It also determines whether the family starts to relax or prepares for the worst. Here are a few devilish details that can tip the scales.

Not Anticipating the Needs of Families

Bring extra napkins right away. Be ready with an extra spoon. Leave a clean, damp cloth when there's a child in a high chair. Consider wet naps for after-dinner cleanup of sticky faces. What are you pretending not to know about taking children to out to eat?

No Children's Menus

Adults appreciate knowing what you have in children's portions and children appreciate having something just for them. Children's menus can be as simple or elaborate as you choose, but keep them consistent with the look and theme of your restaurant.

No Provisions to Keep Children Amused

Children always need to be doing something. Coloring books are inexpensive and easy to get from specialty/novelty houses. Even a blank piece of paper and a pencil will work. There's no end to the possible ways to amuse children, but be sure you have *something* readily at hand. Kids will run rampant in the dining room if they have no other acceptable (to them) play option!

Not Listening to Parents

People know what their children like and don't like; what they will and won't do. They'll tell you ... but you must ask (and pay attention to their answers). Not only will they appreciate your concern, but you can gain some free market research in the process.

Not Giving Youngsters Something to Do Immediately

Children are either eating, sleeping or playing. Since they won't go to sleep when you seat them, get something in their hands. At least give kids some crackers to throw around until their meals arrive.

Leaving the Place Setting in Front of Small Children

Parents know their children's capacity for handling utensils. Often youngsters can make do with just a spoon. Never leave a two-year old alone with a steak knife! Even if the child can safely handle a full set of silverware, let the parents decide what to leave with their kids. They'll appreciate your awareness and concern.

No Bibs Available
While many families will bring their youngster's favorite bib with them, be sure to have a few bibs readily available if needed ... and be sure all your staff knows where to find them.

Tall Glasses for Children's Beverages
Unless you want to spend half the meal cleaning up spills, give children something they aren't likely to turn over! Use a low, broad-based glass and a short (flexible) straw with children's beverages.

Taking a Long Time to Settle the Check
By the end of the meal, the children are usually becoming restless and harder to control. When the kids are ready to go, the family's ready to go. Settle the check within two minutes. The parents (and the rest of the dining room) will thank you.

Service Slip-ups

Serving a family has a different pace and different requirements than a party of adults. How well you deal with some of these small points will determine the success of your efforts.

Lack of Concern for the Well-Being of the Children
Parents appreciate people who appreciate their children and children like places that like them. Since the children often decide where the family dines, treat them with the same respect you give your adult guests. Parents will judge own their dining experience by how sensitively you handle the needs of their family.

Not Serving Children First
Be sure the youngsters get their food before the adults. It will keep their fingers out of the parent's meals!

Expecting Adult Behavior from Children
You can count on children to behave childishly! Don't pretend they can be otherwise. If you find yourself losing your composure just step back, take a deep breath and relax. Let yourself be touched by their innocence and energy.

If you can't shake your irritation, have someone else serve the table. Children are very sensitive and will pick up on your upset. They won't know why, but they'll remember they didn't have a good time at your restaurant. When their parents suggest dining in your establishment, the children won't want to come back.

Not Properly Taking Care of the Adults
Parents don't lose their appreciation of a good time just because they have their children with them. The youngsters may influence where the family eats, but the adults drive the car, pay the check and judge their dining experience by adult standards.

Inability to Heat Baby Food or a Baby's Bottle
This is not an uncommon request if you cater to families, so work it out with the kitchen. All it takes is a microwave or a pot of warm water and a few minutes. Knowing what to do will keep you from flinching when asked for this service. If you want to pick up a few points, make the offer before the guest even asks.

No Side Bowls or Plates for Sharing
The children may want to try some of whatever their parents are having. Provide a convenient way to give the children a taste. A side plate with the parents' meal shows your awareness of what it's like to take the family out to dinner.

Not Cleaning Under the Table
When the kids leave, count on a floor full of french fries, cracker wrappers and other assorted debris. The next guest at the table won't appreciate slipping in someone else's trash. A carpet sweeper or cordless dust buster will make this task easier and faster.

Poor Practices

To be truly responsive to the needs of families, you must allow for some special requirements. If your policies and practices are too rigid to accommodate these needs, you won't become the restaurant of choice for the family. If you can avoid the problems here, you're on your way toward developing a strong source of business.

No Plan to Handle Breast Feeding
This need will arise and your staff must know how you want to handle it. Remember a nursing baby doesn't have any other meal options! Handling the request smoothly avoids an uncomfortable situation for both the mother and your other guests.

No Healthy Menu Options for Children
Go the extra mile. Move beyond typical "junk food" or fried choices when designing a menu for children. The kids can handle it and their parents will appreciate your thoughtfulness.

Pricing Yourself out of the Market

For perspective, calculate your average check per family instead of just your average check per person. Your individual prices may be reasonable, but if it costs $120 for a family of four to have dinner, you won't be serving many families!

Not Allowing for Food Preferences of Children

Youngsters are not very trendy. They'll make a fuss if you don't have white bread or un-seeded rolls for their sandwiches. There are some choices you almost *have* to offer, but give your children's menu some thought. You can have signature items for children as easily as you can have signature items for adults.

No Provisions for Diaper Changing

When diapers need to be changed, they will be changed. I've seen it done on a restroom counter or even on a table in the dining room! Each restroom needs a shelf wide enough for this purpose. Using the countertop by the sink irritates other guests. A separate covered trash can for dirty diapers is also worth considering.

Bonus Points

Everybody likes pleasant surprises. These little unexpected touches are opportunities to improve your score and put your guests in a better mood. They help make up for any lapses in the operation and give people something to talk about to their friends.

Treasure Chest

Everybody has coloring books, but Angus Barn in Raleigh, NC has a Treasure Chest of assorted playthings. With parental permission, they'll take children away from the table and let them make their own choice. They say both the parents and the kids need a break.

Diaper Changing Tables

If a parent has to change a diaper, the counter at the sink is *not* an appropriate location. A changing table can be easily wall-mounted to save space. One operator I know suggested mounting it on the wall in the handicapped stall so the changing happens out of sight.

Those who use it (and even those who don't) will appreciate your thoughtfulness. If you install a changing table, remember to put one in the men's room as well. Include a separate, covered waste container for the soiled diapers.

For a real bonus, have some spare disposable diapers in different sizes on hand. Most parents come prepared, but if an emergency arises, it's hard to improvise.

Separate Area for Nursing

Knowing how you will handle this question when it comes up is good, but a comfortable area set aside for nursing mothers is even better. Nursing babies in public is more common than it used to be. Still, it can be a delicate situation for both for the mother and your other guests. If possible, a separate room with a comfortable armchair neatly resolves the situation to everyone's delight.

Routinely (And Quickly) Checking for Forgotten Articles

It's not that the family will never recover the lost items, it's more a recognition that families don't need the inconvenience of having to return for forgotten items. They will appreciate and remember that you found that favorite toy that rolled behind the plant, particularly when it's back before the youngster throws a tantrum about it!

Highchairs on Wheels

Particularly in restaurants where the parents have to wait in line for their food, rolling high chairs by the front door are a definite plus. Parents can place their small children in the chair and keep them under control while waiting and all the way to the table.

Stands for Infant Carriers

Molded infant carriers are common but they don't usually fit on dining chairs, they're dangerous to put on the floor and awkward on top of the table. Some high chairs can be inverted to hold an infant carrier securely. They're worth a look.

Wet Towels

Children's hands are always dirty. If you provide a way to clean sticky hands at the table, you'll win the undying appreciation of the parents. It's hard enough to take a group of children out to eat without having to shuttle them to the restrooms for a cleanup. The solution can be as easy as packaged Wet-Naps or as classic as warm, damp washcloths.

"Give 'Em!"

Children love presents. A memento of their meal (and of your restaurant) can do wonders for developing loyalty in the younger set. Just look at what McDonald's has done with the Happy Meal! Call it bribery if you like, but it works!

15
Disabled
Disasters

Legendary operators always offer the same level of excellent service to every guests. If you've been providing indifferent service to the disabled, it's time to take another look at your style. The Americans with Disabilities Act (ADA) requires all restaurateurs to accommodate the needs of disabled guests.

Disabled diners are people, too. They have some extreme challenges in their lives and are among the most courageous people on the planet. All they ask is the same respect and opportunities for life that able-bodied people enjoy.

Dining out is one of life's pleasures. Making the restaurant experience part of their lives is a special service you can provide. If you give them the respect they deserve, they can be extremely loyal and enthusiastic guests. I suspect your other diners will notice the compassion with which you treat the disabled and view you more favorably for it.

So while disabled diners are just people like anyone else, they do have different needs than able-bodied patrons. Equal treatment doesn't mean treating them just like every other guest. Giving equal treatment to disabled patrons means providing them with a dining experience of equal quality.

Universal Irritants

Despite their particular disabilities, all disabled people I spoke with mentioned the following irritations in restaurants:

Condescending Tone from the Staff

Disabled persons are not second class citizens. They are just people with a few more obstacles than the rest of us. Treat them with respect and courtesy and be aware of the words you use when you speak to them. These are responsible – even heroic – adults. When you see them that way, it all works more easily. Your real message is always carried in your tone of voice, not your words.

Impatience

Disabled diners don't enjoy many advantages that able-bodied people take for granted and communicating with the disabled is often more difficult. The pace of service for a disabled diner takes different timing than most of your parties.

When serving a disabled diner, just relax and let your heart go out to them. Remember, good service is defined from *their* perspective, not from yours. If you become impatient, it only shows your lack of understanding and lack of professionalism.

Taking a Roundabout Route to the Table

Some disabled persons have a more difficult time moving around. It is inconsiderate and embarrassing to make them run through an obstacle course to get to a table in the back of the dining room. Whenever possible, seat disabled parties near the entrance.

Talking in a Louder Voice

There's an annoying tendency to increase the volume of your voice when talking to the disabled. Modulate. Blind guests or patrons in wheelchairs are not hard of hearing and guests who are deaf can't hear you anyway! Raising your voice only calls attention to the diner and makes them more uncomfortable.

Seating Other Parties Ahead of Disabled Parties

Treating everybody equally well means that all guests receive the same level of attention. There is never a good reason for making a disabled party wait while you seat diners who arrived after them.

Wheelchair Wickedness

Most local codes require all facilities to be accessible to persons in wheelchairs. Besides physical access, there are a few other facts about dining in a wheelchair that you should be aware of.

No Access Ramps

You don't make able-bodied guests climb over a wall to get in. Why would you make it impossible for a chair-bound diner to enter your establishment? Even if you are grand fathered on this from a code perspective, adding an access ramp will make it easier for elderly diners and children. If you receive deliveries through the front door, think how much easier it is to bring a hand truck up a ramp instead of up the steps.

Undersized Restrooms

Disabled diners are as likely to use your restrooms as anyone else. Compact restrooms can be difficult for wheelchairs to maneuver in. Put yourself in their position. How welcome would you feel in a place where you couldn't use the restroom? If your public restrooms are too small to accommodate a wheelchair easily, look for options. Perhaps there's another toilet in the building you could use for a single occupant in a wheelchair.

Inaccessible Tables

You need at least one table that can comfortably accommodate a wheelchair, preferably near the door. Booths may be more efficient seating for most people, but they're extremely awkward for a diner in a wheelchair. A chair-bound guest likely can't slide into a booth. Unless they make a specific request, don't even suggest it.

Placing a wheelchair at the end of a booth table will usually put the chair in the middle of a traffic lane. Only tables where you can remove a conventional chair will give wheelchair diners the feeling of equal treatment.

Pushing the Chair Without Permission

Just because someone is in a wheelchair doesn't mean they are incompetent. Disabled individuals are very proud (and protective) of their independence and resent your trying to help them, no matter how well-intentioned your motives. Unless they ask for help, escort guests in wheelchairs to the table as you would any other diner.

Seating in the Back of the Dining Room

The best seating for diners in wheelchairs is close to the door. It is difficult to maneuver a chair through most restaurant traffic lanes. Trying to seat a wheelchair diner in the back of the dining room can inconvenience every guest seated along the aisle and call undue attention to the disabled person. Make it as easy as possible for everyone and minimize the travel distance to the table.

Insufficient Space for Chairs

Narrow traffic lanes and small lobbies are difficult to negotiate in a wheelchair. Look at your layout to see if a simple rearrangement would make it easier for a wheelchair diner to get around. Have a plan for where you will seat a chair-bound patron and the route you will take to get there. Then be sure every front of the house staff member knows the drill.

Sightless Oversights

Blind guests (or those with reduced vision) are loyal patrons of those restaurants that understand and respond to their needs. Here are a few common errors to avoid if you want to attract these steady guests.

Petting the Guide Dog
Guide dogs for the blind are highly trained, hard-working animals who are on the job when they're in your restaurant. Train your staff never to interact with the guide dog like it's a pet or another friendly puppy. Be friendly to the blind guest, not the dog.

Unwillingness to Read Menu and Prices
Not all restaurants have Braille menus (and only a small percentage of the blind read Braille), but every restaurant has someone who can read. Without one or the other, how is a blind patron supposed to know what to order? Table service restaurants generally do a better job of this than quick service operations or cafeterias. Be sensitive to the problem and have enough compassion to read your menu board and prices. (This is another case for having a shorter menu!)

Talking to a Sighted Companion Instead of the Blind Patron
Don't treat a blind guest like a non-person. Nobody likes to be ignored. Respectful service – for anyone – requires speaking to them directly and courteously. It doesn't matter if the guest can't see your face. They'll know when you're focused on them and when your attention is elsewhere. Give *all* guests your undistracted attention.

Refusing to Admit a Service Dog
Most local ordinances require you to admit guide dogs for the blind and other service animals. Even health department regulations, which normally prohibit animals in foodservice establishments, make an exception for guide dogs. Use your head and don't give anyone a hard time. Remember you're not talking about an ordinary animal, you are talking about someone's eyes. Besides, guide dogs are better behaved than children (and many of your guests!)

Seating at a Table with Dim Lighting
Many visually-impaired people are not completely blind. With a reasonable amount of light, they can function in a nearly normal fashion. When seating a blind patron, choose a well-lighted table close to the door. They'll appreciate your understanding.

Giving Blind Patrons the Wrong Change

It's a sad commentary, but apparently there are lesser life-forms who will actually short-change a blind person. When settling the check in cash, ask the blind guest if they'd prefer their change all in ones. Many would ask you to do it anyway, but by bringing up the subject first, you show your awareness of their needs.

Deaf Displeasures

Guests with impaired hearing don't appear much different from other guests so it's easy to forget they need special consideration. To avoid offending deaf diners, be aware of the following details:

Refusing to Admit Hearing Dog

Some deaf persons have specially trained dogs who help them live more productive lives. If they bring the dog into the restaurant, give the animal the same respect you would a guide dog for the blind. The same laws and exceptions apply to hearing dogs.

Not Facing a Deaf Person When Talking to Them

Many deaf persons are very skilled lip-readers and you can readily communicate with them. When talking to a deaf diner, face them squarely and speak in a normal voice. After all, how is a deaf diner going to read your lips if they can't see your face? Talk a little slower than your normal pace so they can follow you. They'll respond either by pointing to items or with a note.

Bonus Points

Braille Menus or Staff Member Who Can Sign

If a guest spoke another language, you'd try to get someone who could translate, wouldn't you? At the least, you'd want them to have a menu they could read. Why not extend the same courtesy to deaf or blind guests? Most towns have a local agency who provides services for the blind. Ask them to translate your menu to Braille ... or record the menu so a blind patron can listen at their own pace.

If you have someone on your staff who knows sign language, you'll open an entirely new dining experience for deaf guests. There are many people who learned to sign to communicate with hearing-impaired friends or family. Ask your staff if anyone has this skill.

16
Teenage Turnoffs

Y ou can love 'em or hate 'em, but you can't deny that teenagers are your future consumers. They may even be a big part of your business already. Teens are at an age when they're developing the habits that will carry them into adulthood. If you understand their needs and treat them well, dining in your restaurant could be a habit that stays with them for years.

If you need a more immediate incentive, here are a few more points to ponder. In most families, the teenagers are the ones who decide where family goes out to dinner. Parents often make calculating the tip an exercise in practical mathematics, so teens may decide how much of a tip the family will leave. Teenagers will patronize your restaurant with their parents, in groups with their peers or on dinner dates. Each situation has slightly different problems and opportunities.

Don't make the mistake of treating teenagers like children. Yes, they are new to adult ways, but they're as aware and observant as any adult diners. Forget the idea that all they know about is fast food and pizza. Many of today's teens have extensive dining-out experience in a wide range of restaurants. And never think teens don't have their own opinions about things. You may be surprised at what they like and dislike about restaurants.

Attitude Annoyances

As you might expect, a major adolescent complaint about restaurants has to do with the attitude of restaurant staff toward teens.

Different Treatment for Adults and Teens

There are no second class citizens in a great restaurant. Often teens receive incomplete service. Perhaps servers don't think teenagers will know the difference, but believe me, they know. Unless there are other mitigating factors (like you have the killer enchiladas in town), teens won't patronize your restaurant if you treat them poorly. When it's time for the family to go out, your establishment won't be in the running, either.

Obvious Sense of Displeasure When a Teen Party Arrives
Teenagers can always tell what you're thinking. If you see teens as pests, they'll react to you with annoyance. On the other hand, if you welcome teen parties and make the dining experience pleasant for them, you help instill the habit of dining out as a satisfying activity.

Seating Adult Parties Ahead of Teens
Escort guests to the table in the order of their arrival. Period. Many restaurants discriminate against teenage parties. Maybe they think the teens don't care. Perhaps they feel adults are more important patrons. Maybe they think they'll insult the adults if they seat the younger group first. These notions are all misguided. Good service is equal service, regardless of age.

Assigning Inexperienced Staff to Teen Tables
Often a restaurant will assign their least experienced staff serve parties of teenagers. The rationale, I suppose, is that the teens won't know the difference. Wrong! They not only notice, but they resent the inference that they aren't worth your best efforts. Teens don't come to your restaurant to provide training to your new servers. Don't reassign stations for groups of teen diners.

Asking the Parents for the Teen's Order
You're being rude any time you don't speak directly to a guest. Age, sex or physical condition has nothing to do with good service. Teens are particularly sensitive to poor treatment because they're so used to getting it, but they're not children and will resent your treating them that way. They know what they want. Always address them directly and with the same respect you give their parents.

No Substitutions
Younger diner's tastes are different from those of your adult patrons. Teens will often request substitutions from your standard fare. Give them the same consideration you would offer adult diners. After all, if you won't give them what they want, they'll find another restaurant that will!

No Attempt to Make Suggestions or Explanations
Many items on your menu may be unfamiliar to your teen patrons. They also may be uncertain about which foods go well together. Young diners appreciate helpful suggestions as much as any of your other patrons. Don't talk down to them or become annoyed if they ask endless questions about your menu. Remember, you're helping educate them about the joys of dining out.

AND WHAT YOU CAN DO ABOUT IT 237

Failure to Bring Food to the Table Quickly

Teenagers are active and eat a lot. As you would with younger children, get some food in front of them quickly. If you have a basket of an item (like tortilla chips) on the table, keep it re-supplied throughout the meal. If teens don't have something to do, they will *find* something to do!

Impatience with Limited Funds

Do you remember how it was when you were a teenager and low on money? More than once, I recall taking up a collection at a gas station to put a few more drops into the tank! Teenagers still find themselves short on cash. If a teen chooses to spend their last dollars in your restaurant, don't lose patience if you need to adjust the order to meet the funds available. The situation is touching proof of the loyalty of your young diners.

Not Showing Any Personal Interest

Teens are still learning social skills and may be a little nervous when they dine out. Staff members who are abrupt or appear uninterested in providing good service offend all diners. Take a personal interest in helping teenagers have a pleasant and comfortable experience. They'll appreciate your caring and become enthusiastic regulars.

Not Listening When Addressed by Teens

Talking to someone who isn't listening will create rage in even the most reasonable person. Any time a guest is talking to you, drop all other thoughts from your mind. Hear what they are saying, but pay particular attention to what they *mean*. Teenagers are very sensitive to your lack of presence. You can't fool them and they surely won't appreciate your attitude.

Shortchanging Teens

Some people try to take advantage of teens' inexperience. I've seen adults take a $20 bill from a young patron and only return change for $10. They insisted the youngster was lying about giving them a larger bill. Teens are still learning how to stand up for their rights and a belligerent adult can either intimidate them or trigger a severe push-back reaction.

Before you try to make a quick profit this way, remember teens talk to each other ... a lot. The word will travel quickly and can cost you more than just the business of the high school crowd. Once you get the reputation for being a ripoff, it's hard to recover. What goes around, comes around.

No Sense of Humor

The unexpected is routine in the restaurant business, more so with a party of teens. A sense of humor will help you provide a more memorable service to younger diners. They appreciate people who are comfortable enough to joke with them. A little levity can make the dining experience more enjoyable for everyone.

Menu Mistakes

Teens know what they like and what they don't. Here are a few menu errors that irritate younger patrons.

Limited Menu Choices

Teens are not particularly adventurous diners, but they still like to have choices and they *will* experiment with new items. You can help expand their culinary horizons with helpful suggestions. To attract more of their business, give them a variety of interesting dishes from which to choose.

Self-Serve Food Bars

Teens are aware of the sanitation dangers of food bars. The young people I spoke with didn't like salad bars because they saw too many people mishandling food. If you have a salad or food bar, do it right. Be sure someone continually supervises its operation. Clean up spills promptly. Don't pour new product on top of old product. Change serving utensils when you change food containers. *All* your guests will appreciate your concern.

Boring Beverage and Dessert Choices

The adolescent years are a time to experiment and discover. Don't assume teens only want to drink soft drinks. If you have something worth trying, you can count on teens for a dessert order every time! Give as much thought to offering interesting beverage and dessert choices as you do to writing your entrée menu. With a little bit of thought, you can increase your sales from the teen market and give them a more enjoyable experience.

Atmosphere Aggravations

Teens are sensitive to what's going on around them in a restaurant. Here are several details they find particularly irritating.

Inappropriate Background Music

Many teens don't like background music from a radio. They hear radio all day and think restaurants should offer something unique. Neither do they find heavy metal or rap music an appealing choice. If you draw (or want to draw) a teen market, consider classic rock.

Noisy Video Games

Contrary to what you might think, an incessant din from video games annoys teen diners. They like having video games accessible in the restaurant, but they don't like the noise intruding on their meal. If you offer video games, soundproof the game room. All your patrons will appreciate the gesture.

Dim Lights

Because they live active lives, dimly-lit dining rooms have little appeal to teens. They prefer brighter lighting, perhaps so they can see what's happening around them. A higher lighting level can also shift the focus away from the table, where there may be some social awkwardness. To make dining attractive for younger diners, keep the lights up or seat them in more brightly lit areas.

Dirty Restaurant

Teens are hyper-sensitive to cleanliness and sanitation. They notice the clutter, dirt, stains, dirty restrooms, soiled seating and the poor sanitation habits of your staff. In short, they're just like any of your other guests, so don't think you can get away with anything. Teens won't patronize restaurants they don't trust to be safe.

No Uniforms

You won't make teen diners more comfortable by allowing your young staff to wear their regular clothes at work. Teens think that a uniformed staff looks more professional. They feel better being served by someone in a clean uniform than by a worker in a t-shirt and jeans. Workers in uniform, particularly younger ones, also tend to show more pride in their behavior and their work.

Bonus Points

Everybody likes pleasant surprises, especially teens who rarely see people truly concerned with their needs. These little unexpected touches will endear your restaurant to teenage diners. They will have a reason to recommend you when the family is dining out and provide something to talk about to their friends.

Free Gum after the Meal
You give mints to the adults after the meal, why not give gum to teenagers? If you really want to make some points, make it bubble gum! Plan B is a "Trick or Treat" approach where you offer them a choice from a basket of assorted goodies.

Bottled Sodas
As you might expect, teens are connoisseurs of soft drinks. They appreciate the sharper carbonation of bottled sodas over the post mix product.

Something to Look At
Teens thrive on visual stimulation and enjoy interesting things to look at. They like restaurants with "a lot of junk" on the walls, TV sets, windows on the street – anything that is highly visual.

Souvenirs
Teens will prize keepsake glasses with your restaurant's logo. They are collectors and look for places where they can add to their accumulation of memorabilia. Tie the glass in with a signature drink that enhances your establishment's image (and profitability).

Free Beverage Refills
Adolescents have a continual thirst. They appreciate restaurants that recognize this need with prompt (free) beverage refills. The initial price of the drink is only a partial consideration. You'll gain points by charging a little more for a drink and giving free refills. You can do even better by making the cup a souvenir of your restaurant.

Unusual Desserts
Teenage guests love anything sweet. They are enthusiastic about restaurants with many different desserts from which to choose. So offer interesting desserts with clever names and you'll increase your teen patronage as you build dessert sales.

Cool T-Shirts
Hard Rock Café is hot with teens because they have a distinctive t-shirt everybody wants. Many other restaurants built their fame with a distinctive logo and a well-merchandised line of clothing. Eskimo Joe's in Stillwater, Oklahoma even has a four-color, 32-page clothing catalog published twice a year. If you want teens to think about your restaurant, develop a line of great t-shirts.

Mocktails

Don't automatically assume teens only want soft drinks. They love having a range of beverage choices as diverse as what's available to adult diners. The same alcohol-free signature items that appeal to adults can give teenage diners a new range of beverage choices ... and increase your sales.

Sensitivity to Conversational Stalemate

When teenage couples go out for dinner, they often find themselves caught in a socially awkward situation when nobody at the table can think of anything to say. So they end up just staring at each other in silence. I'm sure you can remember these uncomfortable social deadlocks when you were growing up.

Be sensitive to this situation. When you sense an impasse, stop by the table to make a comment or suggestion. That will loosen up the situation, make young guests more comfortable and help salvage what could otherwise become a disastrous evening.

Exhibition Cooking

Young diners are very sensitive to how you prepare their food. They're also curious about the process, so exhibition kitchens are a real attraction. If you sense your teenage diners are restless (and if your layout permits), offer them a quick behind-the-scenes tour of the restaurant. They soak up new experiences like sponges.

You can use the excursion to point out what makes your restaurant different from your competition. Educate them about what they should be looking for when they go to restaurants. Teens love to have something to tell their friends about. It can't hurt to have them talking about what a great place you have.

Attentive, Respectful Service

In the end, teenagers just want the same responsive service that any other guest expects. They don't want to be treated like children or second-class citizens. They appreciate friendly staff who show a genuine concern for their well-being and enjoyment.

17
Elderly Irritations

Socially and personally, dining is as much part of a satisfying life for seniors as for any of your other guests. Older diners grew up when standards of service were higher than those typically found today and their expectations are higher. They know what should happen, they know what they want and they know when they don't get it.

Seniors are more vocal than younger diners. They're more likely to speak up, not because they're more critical but because they're not afraid to ask for what they want. They won't tip for service they didn't receive. In short, they can be "tough customers" who demand nothing less than your best efforts. Your ability to meet the expectations of senior diners is a good measure of your professional skill.

Seniors' expectations aren't unreasonable. They simply want the same friendly, efficient service as other diners. They appreciate restaurants that understand and satisfy their particular needs. You don't get many second chances with older diners. They figure you should know what you're doing. If you don't, they'll find another place that does.

With good reason, older diners have more concern for their personal safety and are sensitive to potential risks. They're less likely to dine in the evenings, since physiological changes to their eyes often make driving after dark more difficult.

Still, senior diners can be a valuable source of business. Their funds are often limited, but they're not afraid to spend their money with those who earn it and they can fill your restaurant when it would otherwise sit empty. They are intensely loyal to establishments that treat them well. They thrive on respectful service and gratitude for their patronage.

To serve this growing market properly, you and your staff must be aware that senior diners aren't just older versions of your younger patrons. There are some basic changes, both in physiology and motive, that make senior diners unique.

The graying of the baby-boomers is upon us, so you may want to consider some adjustments in your operation to be more responsive to the needs of older guests. Often what's good for older diners turns out to be a service to younger diners as well. Here are some details you should know to be more responsive to seniors.

Terrible Treatment

Older diners have a wealth of experience and know good service when they get it. They also know when you're treating them poorly and they are not afraid to tell you about it.

Waiting in Line

Seniors don't have the physical stamina to stand for long periods so they hate to wait in a line. If you must ask an older diner to wait, find them a seat and make them comfortable. Offer something to drink and keep them informed of the status of their wait. If your service system requires guests to carry their own food to the table, offer to carry the tray for older guests.

Calling Seniors by Their First Names

Your Mom knew had it right when she told you to respect your elders. Seniors deserve respect, including addressing them as "Mr., Mrs. or Miss." Never address an elderly patron by their first name unless they've asked you to do so. [Note: In the south, "Miss Alice" is considered respectful.] Remember, seniors grant the first-name permission on a person-by-person basis. Just because one server has the privilege doesn't mean everyone on the staff has permission. When in doubt, err on the side of formality.

Seating Other Parties Before Older Diners

Some greeters ignore seniors and give preferential treatment to younger parties, perhaps thinking they'll generate more sales for the restaurant. Nobody likes to be treated like a second class citizen, particularly older diners who deserve more deference. Remember that elders find it physically difficult to stand around waiting for seating – don't make them wait any longer than necessary.

Seating Seniors Beside Loud Groups

Families with children and groups of teenagers usually create more noise than other diners. Elders find loud noises disorienting and stressful. A sensitive greeter will make it a point to seat seniors at well-lighted tables away from loud groups.

Uncertainty Where to Go or What to Do
Seniors don't like to feel incompetent or out of control. Who does? They want to know where they're supposed to go and what they're expected to do. Should they wait for a greeter or seat themselves? Which way is the non-smoking section? Ideally, the greeter will be at the door when guests arrive, but cover yourself with clear signs for the times when the staff may be elsewhere.

Appearing to Make Fun of Elder Diners
Seniors face problems younger people can only imagine. Older people are doing the best they can and are very sensitive to what they perceive as ridicule. It's inexcusable to appear to joke about the infirmities or limitations of any guest. Don't permit any member of your staff to engage in this thoughtless behavior.

Talking Down to Older Guests
Just because someone is old doesn't mean they're stupid. Quite the opposite is usually true. Always treat older diners with respect and courtesy. Remember the message is carried more by your tone of voice than your words. Avoid sarcasm and innuendo in your choice of words and inflection.

Talking More Loudly to Seniors
Many people have an annoying tendency to increase the volume of their voices when talking to elderly people. Keep your voice at a reasonable level. If a senior diner has a hearing problem, they'll tell you. Raising your voice only calls attention to the diner and makes them self-conscious.

Impatience
Older people live at a slower pace. Their thought processes may slow down and many tasks simply take more time. When you think about it, why would an older person be in a hurry anyway? Your skill as a foodservice professional is measured by your ability to delight *all* your guests, not just diners of your age group. If you become impatient, you'll only show your immaturity.

Atmosphere Irritations

Because of natural changes in the body, elderly diners are more sensitive to extremes of sight, sound and touch than your average patron. Recognition of these sensitivities helps provide seniors with a more pleasant meal.

Seating Seniors in Drafts
Drafts are uncomfortable for any guest, but are particularly bothersome to seniors. Due to changes in the tactile responses of the skin, older diners don't tolerate extremes of temperature as well as younger patrons. Pay particular attention to the temperature and humidity conditions in your dining room when selecting seats for older guests.

Not Enough Light to Read the Menu
Guests can't order what they can't see. Vision changes as people get older and compassionate operators allow for the visual limitations of their elder patrons. To make it easier, you can raise the lighting level or use larger type on the menu. Menus on matte finish papers are easier to read than those on glossy stock. Paper or ink color combinations also affect the readability of your menu. If the menu you use for the public is difficult for senior diners to read, it may be worth making a special menu for them.

Noisy Dining Rooms
Many elders experience a loss of tone sensitivity in higher ranges, causing sounds to converge. Poor acoustics in the restaurant only increases the stress on seniors. In the extreme, harsh acoustics will cause older diners never to return.

Menu Missteps

Your menu is the operating plan for your restaurant. If you want your establishment to attract older diners, be sure your menu provides the items they want in the way they want them.

Menu Items Unavailable in Smaller Portions
Older diners just don't eat as much food as they once did, so huge portions and doggie bags are less attractive. While price is always a consideration for people on a fixed income, the waste of food is equally unnerving. Offer several of your entrées in smaller portions and you'll be doing a favor for all your guests.

Lack of Menu Variety
As their options for activity decrease, the lives of elders can take on a certain sameness. Though they may choose to order the same item most times they dine, seniors enjoy the ability to choose their meal from a range of interesting selections.

No Familiar Foods on the Menu

Seniors like the comfort of familiar foods. They will try new items, but aren't drawn to trendy menus offering entrée combinations that seem strange to them.

Items Covered with Sauce, Gravy or Dressing

Older digestive systems don't handle fat as easily as younger ones. Food with excessive sauce is difficult for seniors to digest. Offering more low fat entrées on your menu and serving sauces on the side will better meet their needs. It also will respond to the growing health-consciousness of the public. This is an example of something good for older diners being a service to younger folks as well.

Highly-Seasoned Food

Most elder diners don't like foods that are extremely spicy because their digestive systems can be easily upset. If you have spicy items on your menu, warn seniors what to expect when they order. What may not seem spicy to you may still irritate an older guest.

Uncut Sandwiches

Seniors often have trouble cutting and eating food. Even sandwiches that are cut in half can be a problem. If possible, cut sandwiches for older guests into at least four pieces. The presentation can be attractive and your guests will have a more enjoyable time. Women and children also might appreciate this gesture.

Menu Items in Large Pieces

A menu composed only of soft foods will not interest most seniors. Still, cutting, chewing and swallowing are often more difficult for elderly people. Entrées with smaller pieces of meat are more appropriate choices. If you don't already have such items on the menu, offer to have the kitchen cut the food to a more manageable size. It will show your awareness and concern.

Prices Beyond the Budget

Many seniors live on a fixed income and simply can't afford the prices at many establishments. Still, they enjoy dining out as a social and personal experience. Many prefer eating in restaurants to cooking at home.

To be more attractive and accessible to older diners, offer a senior menu or discount program. This is as much an acknowledgment of the older diner's importance to your business as it is a cost savings. Seniors appreciate both motives. There's no reason you can't offer lower-priced options to everyone at certain times of the day.

Bonus Points

Everybody likes pleasant surprises and none so more than seniors. These little unexpected touches are opportunities to improve your score and put your older guests in a better mood.

Manager Contact
Older people always like to know who is in charge and love to receive personal attention from "the boss." They favor restaurants where the owner or manager actively works the floor.

Escort to the Car
Seniors, especially women, have concern for their personal safety. They appreciate an escort to their cars in the evening. If you choose to offer this service, be sure to ask permission before taking action. Elderly women are often suspicious of strangers who offer to help, though, so it will put them at ease if their escort is obviously on the restaurant's staff (i.e. in uniform).

Prompt Resolution of Complaints
Never negotiate a guest's complaint. The only approach that will work is to apologize for the situation and fix it immediately. Don't ask the guest what they want you to do – it will put them on the spot and make them uncomfortable.

When you understand the nature and source of the problem, propose a generous solution. Remember you're not just solving a problem, you're making an investment in securing a regular patron.

Benefit of a Doubt Stance
A wonderful woman in her 70's told me of going to a restaurant near her home for lunch. When the check arrived, she realized she'd left her wallet at home. She told the manager of her plight and was delighted when he trusted her to come back later to settle the bill. The point is that you can usually trust seniors. Give them the benefit of the doubt and you can make a friend for life.

Take-Home Menu
Many seniors don't cook, but still like to eat at home. Going to the market is often inconvenient, so they appreciate the ability to get restaurant meals to go. An extensive menu of items available for take-home service can be very attractive to seniors. If you really want to serve the older market, consider a delivery service.

Location Within Walking Distance

Strictly speaking, this isn't a case of "location, location, location" ... but many elderly people don't drive and prefer to patronize restaurants within walking distance of their homes. You can't move your business, but you *can* – and should – actively market yourself to seniors living in the neighborhood.

Single-Priced Buffet

Because of their fixed incomes, seniors like to know in advance what their meals will cost. If your concept lends itself to this format, offering a set price buffet or fixed-price menu will make you more popular with the older set. Make the fixed price meal available during your slower hours when you have excess capacity. Since seniors eat less and go out as much for the social contact as for the meal, you're not taking much of a risk.

Respectful Service

Unfortunately, our society often ignores senior citizens. This creates the opportunity for your restaurant to give seniors the recognition and respect denied to them elsewhere. While they have some special needs, older diners want the same enjoyable dining experience as any other guest in your restaurant. If you are compassionate enough to serve seniors with courtesy and respect, they can become your most loyal guests.

18
Management Mistakes

In the words of Walt Kelly's swamp philosopher, Pogo, "We have met the enemy and he is us!" The sad truth is that most the problems that occupy your time are problems of your own creation. It's not that you're not trying to make your job more difficult, you've just lost perspective on what's important to the success of your operation.

The problem isn't really your fault. You learned "how to do it" from those who preceded you ... who, in turn, learned the business from *their* predecessors. This long line passed down some wonderful skills and traditions. It also passed along a way of doing business derived in response to needs and conditions far removed from those of today. You do it the way you do it because you've always done it that way.

Many restaurateurs operate with the mentality of a policeman: always watching for people trying to get away with something. They create a web of rules and policies to maintain order and find more ways to say "no" than to say "yes." They develop procedures that are efficient for the restaurant but often frustrating for their guests.

It's time to wake up and get serious. If what you've been doing doesn't work for your guests, more of the same won't solve the problem. Take a hard look at your operation and see if you have created any of these problems for yourself:

Dense Decisions

Many restaurant policies are well-intentioned but ill-advised. Any time your priority is to make the experience easier for the restaurant or the staff instead of easier for the guest, you are asking for problems.

No Substitutions

Service guru Peter Glen suggested that the way to make guests happy is to find out what they want, find out how they want it, and give it to them just that way. If you refuse to make even reasonable substitutions, the requirements of the restaurant are obviously more important than the desires of your guests.

Does your staff think substitutions are an imposition? If they do, you're just asking for unhappy guests. Not all substitutions are practical, of course, but when you can't do what the guest asks, tell them what you *can* to ... then do it with a smile.

Not Accepting Credit Cards

Some restaurants still have a policy against accepting credit cards in general or a specific credit card in particular. Management has the right to make this decision, of course, but many diners use different credit cards for business occasions than they do for personal ones. Some guests won't patronize your restaurant if they can't use their credit card of choice.

No Separate Checks

If you want delighted guests, make it as easy as possible for them. There are many reasons why a party might want separate checks. It may require additional time for your staff, but that's not a valid reason to refuse. Fortunately, electronic point-of-sale systems make separate checks much easier.

At the beginning of the meal, ask large parties if they prefer separate checks and there will be trauma (and less work to do) later. If orders need to be placed separately, work with the kitchen staff to develop a system where all entrées for the table can be ready simultaneously.

If a guest changes their mind about a choice, take it in stride. It's not worth losing your composure over human nature. Most guests will remember and appreciate your patience. Besides, in my experience, the tips were always better with separate checks!

Minimum Charges

Most minimums are for the benefit of the house instead of for the benefit of the guest, so policies of this sort are risky. Many diners object to minimum charges, especially when imposed on families with children. If you have a minimum charge policy, be sure your staff understands *why* you have it and reach a consensus about when they should (and shouldn't) insist on the minimum charge.

Charging More for the Same Portion at Dinner

People usually expect to pay more for their evening meal. However, when the same size portion has a higher price in the evening than in the afternoon, guests can feel cheated. If you have similar items available at lunch and dinner, offer them in a different presentation or portion size to avoid the impression of exploiting your guests.

AND WHAT YOU CAN DO ABOUT IT

Opening Late or Closing Early Contrary to Posted Hours

You can never win an argument with a guest ... particularly about whose watch is right! To give everyone a break, simply play it safe and avoid the problem in the first place. Open the doors at least ten minutes ahead of schedule and don't lock up until at least ten minutes past your posted closing time.

Establish clear guidelines for your staff about how you will handle guests who want service outside regular hours, but be sure you provide full services during your posted hours. Scheduled closing time is *not* the hour your staff should expect to go home! If this isn't made clear to your team, guests who arrive just before closing are likely to feel some hostility.

An Automatic Service Charge and Indifferent Service

The debate over service charges vs. tipping probably will always be with us, but one thing for sure: if guests feel forced to pay for a level of service they didn't receive, they won't be anxious to return.

Not Allowing Transfer of a Bar Check to the Dining Room

Picture this: it's a busy Saturday night and the restaurant is jammed. People are waiting in every available corner. The dining room is mobbed. A couple has been sitting in the bar for well over an hour, sipping wine and waiting for their table.

Suddenly the greeter appears to tell them their table's ready. She's in a rush because there are so many other guests waiting and the manager is pushing her to get somebody on that empty table. The couple is hungry, so they start toward the dining room and ask the greeter to just have their bar tab transferred into the dining room. The greeter says they can't do it. Now what?

The couple can't leave the bar until they find their cocktail server, get the check, give them the credit card, wait for it to be processed and sign the charge form. This is going to take a little time.

What does the greeter do while all this is unfolding? Does she seat the wife alone and make the husband try to locate his bride somewhere in the dining room later? Does she stand around while the husband closes out the bar check?

Meanwhile, a table sits empty in the dining room and the manager fumes while other guests are wait to be seated. Do you see the problem? Never waste time solving a problem you can eliminate. Do everybody a favor and change your system to allow guests to transfer bar checks into the dining room.

Unexpected Charges

Be aware of the customs in your area and don't surprise your guests with charges they don't expect. For example, if you operate a Chinese restaurant and all other Chinese restaurants in your area include rice in the price of their meals, don't have a separate charge for rice without letting your guests know in advance.

Not Allowing Guests to Take Home Uneaten Food

People are becoming more aware of waste. As prices rise, many diners are doing all they can to get the most value for their dollars. Other guests are just enthusiastic about your food. Any of these motives may cause a guest to ask for the leftovers.

You'll create suspicion if you don't allow them to take home items from the table they have paid for. For example, most guests know you shouldn't reuse rolls. If you refuse to let them take the extra rolls home, they'll logically wonder what you plan to do with the rolls! You don't need rumors like this in the community. Do all you can to minimize leftovers at the table, and comply with guests' requests.

Control Collapses

Management is responsible for the efficient operation of the business. When you don't maintain a sense of order in your restaurant, guests don't feel comfortable.

"Who's in Charge Here?"

Nobody likes to walk into a restaurant that's operating in chaos. If your guests experience confusion in your dining room, you'll start losing points at once. When your staff is "in the weeds," you must be on the floor keeping the panic from affecting your guests.

Crimes Against Guests

You are responsible to protect your guests' safety while they're on your premises. Whether this is a legal requirement or just part of good hospitality depends on the circumstances. Still, if someone is assaulted in your restaurant – or worried they *might* be assaulted in your restaurant – they won't be back.

Talk with other operators in your area. Find out what crime-related problems they've been having and what they're doing about it, then make sure you are doing at least as much as they are. Anything less is negligence and can create legal issues for you should there be an incident in the future.

Any Sort of Bother for the Guest
Nobody wants a hassle when they go out to eat and there's no way to win a dispute with a guest. Give your staff the authority to do whatever they feel is necessary to correct irritations on the spot. If they spill food on a guest, they should be able to pay for the cleaning without making the guest wait for management approval.

If your staff thinks protecting the house is more important than doing what is right for the guest, the diner's cleaning bill might not be paid at all and the person will be lost forever!

Failure to Resolve a Complaint Promptly
Always resolve complaints in the guest's favor – issues don't resolve themselves any other way. There's no negotiation when if comes to correcting a guest annoyance. The only approach that will work is to apologize for the situation and fix it immediately.

Don't ask the guest what they want you to do – it puts them on the spot and makes them uncomfortable. Once you grasp the nature and source of the problem, propose a generous solution that will make the guest happy. Remember you're not just solving a problem, you're making an investment in securing a regular patron.

Failure to Respond to Written Complaints or Compliments
Of all guests who have a problem, statistically only one in twenty-five will care enough to tell you about it. The rest just go away and most of them won't come back. A written complaint (or compliment) is a rare gesture of caring. Respond promptly, appropriately and personally. Guests appreciate your acknowledging their message.

Making the Guest Feel Wrong, Stupid or Clumsy
This is a most uncomfortable feeling for people. It happens when your staff operates from their personal notions of what is right and what is wrong. Right and wrong are concepts, not absolutes. What's right for you may not seem right to someone else.

In the restaurant business, the only values that matter are those of the guest. Never do anything that would cause a guest to feel wrong, stupid or clumsy. Watch your tone of voice when a guest does or says something you think is inane. Your patrons don't know your rules and customs, nor should they have to.

There are lots of places people can go to receive abuse and hostility. Make your restaurant an oasis of hospitality in an otherwise harsh world and you will draw business like a magnet!

Failure to Maintain Order

Fortunately, most guests are reasonably well-behaved in public, but there are exceptions, particularly if people have been over-served alcohol. You *are* in business to help diners enjoy themselves, but there are practical limits to the behavior you can tolerate. Your first loyalty must be to your staff and the majority of your guests.

When a particular guest or a group is being abusive to your staff or disrupting the experience for other diners, management has a responsibility to address it. The most effective intervention always comes from within the group itself.

Toward that end, the most non-confrontational approach is to talk with the offender or the party host privately and make them aware of the problem. Have the server call them away from the table to take a telephone call, and politely ask them to tone it down.

In the case of a group, suggest relocating the party to a more private area if possible. In most cases you don't want to issue an ultimatum but you *should* endeavor to have an adult discussion in an honest attempt to reach an amiable solution.

Most people will comply, but if they ignore repeated requests to modify their behavior, you must then ask them to leave as firmly and diplomatically as you can. Better to upset one party than to alienate a room full of well-behaved patrons.

Failure to Apologize for an Error

If you don't apologize immediately for every error, oversight or difficulty experienced by the guest, they may think you don't care. You don't have to admit guilt to apologize – just acknowledging you're sorry the situation was an upset will help.

Disturbances In the Dining Room or Bar

You can't always prevent disturbances from happening, but you always control of how you handle them when they arise. When you have a disruption in your restaurant, management or staff must resolve it immediately and discretely.

Jaundiced Judgement

Even with an enlightened perspective and proper priorities, your judgement is still an important factor in guest gratification. Here are some examples:

Not Enough Staff to Provide Good Service

If guest gratification is your most important job, you must have enough staff on the floor to do the job. I've been in many restaurants that failed to provide responsive service because they were short-staffed by choice. They ruined the evening for most of their guests just to save two bucks an hour by having one less server on the schedule! Wake up to reality and start to think of labor as a profit center, not an operating cost.

Greed

In the movie "Wall Street," Michael Douglas (as the character Gordon Gekko) rhapsodizes that "greed is good." His logic may have fit the film, but it's dangerous in our business. So what do I mean by greed? Greed is all about what's in it for you.

Greed is a concerted effort to maximize revenue by trying to pry the most money you can from every patron's wallet. Greed is a one-way flow of cash – to you – with hardly a passing thought of sharing the wealth. Greed comes from insecurity, a belief there's not enough to go around and you'd better grab yours while you can. What you obsess about often comes to pass.

When you're running scared, it reflects in the way you run your restaurant which impacts how your guests are treated, which, in turn, determines whether they come back or not. Greed will kill your spirit and ultimately it will kill your business.

The best way to maximize income is to stay in business a long time. Relax, do a better job than necessary and trust if you consistently delight your guests, earn their trust and always work in their best interests, they will continue to support you over competitors who are only out for themselves.

In short, leave some money on the table. Don't try to get every dollar you can tonight. Rather, show guests a great time at a fair price and leave them a little spare change so they can afford to visit you again.

Serving Minors or Intoxicated Persons

Serving drunks puts your liquor license in danger. It also encourages inebriates to stay in your restaurant, driving away the very business you want to cultivate – those who go out for a drink to be sociable, not to get drunk.

Serving minors is also making a bet you can't afford to lose: your liquor license. These practices can foster an bad reputation and discourage the patronage of more responsible guests.

Sudden Changes in Operating Style

Unless your restaurant is in serious trouble and needs a complete change of concept, don't do anything rash. Evolution will keep you prosperous, revolution will confuse your market. (McDonald's isn't the same place that sold 15¢ hamburgers. When did they change?) The marketing battle is fought between the ears. To be successful, you must occupy a memorable place in the minds of your market. Sudden changes will most likely be confusing and they'll forget you.

Uncorrected Complaints

If someone cares enough to complain, care enough to listen. If you care enough to listen, care enough to do something about it. If you can't solve the problem, tell them what you *can* do to make their experience more pleasant. You'll only hurt your reputation if you let a guest detail their complaint without really listening.

Others always know when you're not paying attention and it will enrage them even more. They'll likely interpret your lack of interest to mean you don't care (and they'll probably be right!) On the other hand, if people sense you are really listening and sincerely want to solve any problems in the restaurant, they'll give you all kinds of helpful hints.

Your openness will dissolve their frustration and they'll leave your establishment feeling well cared-for. It's a lot easier to discover problems this way than to track them all down by yourself.

Conducting Business in the Dining Room

I was once in a coffee shop where an Avon representative had set up her office at a table in the middle of the dining room. For almost an hour, there was a steady stream of people in and out of the dining room to drop off orders. It was obvious they weren't there to eat and I found the experience extremely distracting. Our guests must be able to meet at the restaurant to talk business, of course, but it's also reasonable to expect they will do it over a meal!

Different Rules for the Owner

We were having dinner in the non-smoking section of a restaurant where my family knew the owner. After dinner, the owner visited with us at the table for a few minutes. She lit a cigarette and puffed away throughout the conversation. She never asked our permission. Since she bought us after-dinner drinks, it was awkward to ask her to put out the cigarette, but everyone at the table was uncomfortable as were diners at adjoining seats. Smoking in restaurants may be gone but owners who feel they're above the rules are still with us.

Tolerating Incompetence

Seek out positive attitudes, but hire for skill and willingness to learn. An incompetent person with a great attitude is still a substandard performer. You have a responsibility to develop every staff member to their full potential, of course ... and when the work performance isn't there, you also have a responsibility to your other workers to keep the playing field clear.

The operable question is, "Can I live with it?" If you can, limit their duties and keep coaching. When you reach a point where you can't live with it, either move them into a job that better fits their skill set and aptitude or free up their future for something that will be a better fit for them. If you make a mess in the process, clean it up and get on with your life.

Diabolical Details

Since *all* details are diabolical, this section title may be redundant,. Still, there are important points that don't fit neatly anywhere else:

Empty Dining Rooms or Lounges

People want to be where the action is, so they can feel self-conscious when they're the only people in the restaurant. Because you can't always have a full house, the most effective defense is good design. Break the dining room into smaller seating areas with half walls and dividers. Your design might create platforms or level changes. If possible, create some private dining rooms that open into the main seating area. Your goal is to design the room so it will always feel full, regardless of the number of guests who may be in it.

Driving Company Vehicles Inconsiderately

When your trucks are on the road and your name is on the side, your reputation is on display. When your staff drives with courtesy and consideration, it reflects positively on your restaurant. If your truck is spreading terror on the road, expect other drivers to draw a conclusion about how you run your business.

Carefully coach your drivers on the importance of courtesy and highway etiquette. Be sure they fully understand their responsibility as ambassadors for your brand. It may be helpful to paint your telephone number on the vehicle and ask for comments on how your drivers are doing, if only to make your drivers think twice before doing something inconsiderate.

Banquets, Receptions or Coffee Breaks That Start Late

You can be early, but never late. Plan to have functions set and ready to go at least fifteen minutes before the scheduled start time. That will keep the client from getting nervous and avoids errors from last-minute scrambles. Besides, someone will always be early and it's unprofessional to let them "catch you in your underwear" as they watch you madly trying to get set up!

Not Receiving Value

When patrons pay top dollar for quality food and beverage and don't get it, they go away mad. This is a question of value and it's very simple - if you don't give people what they've paid for, they won't return. Remember that value is determined by the guest's perceptions and standards, not yours! To assure guests receive value, always give them *more* than they expected. Find out what they want and how they want it, then give it to them just that way ... with a little something extra.

Suspicion of Drug Activity

It doesn't have to be proven. Just the rumor of drug activity in your restaurant can damage your business. The best defense is a good offense. Take a proactive stance against drugs in the workplace. Screen all job applicants thoroughly. Conduct random drug tests if your state law permits it. Support local anti-drug efforts in your community. Treat all members of your staff the same, managers and staff alike. Don't give rumors a reason to start.

Company Vehicles in Poor Condition or Spewing Smoke

Just as people draw conclusions about the cleanliness of your kitchen from the cleanliness of your restrooms, they reach similar opinions from the condition of your trucks. Everything the public sees with your name on it either helps or hurts your brand and makes a statement. This detail is particularly applicable to caterers. If potential guests would feel embarrassed to have your trucks seen in front of their house, they'll call someone else.

Store Labels or Price Stickers

Once something gets into your restaurant, it becomes part of your operation. There are many sources for the myriad items we use in the industry every day and you may bring items onto the premises that have labels or stickers from another enterprise. No matter how urgently you need to put something into service, take the time to remove labels and price tags. They'll only remind your guests of another place when you want them focused on yours.

Leaky Take-out Containers
It takes more than price to make a take-out container work. Before you commit to buy a large quantity of a container, test samples of it on all items you plan to offer for take-out. Make sure you don't risk irate guests by having your famous Fettuccine alla Puttanesca dripping all over the back seat of their Volvo!

No Working AV Equipment for Meetings
Having a house TV, DVD player, data projector, etc. can help you attract meeting business, but if the equipment doesn't work, the meeting won't work. Test out all equipment and connections well before the start of the meeting to give yourself enough time to remedy any problems before your clients arrive.

Handling Lost and Found Articles Inconsiderately
Leaving personal property in a restaurant is bad enough. Having that property abused or mishandled is worse. When you find a lost article, remember that it's someone's personal property. Treat it with respect until they pick it up. If you can locate them, call to let them know you've found their property. If you really want to pick up points, deliver it to them along with a coupon for a free dessert to make up for any inconvenience (no matter who was at fault).

Tip Jar in a Self Service Restaurant
How rude! Why not just put out a begging bowl? The staff of a restaurant where food is ordered and picked up at the counter really hasn't done much to earn a tip. Your guests will resent your asking for (or expecting) gratuities.

Excessively High Prices
High prices don't automatically mean you're trying to gouge your guests, but if your prices are unreasonable for the items offered, that is another issue. As the economy changes, people's habits change along with it. If sales are declining because guests can't afford the cost of dining in your restaurant, do something about it. Adjust your menu to offer more reasonably-priced entrées that still have a good profit margin. Offer a smaller portion at a lower price. Stay in touch with what your market wants ... and give it to them.

System Breakdowns
Guests become annoyed when you have no one who knows how to change the cash register tape or reboot the computer. (You can count on this to happen in the midst of the rush!) Include these items in every staff member's basic training to be sure the operation doesn't grind to a halt at a critical time.

The same problem comes up if you have no manual backup systems when the computer goes down. There's no question that electronic point-of-sale systems offer significant advantages, but everything electronic is vulnerable to power surges and unexplained crashes.

To avoid lapses in guest service when the inevitable happens, have a solid manual system ready to go. Train your staff in how it works and pull announced drills so they won't panic when they have to manage the transition from and to your computerized system.

Passively Promoting the Competition

I was having a late lunch in a midscale table service restaurant. As I waited for my broiled fish, I watched the managers bring in bags of food from Pizza Hut. They sat happily in the back of the dining room and ate lunch! It made me wonder what they knew about their kitchen that I didn't! I don't know if there's any connection, but the restaurant is no longer in business.

Website Weirdness

The Internet is quickly replacing the Yellow Pages as the place people get their information, meaning you must have a functional website. Your website may not be a reason guests don't come back, but it can surely be a reason they don't show up in the first place!

I don't profess to be an expert in web design so I talked with Joel Cohen of RestaurantMarketing.com about what works and what irks. Between the two of us we came up with this short list of the good, the bad and the ugly of restaurant websites.

No Basic Information on the Home Page

The whole point of having a website is to make it easy for potential patrons to find basic information about your restaurant, feel good about what they see and decide to give you a try. Toward that end, your site should answer these basic questions:

- Who are you? (name)
- What are you known for? (positioning statement)
- Where are you?
- How do I get there?
- How do I contact you?
- When are you open?
- What do you serve?
- What will it cost?
- What is your reservations policy?

At least the contact information should be prominently presented "above the fold," so prospective guests don't have to scroll down to find it. Keep it all up to date and don't let your web designer bury it behind a 30-second Flash introduction with music.

Outdated Menu

Make sure your online menu bears at least a passing resemblance to the food served in your restaurant. It takes a few minutes to update a menu online, but in a business where success depends on meeting and exceeding expectations, you'd best make sure those initial expectations are based on reality. If you change your menu daily, change your website daily, too.

Multi-Page Menu

Often less is more. If your menu is extensive, most people will tune out before they absorb it all (they didn't look you up to become a student of your menu!) In this instance, you can accomplish what you need by posting a Sampler Menu – noted as such – that lists your most popular items in various categories.

PDF Menus

These seem to be common practice. They present no problem when the site is accessed from a desktop computer, but can be awkward or even unworkable from a smart phone or tablet. Have your menu coded so it can be a web page, not an attachment.

Unpriced Menus

The idea behind prices on the website is to give prospective guests an idea of how much money they are likely to spend when they dine with you. If you find it impractical to list current prices for every item on the menu, at least provide the typical price range. For example, if your site advises readers that entrées are generally between $18-26, they won't be shocked when you present the menu at the table.

Difficult to Understand or Navigate

Finding information on your site should be intuitive and minimize the number of clicks necessary to find necessary information. This calls for clear headings and the appropriate use of "white space" to keep the pages looking clean and uncluttered. Don't use page backgrounds, they can make the text look muddy. Also make sure your fonts are uncomplicated and large enough to read, particularly on the small screen of a smart phone.

Site Doesn't Feel Like the Restaurant
The website should evoke the feel of your restaurant. This means using colors, textures and fonts similar to your interior decor. It means the tone of the text (formal, casual, irreverent) reflects the degree of formality guests will encounter when they walk through the door.

Annoying Gimmicks
Like television ads that win industry awards but don't result in increased sales, websites are often designed by techies who produce work to impress their peers rather than address the real needs of the client. The result can be sites that use all the latest bells and whistles. They look cool but aren't always user-friendly and don't generate trial from first-timers.

It's best to avoid anything written in Flash (it won't work on many tablets and smart phones). Likewise, steer clear of a sound track, especially one that starts automatically when the site is opened and has no obvious mute button. YouTube-like movie clips can also be overkill way unless there is a clear guest-oriented point to them.

Poor Use of Photos
Your website must have photos of course, but there are effective and ineffective ways to use graphic images. Here are a few important considerations when deciding which ones to use:

If the exterior of your restaurant is amazing and is a magnet to attracting drive-by customers, DO include it on the home page.

DON'T use stock photographs. They aren't unique and your menu items won't look like that anyway!

DO hire a professional to take photos of your restaurant and a professional food stylist to capture the look and feel of your signature dishes.

DON'T use photos of empty dining rooms or bars. They come across as cold and impersonal.

DO include photos of real (local) people dining and having fun in your restaurant. That makes it easier for would-be guests to picture themselves in that environment.

DO include photo(s) of the owner(s) to personalize the restaurant.

DON'T include a link to your website designer. The site is there to promote you, not the designer.

Spelling/Grammar Errors

Ours is a business of details and poor grammar and typos in your copy won't make potential guests feel more confident about how well you run your operation. Don't trust your own eye, particularly if you wrote the original copy. Have the copy reviewed by several other readers before you upload it (and again after you do!)

Not Mobile Friendly

Given that the smart phone is becoming the new Yellow Pages, your site must be legible on the small screen and easily navigable by touch. This may mean designing an entirely separate mobile site.

Bonus Points

Everybody likes pleasant surprises. These little unexpected touches are opportunities to improve your score and put your guests in a better mood. They help make up for any lapses in the operation and give people something to talk about to their friends.

"The Answer Is Yes. What's the Question?"

If you want to eliminate most guest relations problems before they start, adopt this simple management policy long espoused by "Coach" Don Smith. It's a simple way to say that the guest is always right, even when they are wrong. It acknowledges you can never win an argument with a guest, so don't even try. It keeps the emphasis on assuring guests have an enjoyable experience in your restaurant. It's a policy well worth adopting. What have you got to lose but unhappy patrons?

Service Guarantee

Service guarantees are the natural result of a guest-oriented business posture. When you offer an unconditional service guarantee, you pledge to do whatever is necessary to assure your guests have a wonderful experience in your restaurant. It is going to cost you some money to carry out an effective service guarantee, but the idea may not be as radical as it sounds.

If guests aren't having a good time, it is already costing you money, you just don't know how much. Paying off on the guarantee will quickly point out the breakdowns in your system so you can correct them. Just don't let paying off on the guarantee become a substitute for providing good service in the first place.

There are many elements of guest satisfaction that are beyond your control, but if patrons don't enjoy themselves, they're going have a bad memory of the experience. Since you are going to take the hit anyway, what have you got to lose by taking responsibility?

Environmental Consciousness

Environment concern is increasing and restaurants are targets of criticism from many consumer groups, often with cause. If you're not part of the solution, you're part of the problem. Recycle as much as you can and reduce your use of chemicals. Get your staff involved in finding ways to be more responsive to environmental concerns. Be sure your guests know you care and are doing something to help. It can't hurt.

Conspicuous Support of Local Charities

Your success comes from the support of your local community and the more you give, the more you'll get. If you only *take* from the community and never give anything back, you're an opportunist. Share your success and you will attract more of it. Be a good citizen. What goes around, comes around.

Making a Big Deal of Special Occasions

When people go to restaurants to celebrate special occasions, they want a festive time. If you're going to help them celebrate, do it right! Be consistent with the theme and tone of your restaurant, but be careful not to unduly disturb other diners.

You should know what your competition is doing for similar events and be do something uniquely different. Sparklers on the cake? A special song or a gift from the restaurant? Talk it over with your staff and see what you can collectively come up with to make your place the restaurant of choice for special occasions.

Frequent Diner Plan

A simple fact of human nature is that people will do what they're rewarded for. If you make it worthwhile for them to return to your restaurant, guests are more likely to return. A frequent diner plan has several advantages, chief among them that repeated visits help develop the habit of dining in your restaurant.

You can often use the plan as a way to direct business into periods when you have excess capacity and the data developed can allow you to flag MIAs – previously regular patrons whose frequency has fallen off. The most effective plans create an incentive to return. Instead of a straight discount, offer a percentage of tonight's check as a credit against a future meal.

Owner or Manager On the Floor

Train your staff and let them be stars. Even with a room full of stars, you should spend more time on the floor talking with your guests than in your office pushing paper. There's no substitute for personal presence and everybody enjoys knowing "the boss."

Something for Nothing

People love something for nothing and upscale restaurants don't have an exclusive hold on this touch. I remember having breakfast at Lou Mitchell's in Chicago. Halfway through the meal they brought a little frozen yogurt with strawberries as a palate cleanser ... at breakfast! I was impressed.

Mike Hurst, owner of 15th Street Fisheries restaurant in Fort Lauderdale regularly gave out free samples of potential new menu items. His guests are delighted. The unexpected extra is a wonderful gesture of hospitality that not only helps your patrons try something new but gives them something to talk to their friends about.

Selection of Reading Glasses

It's hell when you pass 40! For your guests who need a little optical assistance and forget their reading glasses, being able to help them out is a nice touch. Reading glasses in standard prescriptions are readily available in most pharmacies. Present the selection in a good-looking lined wooden box. Your guests will appreciate and remember this unexpected amenity.

Pictures or Sketches of Guests on the Walls

The theme from the old TV show Cheers talks about "a place where everybody knows your name." People love to feel like they belong and nothing makes that statement quite like posting their picture in the restaurant. It's a memorable gesture to acknowledge your regulars this way and has more impact than photos of the owner with celebrity guests.

If you choose to memorialize your regular guests this way, have some definite selection standards for enshrinement. Then, make a ceremony of placing the person's picture on the wall.

Free Coffee for Waiting Breakfast Guests

If you can help get someone's day off to a good start, you've done them a real favor. Timing is critical during the breakfast period, so anything that makes a delay less painful is a good move. Offering free coffee to a guest that has to wait is a small gesture that will yield big returns in guest satisfaction.

Thank-You Notes

If you have a guest's telephone number, you can find their address in an online reverse directory. Imagine the impact of a polite handwritten note thanking them for dining with you! People never receive all the gratitude they deserve. Show them you appreciate their patronage and you'll stay in their minds.

Striking Logo Used Tastefully

Image is everything, so create a distinctive logo. Look at the impact the Hard Rock Café has received from the widespread use of its logo! The more times you can put it in front of your guests, the more they'll associate the image with the quality of their experience. This can work to your benefit if guests are enjoying themselves.

Singing a Song Other than "Happy Birthday to You"

I think anyone who sings this tired standard in a public place should be shot! Show a little originality! The traditional birthday song is what your competitors (and five-year-olds) sing. Your guests are immune to it.

Get their attention with something short and personalized to your restaurant. If it's a song, make it one your staff enjoys singing. It is unsettling to see people singing when their hearts aren't in it. If you do it well, guests will automatically think of your restaurant for their next special occasion.

Special Events and Promotions

It doesn't matter what the events are or even if they are profitable. The goal is to break the routine for both your guests and your staff. Special events and promotions create a sense that something is happening at your restaurant and people like to be where things are happening. If you tie these events to a charitable cause, you can do some good for others simultaneously while you gain valuable free publicity for your restaurant.

Hot Towels

There's nothing like beginning and ending a meal feeling clean and content. Japanese restaurants have traditionally offered hot towels at the beginning of the meal. Why not you? Consider the gesture at the end of the meal as well. You could be as formal as finger bowls with fresh towels or as informal as packaged Wet-Naps.

The Japanese approach of a hot washcloth is easy to do and makes a wonderful impression on your guests, particularly if your menu includes finger foods like ribs, fried chicken or corn on the cob.

Classic Take-out Packaging

If you enjoy a significant take-out business (or would like to), spend some money on customized packaging. Your containers can be an effective image-building tool, particularly with corporate clients. Making this investment can change packaging from a cost item to a profit center.

Unexpected Touches

Find a way to do a better job with something ordinary. For example, when you order coffee at Hudson's Bar & Grill in San Luis Obispo, California, it comes with a cinnamon stick, chocolate chips and fresh cream ... and priced like regular coffee! Lambert's Café in Sikeston, Missouri has a reputation for "throwed rolls," a unique way of passing out the bread!

The advantage of making a point of difference out of common items is that guests will think of you time they dine at another restaurant. So what does every restaurant have? Salad, napkins, water, bread, beer, wine ...

Reading Material for Unaccompanied Diners

Solo diners don't have the conversation of dining companions to occupy their time during lulls in the meal. Often they'll bring a book, newspaper or tablet computer with them. If you attract (or want to attract) solo diners, have some reading material available and train your staff to offer it discretely.

Calculator with the Check

Parties of singles with a common check especially appreciate this touch. Groups of women also seem driven to create a painstakingly equitable cost split. Even if there's no entrée cost to divide, many people appreciate a little help with calculating the tip. Credit card-sized calculators are inexpensive and easy to attach to a tray or check folder. It's another small point of difference.

Cheerful Handling of Special Requests

This is where stories of legendary service come from. If a guest wants something you don't normally offer and you go to the grocery store to get it for them, you'll have a friend for life.

The possibilities are endless once you decide that your only real job is to make sure your guests are delighted! You can't buy the kind of publicity and word-of-mouth you earn just by going out of your way for a guest. After all, this *is* the hospitality industry!

Closing Comments

Does your head hurt? That's a lot of material to digest and it may have you wondering just what to do and where to start. I can help ...

Put this Material to Work

Use this book to raise your awareness and perspective. For example, you may not have considered that bright red nail polish on the hands of a waitress bothers some people. Knowing that, it might be prudent to have your waitresses avoid bright red nail polish. On the other hand, you might feel bright red nail polish is an important part of your image and choose to do nothing. If so, at least you'd be aware of the potential reactions to your decision.

Often you'll have a dilemma. For example, it will bother some people if you don't take reservations; it will bother others if you do. In the absence of a state mandate, going entirely non-smoking will attract a particular segment of the market and drive away some of your regular patrons. In each solution lie the seeds of another potential problem.

Life is like that. This book is not a blueprint on what you *should* do, it only suggests what you *could* do. It offers insights into why guests may have an enjoyable experience or a miserable one. It can help you understand why you've been popular and give you ideas on how you could be even more successful.

Get the Message to Your Staff

Correcting and eliminating guest distractions is a five step process. You don't have to approach it this rigidly, but you must be sure to cover all the steps.

Raise Awareness

Be sure your staff understands *what* the points of guest irritation are and *why* they're important. As a simple solution, consider posting ten of these points on your staff bulletin board each week. (That'll give you twenty years worth!) They points may not be anything you haven't told your crew before, but hearing it from an outside source shows you aren't the only one who thinks details are critical.

A list of negative points seems to provide the most impact. If you present everything in terms of what people *should* do, it sounds like a sermon. I found that just giving the list without the lecture was an effective and painless way to raise staff awareness.

With a sharp crew and a supportive working climate, this may be all you have to do. Some problems are more elusive and I suggest you bring up these points for discussion at your staff meetings.

Establish Perspective

To what extent does your staff agree or disagree with the particular point. To what extent does the problem exist in your restaurant now? What is the potential financial impact of ignoring it?

It's important they understand *why* the point can be a distraction to your guests and *how* distractions affect the experience your guests have in the restaurant. Make sure they also grasp *why* it's important that your guests enjoy themselves. Let your crew know what's in it for them when they sweat the details.

Identify Causes

When you identify an issue, the next step is to determine *why* the problem exists in the first place. It's also appropriate to establish *what* results you hope to achieve. Get your staff involved. Focus on breakdowns in your system and not on problems with individuals.

For example, delays at a particular station in the kitchen may be due to an unbalanced menu, inadequate equipment or incomplete training. Search for the *why* not the *who*. If you assign blame to an individual, you won't be addressing the real cause of the problem and you'll never hear another suggestion from your staff!

Take Action

Once you've narrowed down the cause of the problem, ask your staff how they might go about correcting the situation. Listen respectfully to what they have to say. The ingenuity of your crew may surprise you. Better yet, you won't have to solve the problem by yourself. You also won't have to force your solution on anyone.

When a plan of action is determined, assign responsibility for its implementation. Be clear about *who* is going to do it, *when* it needs to happen and *where* the action will be taken. The plan must address *what* equipment or training will be required and *how* you'll be able to tell when the problem is effectively under control.

A Word of Caution:

If you try to specify exactly *how* the results must be achieved, you risk negating the creativity and enthusiasm of your staff.

Coach Consistently

Coaching is the place to deal with *how* the results are being achieved. Coaching is more powerful than management because it requires a presumption that the worker is basically capable. Coaching includes monitoring as well as recognizing and rewarding successful efforts.

Approaching your staff as a coach instead of a cop is more enjoyable for everyone. You'll also achieve better results with less effort and stress. Think about it.

As your staff becomes more involved in the problem-solving process, their personal levels of well-being will rise and they'll find it easy to take better care of your guests. The better treatment your guests receive, the more often they'll return. The more they return, the more profit you make. In short, everybody wins!

Create Points of Difference

Every time one of these annoyances arises in a competitor's operation and not in yours, it creates a point of difference. Coach your staff on how to educate your guests about the exceptional job you are doing for them. This is what creates positive word-of-mouth. Here's an example of how you can use trivia to your advantage:

When I opened my first restaurant in 1976, plate garnishing was still an afterthought in most restaurants. By contrast, we were dressing our plates with the colorful arrangements of fruit more common today.

When we presented a plate to the guest, we usually received a spontaneous positive reaction. At that point, the waiter might chuckle and say "Isn't it refreshing to see a plate that's not covered with parsley?" When that same guest next dined with my competitors, their plate would invariably arrive covered with parsley.

Do you think they noticed? Who do you think they thought of? What do you think they said to their dining companions? How do you think my restaurant looked by comparison? I have many more examples but you get the point.

Our sales that first year sales were over 60% higher than comparable operations in our market! We were the topic of enthusiastic conversation among our guests because we created and exploited small points of difference. We educated our guests about why they dined with us and gave them something to talk about!

A 60% increase may not seem real to you, but what if you could increase your volume even 10% at almost no cost? Think about it. There are a wealth of profit-making opportunities in this book, provided you're willing to **Do the Work!**

Make a Statement

At the risk of sounding self-serving, my last suggestion is that you put your money where your mouth is. Your staff will believe what you *do* before they'll believe what you *say*. If you're truly serious about developing legendary guest service, I urge you to put something tangible in everyone's hands.

The least expensive option for the service staff is my pocket-sized book, *50 Tips to Improve Your Tips: The Service Pro's Guide to Delighting Diners*. Your servers, managers and key supervisors should each have a copy of 50 Tips.

In addition, everyone on your leadership team should have a copy of *Restaurant Basics Revisited*. Why? Because details are insidious. They're always lurking in the shadows, ready to trip you up.

Staying on top of the details is an ongoing process, not the subject of a one-hour staff meeting. Issue the books like you issue uniforms and you'll assure your staff will always have access to these reminders.

Whether you explore the book option or not, I urge you to start an ongoing coaching program with regular homework. Over time, I guarantee the continual exposure to these trivialities will increase your staff's awareness of the fine points of guest gratification.

The books will cost far less than sending a few of your staff to a even a single training seminar and will gain more long term benefits.

Assigning each member of your crew their own copy of this material delivers a powerful message. Do that and your staff will understand how important they are to your operation and grasp why handling these details effectively is vital to you.

With this material readily at hand, your staff can become more involved in improving your level of guest gratification. Better yet, they'll have reference information that will help them make money for you (and themselves) every day you're in business.

The implications of this gesture are wide-ranging. For example, dishwashers and bussers are typically our highest turnover positions. In my experience, the key to retaining entry level staff is to increase their understanding of how the restaurant works and how they fit into its success.

By including dishwashers and bussers in all aspects of training, you show them how important they are to your organization. The more important they realize they are, the more dedicated they become. The more dedicated they become, the longer they'll stay.

No pressure, but think about it. After all, you have nothing to lose but your turnover.

Now get to work!

Management Resources

There's never enough time or space to treat every topic in the depth it deserves. I recommend the following resources for those readers who wish to explore some of these ideas more deeply. Yes, all these resources are also in my personal professional library and I refer to them frequently.

Bill

HOW TO BECOME THE RESTAURANT OF CHOICE:
A Fresh Look at Service, Hospitality and the Bottom Line
Bill's easy-to-read, common sense look at restaurant service teaches the details of good service. It explores the process by which guests form their opinions of restaurant service and gives a competitive advantage to operators.

SETTING THE TABLE:
The Transforming Power of Hospitality in Business
Danny Meyer shares lessons he's learned developing the business model he calls "enlightened hospitality." This innovative philosophy emphasizes putting the power of hospitality to work in a new and counter-intuitive way.

GUEST-BASED MARKETING:
How to Increase Sales Without Breaking Your Budget
Bill demonstrates that success doesn't come from beating the competition, but from pleasing your guests. He shows how to work from the inside out to build on your strengths and to use the intrinsic advantages you didn't even know you had.

ZINGERMAN'S GUIDE TO GIVING GREAT SERVICE
Based on the principles that made service a bottom-line at Zingerman's, founder Ari Weinzweig lays out the steps they teach their staff on how to give great service.

FROM TURNOVER TO TEAMWORK:
How to Build and Retain a Guest-Oriented Staff
Bill Marvin takes a common-sense approach to why people leave and what can be done about it. Treats such issues as rapport between staff and management, training, salary structure and wages, incentives, performance reviews and disciplinary procedures.

277

THERE'S GOT TO BE AN EASIER WAY TO RUN A BUSINESS:
How to Have a Successful Company ... and a life!
Bill shows you how to have a successful company ... and a life! He suggests common sense alternatives that will allow you to be more effective with less effort ... and get your life back!

LESSONS IN SERVICE FROM CHARLIE TROTTER
Charlie Trotters was a renowned Chicago hot spot, but his reputation was built on a subtle relationship between food, wine, ambiance, and service.

CASHING IN ON COMPLAINTS:
Turning Disappointed Diners Into Gold
Nobody likes to get complaints, but if you know how to mine it, there's gold in those gripes! Bill helps you understand how to deal with – and profit from – the complaints you are sure to receive in the normal course of business.

ZINGERMAN'S GUIDE TO GOOD LEADING, PART 1:
Building a Great Business
Ari Weinzweig examines the basic building blocks of the culture and structure now known as Zingerman's. These approaches are the behind-the-scenes "secret" stuff that goes into making a very special, sustainable business of any kind.

59½ MONEY-MAKING MARKETING IDEAS:
How to Build Volume without Losing Your Shirt
Bill explores ways to build volume that are simpler, more effective, much less risky ... and almost free! The secret is to get existing guests to come back more often and say wonderful things about you to their friends.

ZINGERMAN'S GUIDE TO GOOD LEADING, PART 2:
Being a Better Leader
The second book in the series looks at the leadership style that has helped make Zingerman's such a special place to work and to eat. The book includes their entrepreneurial approach to management and more.

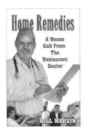

HOME REMEDIES:
A House Call From the Restaurant Doctor
This is some of The Doc's best stuff, taken from the first several years of Bill Marvin's "Home Remedies" newsletter.

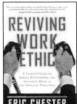

RESTAURANT SERVICE: Beyond the Basics
A how-to guide to the rituals and amenities that make customers feel comfortable and turn a meal into a memorable event, including guidance on table and guest service.

50 TIPS TO IMPROVE YOUR TIPS:
The Service Pro's Guide to Delighting Diners
Bill created this pocket-sized paperback to help your service staff create more personal connection with your patrons and increase their tips while improving service and guest delight. Quantity prices are available.

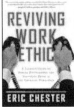

REVIVING WORK ETHIC: A Leader's Guide to Restoring Pride in the Emerging Workforce
Eric Chester takes an incisive look at the entitlement mentality that afflicts many in the emerging workforce and shows readers the specific actions they can take to give their employees a deep commitment to performing excellent work.

50 PROVEN WAYS TO BUILD RESTAURANT SALES & PROFIT
The first in a series, this book contains fifty of the best ideas from the sharpest minds in the hospitality business, capsulized in one to three pages so you can quickly pick up an idea and get back to work.

50 PROVEN WAYS TO ENHANCE GUEST SERVICE
Profitable ideas from Susan Clarke, Barry Cohen, Howard Cutson, Peter Good, Raymond Goodman, Winston Hall, Jim Laube, Bill Main, Phyllis Ann Marshall, Bill Marvin, Rudy Miick and Banger Smith.

WHAT EVERY SERVICE PRO SHOULD KNOW ABOUT PEOPLE (DVD/CD SET)
Bill offers some valuable insights that can help your service staff have more fun on the job, be more confident and relaxed when dealing with the public and be more effective at generating income for both the restaurant and themselves!

50 PROVEN WAYS TO BUILD MORE PROFITABLE MENUS
This collection explores menus and menu design with some great money-making secrets from Barry Cohen, Howard Cutson, Peter Good, Raymond Goodman, Jim Laube, Bill Main, Phyllis Ann Marshall, Bill Marvin, Banger Smith and Ron Yudd.

AT YOUR SERVICE:
A Hands-On Guide to the Professional Dining Room
From the Culinary Institute of America, At Your Service is a comprehensive guide to help professionals learn the ins and outs of running a successful front-of-the-house operation.

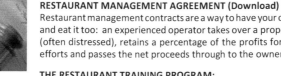

WAITSTAFF TRAINING HANDBOOK:
A Complete Guide to the Proper Steps in Service
The guide covers every aspect of restaurant customer service for the positions of host, waiter or waitress, head waiter, captain, and bus person.

PROTOTYPE STAFF MANUAL & HUMAN RESOURCES MANUAL (Download)
The Human Resources Manual details the company's policies relating to people. The Staff Manual contains all the basic information about the company that every member of the staff needs to be a functioning part of the company culture.

THE ENCYCLOPEDIA OF RESTAURANT TRAINING
An ready-to-use staff training program for all positions in the food service industry. This book shows how to train your employees in the shortest amount of time, and lets you get back to your own job of running a profitable enterprise.

RESTAURANT MANAGEMENT AGREEMENT (Download)
Restaurant management contracts are a way to have your cake and eat it too: an experienced operator takes over a property (often distressed), retains a percentage of the profits for his efforts and passes the net proceeds through to the owner.

THE RESTAURANT TRAINING PROGRAM:
An Employee Training Guide for Managers
This training manual covers safety and sanitation, food production skills and service ability, including standard industry procedures and practices with instructions for customizing to individual restaurant operations.

BRING YOUR "A" GAME TO WORK
Eric Chester reveals the seven essential work ethic values required for success in any job. Every employer sees these values as non-negotiable and yet they have a difficult time finding people who demonstrate these values on the job.

GAMES TRAINERS PLAY
These brilliant offbeat, unexpected, disarming games have one serious mission: to coax even the most reluctant groups to talk, laugh, think, and work together. Page after page of fun, easy-to-plan tear-out exercises to shake up outworn habits.

RUNNING A RESTAURANT FOR DUMMIES
If you're entering the field for the first time or switching to independent restaurants from another style of foodservice, this book can give you a reasonable idea of what you are getting yourself in for.

REMARKABLE SERVICE:
A Guide to Winning and Keeping Customers
The Culinary Institute of America offers tips and tactics on offering consistent, high-quality service in a wide range of dining establishments, from casual and outdoor dining to upscale restaurants and catering operations.

UNIFORM SYSTEM OF ACCOUNTS FOR RESTAURANTS
Don't go into business without it! The Uniform System lays out the standard account classification system used by most restaurant operators allowing you to compare your operating results with those of other similar restaurants.

RESTAURANT FINANCIAL BASICS
This down-to-earth guide focuses on the crucial information busy managers must know-for both day-to-day operations and long-term planning, including cash flow, pricing, budgeting, cost control, equipment accounting, and cash control.

AUDIO CDS OF LIVE SEMINARS

How to Prosper in Tough Times

There's Got to Be an Easier Way to Run a Restaurant!

Cashing in on Complaints

Why Guests Don't Come Back and What You Can Do about It

50 Money-Making Marketing Ideas

Guest-Based Marketing

The Server as an Independent Business Person

Marketing Advantages of the Independent Operator

Retention Is Better than Recruitment

Five Great Ways to Build Sales ... and One Really Lousy One!

(... and there's even more on the website!)

Re-Thinking Restaurants

WHAT IF we suggested you could actually trigger a **contagious resurgence of hospitality** in your own community by delivering the experience of heartfelt caring to every restaurant patron, every time?

WHAT IF we told you we've developed an **elegantly simple system** that provides the logic, methodology and support structure that enables you to operate with **effortless excellence**?

WHAT IF we assure you this approach will give you and your staff a **fulfilling sense of purpose** and the **joyful experience** of enriching the lives of the people you serve?

WHAT IF we made this program so **irresistible** and so **easily affordable** that hospitality could truly become your competitive point of difference in the market?

Would you think, "These people must be crazy!" ... or would you ask, "How can I become part of this?"

A Place of Hospitality™ is a certification and support program that helps independent restaurateurs ...

- re-discover their roots: hospitality itself!
- convey that hospitable mind set to their team
- enjoy more balance in their lives
- put the joy back into serving the public
- level the playing field when competing against the national chains
- develop a sustainable, steadily growing business model built not on discounts and hype but on personal connection and service to the community
- do all this in a way that's both operationally practical and extremely profitable!

Certification as **A Place of Hospitality** recognizes those independent restaurants who have not only made a deep commitment to provide exceptional personal hospitality to every guest ... but who have succeeded at it! This certification cannot be purchased and you cannot pay to keep it – you either deliver every day or you lose it!

The Missing Link

It always seems ironic that the competitive element most responsible for success in the hospitality business ... and the piece most visibly absent ... is hospitality itself!

We're out to fix that – to make hospitality the rule rather than the rare exception, to allow independent restaurants to re-kindle their love of serving others and build their businesses (at full price) with the enthusiastic support of their patrons.

281

The Ripple Effect

Human beings tend to treat others the way they are treated and it has to start somewhere. Who better to trigger a resurgence of hospitality in the world than the hospitality industry itself? Where better to start than your restaurant?

When guests feel well- and personally served, they leave feeling better about life in general and are naturally more considerate of others. Hospitality has a way of paying itself forward. Niceness begets niceness. Courtesy brings more courtesy.

When you are focused on nurturing relationships with your guests rather than simply trying to "sell more stuff," your patrons trust you. When you become their favorite place they will return more often, recommend you to their friends and become fiercely loyal fans. They will stick with you through tough times and rarely quibble about price! The result is higher sales, lower marketing costs, a happier staff and better tips. It is truly a win-win-win situation.

What's the Point?

In addition to the task of re-kindling hospitality in the community, the point of becoming certified as A Place of Hospitality is to grow your business ... not from endless hype and discounting, but from the voluntary, enthusiastic support of the neighborhood ... and it works!

Certified restaurants have consistently generated higher guest satisfaction scores in our online feedback system. Here is the comparative performance for three months earlier this year. While the scores for all Gold Group members (black line) were exceptional, certified operations (top line) consistently out-performed them.

Strong Grades Build Strong Sales

A study by the Harvard Business Review documented that sales grow exponentially as guest feedback scores exceed 4.5. Happier guests spend more money ... because they WANT to!

Certified restaurants report annual sales increases of 10-15% – a few reported their best sales EVER – so even in a down economy, it appears that hospitality is good business.

In fairness, we won't attribute the increase solely to their certification – these are all exceptional operators. But they did say they felt their increased focus on hospitality was a big factor in their sales growth. (It certainly didn't hurt!)

Getting Started

The support resources that make certification as **A Place of Hospitality** practical are part of membership in the Gold Group. Here's just some what you'll have access to as a member:

Weekly Electronic House Call e-Letter
The Restaurant Doctor's weekly e-letter with ideas you can use in your staff and management meetings.

Monthly Interviews with Industry Experts
An audio chat with industry leaders on topics ranging from marketing to management and menu design.

Monthly Roundtable Teleconference
Members get together on the phone to share ideas and discuss items of mutual interest or concern.

Monthly Home Remedies Newsletter
A four-page newsletter with insights, trade secrets and best practices in a short, easy-to-digest format.

FREE Telephone Consulting
Pose your questions directly to recognized industry experts without a meter running.

Online Staff Selection System
A proven system to make the process easier and more effective so you'll get the right people ... the first time!

On-Demand Video Training
24/7 access to online training resources typically only available to national chain operators.

Real-Time Online Guest Feedback System
Know – almost in real time – what your patrons think about their experience of doing business with you.

Food Cost Control System
Know your food cost every day ... without taking an inventory. (Imagine how much better you'll sleep at night!)

... and there are many more resources in development

Gold Group membership is currently about $50 a month. The program is constantly evolving so realistically, that amount may change as we refine the structure and add additional resources to the program. But unlike most other industry support programs, we have a larger purpose than maximizing our own income.

To stay true to our mission of being irresistible and easily affordable, we must offer you as MUCH as we can for as LITTLE as possible! How's THAT for a fresh approach?

Test drive the program risk-free for 90 days and prove to yourself that there is, in fact, a painless process that can help you accomplish "impossible" results and put the passion back into your work at the same time. Then perhaps you will choose to pursue certification as A Place of Hospitality and discover the transforming power of hospitality in your own life!

You've got nothing to lose but your struggle!

Get full details and join the Gold Group at
www.APlaceOfHospitality.com.
Look under "Getting Started."

About the Author

Bill Marvin, aka "The Restaurant Doctor[SM]" is a leading authority on how good restaurants can become great restaurants and an advisor to service-oriented organizations across North America. Bill founded Effortless, Inc., a management research and education company, Prototype Restaurants and Hospitality Masters Press, publishers of the acclaimed Hospitality Masters Series of books.

Bill has earned the designation of Certified Speaking Professional from the National Speakers Association and is a lifetime member of the Council of Hotel and Restaurant Trainers and was one of the first to be certified as a Foodservice Management Professional by the National Restaurant Association.

He started in the industry at the age of 14, washing dishes (by hand!) in a small restaurant on Cape Cod. He went on to earn a degree in Hotel Administration from Cornell University. Bill moved to Colorado in 1984 to design the foodservice system for the U.S. Olympic Training Centers. He and his wife Margene relocated to Gig Harbor, in the Puget Sound area of Washington State, in 1993.

Before joining the Olympic Committee, Bill spent twelve years in the San Francisco Bay Area in a number of roles. He was a supervisor in the management consulting department of an international hospitality consulting firm, developed and operated two restaurants for his own account and started his practice an independent restaurant consultant. In typical Northern California fashion, he also became a commercial hot air balloon pilot and in the fall of 1981, became the first person in history to fly a hot air balloon in China!

He's managed a condominium hotel in the Caribbean, helped run a prestigious New England country club and been a consultant/designer for a national food facilities engineering firm. As a foodservice officer in the U.S. Navy, he also was responsible for operating several enlisted feeding facilities, the largest serving over 20,000 meals a day with a staff of 525 – all pieces in the puzzle of his life.

Bill is a sought-after consultant in the areas of concept development and organizational effectiveness and is a prolific author. In addition to over a dozen well-regarded books focused on the hospitality industry, he writes two weekly e-mail newsletters, offers several subscription series and contributes regularly to trade magazines in various industries. He still has a healthy private consulting practice and logs over 75,000 miles a year delivering corporate keynotes and training programs in North America, Europe and the Pacific Rim.

Bill's final project is to trigger a contagious resurgence of hospitality in the world, starting by helping independent restaurant operators re-discover their roots: hospitality itself! Toward that end he developed a certification and support program called "A Place of Hospitality" that allows operators to enjoy more balance in their lives, put the joy back into serving the public, level the playing field when competing against the national chains, develop a sustainable, steadily growing business model built on personal connection and service to the community not on discounts and hype ... and do all this in a way that is both operationally practical and extremely profitable!

Bill Marvin
The Restaurant Doctor

EFFORTLESS, INC. • PO Box 280 • Gig Harbor, WA 98335 USA

800-767-1055/253-858-9255 • Bill@RestaurantDoctor.com
www.RestaurantDoctor.com • www.APlaceOfHospitality.com

285

Made in the USA
San Bernardino, CA
13 January 2014